895 DAYS THAT CHANGED THE WORLD

to Laurentian University's History Department
which made this book possible

895 DAYS THAT CHANGED THE WORLD

The Presidency of Gerald R. Ford

Graeme S. Mount

with Mark Gauthier

Montreal/New York/London

Black Rose Books No. II342

National Library of Canada Cataloguing in Publication Data

Mount, Graeme S. (Graeme Stewart), 1939-

895 days that changed the world : the presidency of Gerald R. Ford / Graeme Mount

Includes bibliographical references and index.
ISBN: 1-55164-275-1 (bound)   ISBN: 1-55164-274-3 (pbk.)
(alternative ISBNs 9781551642758 [bound]   9781551642741 [pbk.])

1. Ford, Gerald R., 1913- 2. United States--Politics and government--1974-1977.
I. Title. II. Title: Eight hundred ninety-five days that changed the world.

E865.M69 2005   973.925'092   C2005-902389-9

We wish to thank the Gerald Ford Presidential Library, Ann Arbor, Michigan, for permission to reproduce the photographs herein.

Cover design: Associés libres

C.P. 1258	2250 Military Road	99 Wallis Road
Succ. Place du Parc	Tonawanda, NY	London, E9 5LN
Montréal, H2X 4A7	14150	England
Canada	USA	UK

To order books:
In Canada: (phone) 1-800-565-9523 (fax) 1-800-221-9985
email: utpbooks@utpress.utoronto.ca

In United States: (phone) 1-800-283-3572 (fax) 1-651-917-6406

In the UK & Europe: (phone) 44 (0)20 8986-4854 (fax) 44 (0)20 8533-5821
email: order@centralbooks.com

Our Web Site address: http://www.blackrosebooks.net

Printed in Canada

TABLE OF CONTENTS

PHOTOGRAPHS

1. Gerald R. Ford is sworn in as 38th President of the United States by Chief Justice Warren Burger as Mrs. Ford watches, 9 August 1974. *Introduction*

2. President Ford announces his pardon of Richard Nixon from the Oval Office, 8 September 1974. The pardon effectively killed Ford's chances of winning a four year term of his own. *Introduction*

3. President Ford and son Mike play golf, Camp David, Maryland. The 38th President was one of the best athletes ever to occupy the White House. *Introduction*

4. President Ford and Queen Elizabeth dance during the state dinner at the White House in honour of the Queen and Prince Philip, 7 July 1976. Because of the "Special Relationship" between the United States and the United Kingdom, the royal couple went to Washington to celebrate what had been their own country's defeat. *Chapter One*

5. Vice-President Nelson Rockefeller, Queen Elizabeth, and President Ford shared a toast during the Bicentennial Celebrations, July 1976. *Chapter One*

6. Mrs. Ford, Queen Elizabeth, President Ford and the Duke of Edinburgh chat around a table in the White House during the Royal Couple's Bicentennial Visit, July 1976. *Chapter One*

7. President Gerald R. Ford takes a final phone call from Secretary of State Henry Kissinger, bringing him up-to-date on the situation in Vietnam, following a late night meeting in the West Sitting Room with the Secretary and Deputy National Security Adviser Brent Scowcroft, 28 April 1975. *Chapter Five*

8. President Ford meets in the Oval Office with Secretary of State Henry Kissinger and Vice-President Nelson Rockefeller to discuss the American evacuation of Saigon, 28 April 1975. *Chapter Five*

9. Vice-President Nelson Rockefeller, Deputy Assistant for National Security Affairs Brent Scowcroft, and CIA Director William Colby discuss the situation in Vietnam during a break in a meeting of the National Security Council, 24 April 1975. *Chapter Five*

10. President Ford hosts a working luncheon for Indonesian President Suharto at the Laurel Lodge, Camp David, Maryland, 5 July 1975. The Ford-Suharto relationship proved catastrophic in East Timor. *Chapter Seven*

11. Secretary of State Henry Kissinger, Soviet leader Leonid Brezhnev (with translator Victor Sukhodrev at his ear), President Ford, and Soviet Foreign minister Andrei Gromyko during the Helsinki Summit. *Chapter Nine*

12. President Ford had great confidence in his Secretary of State, Henry Kissinger.

13. President Ford, George H.W. Bush (as U.S. envoy to the People's Republic of China), and the President's staff meet Vice-Premier Deng Xiao Ping in Beijing. Ford went to China in order to placate the Chinese leaders who felt offended by his trip to Vladivostok the previous year. *Chapter Eleven*

14. President Ford and Ronald Reagan in Kansas City, Missouri, for the Republican National Convention, 18 August 1976. Reagan disagreed with Ford's policies regarding Panama, China, and the Helsinki Conference, but history has upheld Ford's positions. *Chapters Ten, Twelve, Thirteen*

15. President Ford and former Republican presidential candidate Ronald Reagan display Republican solidarity on the closing night of the Republican National Convention, 19 August 1976. From left to right stand Senator Robert Dole (Ford's vice-presidential running mate), Nancy Reagan, Ronald Reagan, President Ford, Vice-President Rockefeller, Susan Ford (daughter of the President), Betty Ford (wife of the President). *Chapters Ten, Twelve, Thirteen*

16. President Ford and Jimmy Carter meet at the Walnut Street Theater in Philadelphia to debate domestic policy during the first night of the three Ford-Carter debates, 23 September 1976. *Conclusions*

17. President Ford meets with Egyptian President Anwar Sadat in Salzburg, Austria, 2 June 1975. In Salzburg, Sadat made a suggestion which led to an Egyptian-Israeli agreement to withdraw Israeli forces from the westernmost part of the Sinai Peninsula. The Ford-sponsored Sinai Accord, in turn, cleared the way for the Camp David Accord concluded under the auspices of President Carter. *Chapter Fifteen*

18. President Ford was later to claim that the Helsinki Accord led to the end of the Berlin Wall, and his museum in Grand Rapids, Michigan, triumphantly displays pieces of the wall. Tourists, such as these students from Laurentian University, can pose for pictures in front of what had been a European horror. (Taken 12 May 2005 by Graeme S. Mount.) *Chapter Nine*

19. President and Mrs. Ford comfort each other as they watch the election returns 2 November 1976.

1. Gerald R. Ford is sworn in as 38th President, 9 August 1974.

2. President Ford announces his pardon of Richard Nixon, 8 September 1974.

3. President Ford and son Mike play golf, Camp David, Maryland.

4. President Ford and Queen Elizabeth, 7 July 1976.

5. Vice-President Nelson Rockefeller, Queen Elizabeth, and President Ford, during Bicentennial Celebrations, July 1976.

6. Mrs. Ford, Queen Elizabeth, President Ford and the Duke of Edinburgh.

7. President Gerald R. Ford takes a final phone call from Secretary of State Henry Kissinger, 28 April 1975.

8. President Ford meets with Secretary of State Henry Kissinger and Vice-President Nelson Rockefeller, 28 April 1975.

9. Vice-President Nelson Rockefeller, Deputy Assistant for National Security Affairs Brent Scowcroft, and CIA Director William Colby, 24 April 1975.

10. President Ford hosts a working luncheon for Indonesian President Suharto at the Laurel Lodge, Camp David, Maryland, 5 July 1975.

11. Secretary of State Henry Kissinger, Soviet leader Leonid Brezhnev (with translator Victor Sukhodrev at his ear), President Ford, and Soviet Foreign minister Andrei Gromyko.

12. President Ford and Secretary of State, Henry Kissinger.

13. President Ford, George H.W. Bush, China.

14. President Ford and Ronald Reagan.

15. Republican National Convention, 19 August 1976.

16. President Ford and Jimmy Carter debate domestic policy at the Walnut Street Theater in Philadelphia, 23 September 1976.

17. President Ford meets with Egyptian President Anwar Sadat in Salzburg, Austria, 2 June 1975.

18. Students pose before pieces of the Berlin Wall in Grand Rapids, Michigan.

19. President and Mrs. Ford watch the election returns, 2 November 1976.

CHRONOLOGICAL TABLE OF RELEVANT EVENTS

1973

October

Vice-President Spiro Agnew resigns because of criminal activity. President Richard Nixon nominates Gerald Ford, Republican leader in the House of Representatives, to assume the Vice-Presidency under the 25th Amendment to the U.S. Constitution.

1974

25 April

Portuguese coup d'état ousts conservative authoritarian government.

9 August

President Nixon resigns because of criminal activity in connection with the Watergate scandal and flies to California. Ford becomes President of the United States at noon that day when Nixon's resignation takes effect. Nixon's Secretary of State, Henry Kissinger, remains as Secretary of State to President Ford.

18 August

Ford chooses Nelson Rockefeller, former Governor of New York, to assume office under the 25th Amendment as Vice President.

23 November

Ford and Kissinger arrive in Vladivostok for a meeting with Soviet leaders.

1975

April

North Vietnamese forces overrun all South Vietnam.

25 June

Portugal grants independence to Mozambique.

July

Cuba's government agrees to request from Angola's MPLA for assistance. First Cubans reach Angola early in August 1975. National Security Council in Washington agrees that U.S. can transfer operation of the Panama Canal after twenty years.

1 August

The Helsinki Accord is signed.

1 September

Egyptian and Israeli leaders initial the Sinai Accord.

3 November

Brent Scowcroft replaces Henry Kissinger as National Security Adviser.

11 November

Portuguese rule ends in Angola.

20 November

Generalíssimo Francisco Franco, Spanish Head of State since 1939, dies.

December

Ford and Kissinger visit China and Indonesia. Indonesia invades East Timor. Ford nominates George W. Bush to head CIA.

1976

January

Public outrage at CIA misdeeds forces its revamping. President Ford and Vice-President Rockefeller take charge so that change will be limited.

March

Argentina's armed forces oust President Isabel Perón.

July

The U.S. celebrates its Bicentennial. Canadian Prime Minister Pierre Elliott Trudeau attends Economic Summit in Puerto Rico.

18 August

Operation Paul Bunyan takes place in order to reassure South Koreans and warn North Koreans.

2 November

Jimmy Carter defeats President Ford 297:240 in the Electoral College.

December

Bilateral Israeli–Egyptian peace talks begin in Jerusalem.

Secretary of State Kissinger goes to Cape Town for talks with South African Prime Minister Balthazar Johannes Vorster and Rhodesian Prime Minister Ian Smith.

1977

20 January

Jimmy Carter is inaugurated as 39th President of the United States.

INTRODUCTION

With 895 days in office (9 August 1974 to 20 January 1977), Gerald Ford had the second briefest presidency of the 20th century. (Warren Harding died 2 August 1923 on his 882nd day in office.) Yet, the world changed during those 895 days. President Ford's honeymoon with the American people ended abruptly 8 September 1974 when he granted an unconditional pardon to his disgraced predecessor, Richard Nixon, 37th President of the United States. Nevertheless, the world continued to turn, and the Ford administration took initiatives and reacted to events in significant ways. It restored the "special relationship" between the United States and the United Kingdom, which had suffered during Nixon's presidency. The restored relationship facilitated the Reagan administration's support in 1982 for the United Kingdom—a colonial power from Europe—in its war against another republic of the Americas, Argentina. What a contrast this was from the Venezuelan crisis of 1895, when Grover Cleveland's second administration (1893-1897) had chosen to side with another hemispheric nation against the British imperialists! Similarly, Ford's policies on Ireland allowed the Clinton administration (1993-2001) the necessary credibility to mediate the inter-Irish or Anglo-Irish dispute.

Early in 1974, while Nixon still occupied the White House, Portugal had a revolution which led to the termination of decades of authoritarian government at home and centuries of Portuguese colonialism on other continents. Secretary of State Kissinger feared that the arrival of democratic government in Portugal might pave the way for a Communist takeover in the NATO partner whose territory included the Azores, site of an ongoing U.S. military presence in the Azores.[1] The collapse of Portugal's overseas empire led to major changes in Asia and Africa. In East Timor, which Indonesian forces invaded within hours of the departure of President Ford and Secretary of State Kissinger, the consequences proved catastrophic. In Angola, the departure of the Portuguese opened the door to a Cuban presence, which in turn led to a war in Namibia between South African and Cuban forces. Chapter Three demonstrates that that conflict prolonged the adversarial relationship between Cuba and the United States. Independence for Mozambique altered the balance of power on the other side of Africa and convinced Kissinger that government by black Africans in Rhodesia was inevitable. If such was inevitable, Kissinger reasoned, the new government might be less radical and less hostile to U.S. values and interests if it arrived sooner rather than later. Accordingly, Kissinger tried to convince the European-settler government of Rhodesian Prime Minister Ian Smith and the government of Smith's South African allies to begin the transition process. To inaugurate that process, Kissinger went to South Africa in December 1976 for talks with South African President Balthazar Vorster and a meeting with Ian Smith. Chapters Two, Three, Seven and Eight deal with the Portuguese revolution and its consequences.

Ford restored good relations with Canadian Prime Minister Pierre Elliott Trudeau, whom President Nixon had called an "asshole." On the personal level, the two men went together on a ski vacation. More significantly, President Ford played a key role in expanding the annual Economic Summit of influential G–5 nations (France, West Germany, Japan, the United Kingdom, the United States) to become the G–7, with Canada and Italy as additional members.

President Ford's first full year in office, 1975, was one of important developments with long term consequences. The supposed "Peace with Honor" which the Nixon administration had concluded with the government of North Vietnam in 1973—and for which Henry Kissinger won a Nobel Peace Prize—collapsed. In the first four months of 1975, Communist forces occupied the whole of Vietnam, as well as neighbouring Laos and Cambodia. The Ford administration faced a terrible dilemma. President Ford's five immediate predecessors had committed U.S. money and troops to contain Communist forces there, and during the Johnson and Nixon administrations, 47,393 Americans had died in battle.[2] Were such efforts to be in vain? Would history identify Ford as the first U.S. president to lose a war? Would enemies and allies of the U.S. in other parts of Asia and perhaps elsewhere regard the U.S. as an unreliable ally? On the other hand, public opinion in the U.S. had become so hostile to a continued investment of blood and treasure in a seemingly lost cause (the Vietnam War) that it was politically impossible for the Ford administration to send military equipment for, let alone reintroduce combat forces to assist, the beleaguered Saigon-based government of South Vietnam. Chapter Five explains the way the Ford administration coped with this dilemma in the short term.

The most dangerous Asian enemy of the United States was Communist North Korea. Would the regime in Pyongyang assume that U.S. unwillingness to defend South Vietnam indicated an unwillingness to defend South Korea? Had the time come for Kim Il Sung's North Korean government to renew the war which it had launched in 1950 in order to unify the Korean peninsula? That war had ended in 1953 with a cease-fire agreement, and there had never been a peace treaty. Also, would the South Korean government led by President Park Chung Hee in Seoul decide that, given the apparent unreliability of the United States, South Korea should acquire nuclear weapons? Chapter Six explains the manner in which the Ford administration warned North Korea and reassured South Korea. In the process, President Ford managed to avoid both a new war in Asia and nuclear proliferation.

Another Ford decision of 1975 with long term consequences was the decision to proceed with the Helsinki Accord. The Soviet government (led by Leonid Brezhnev) and its Warsaw Pact allies were anxious to improve their credibility and to avoid conflict over boundary settlements imposed by Stalin's government at the end of World War II. To that end, they had been promoting an international conference on European Security and Co-operation. By the time President Ford assumed office, planning had advanced to a point where only a White House indifferent to foreign opinion would reverse course. Ford's was not that kind of White House. Accordingly, high level representatives of the United States, Canada, and all European governments except that of Albania met and concluded the Helsinki Accords. All parties would recognize each other's existing boundaries. This was a concession to the Warsaw Pact countries as it confirmed that Western signatories renounced force to challenge the controversial Oder-Neisse line (Poland's western border) or the absorption of the Baltic states (Estonia, Latvia, Lithuania) into the Soviet Union. In return, all parties agreed to establish fora to monitor human rights and to allow journalists from the other signatory countries to operate on their territory. Henceforth, journalists from West Germany could report events within Communist East Germany and provide an alternative source of credible news to that country's people, trapped as they were behind the Berlin Wall. At the time, the deal seemed so anemic that neither Ford nor Kissinger wanted to emphasize it. Almost 15 years later, however, when wittingly or unwittingly West German journalists had undermined the credibility of the East German government and forced it to open its Western borders, Ford sought to promote the Helsinki Accord as one of his achievements. A piece of the Berlin Wall sits on display at the Gerald Ford Presidential Museum in Grand Rapids, Michigan, as a monument to that triumph. Chapter Ten discusses the role of the Ford administration in reaching the Helsinki Accord.

In November 1975, Spain's perennial head of state, Generalíssimo Francisco Franco, died and the last authoritarian government in Western Europe began its peaceful transition to democracy. With the help of military personnel and equipment supplied by Hitler and Mussolini from 1936 to 1939, Franco had waged a successful rebellion against his country's democratic government. During World War II, Franco had sent Spanish soldiers known as the Blue Division to assist Hitler's forces in their invasion of the Soviet Union, and his diplomats had carried sensitive information to the Axis belligerents in their diplomatic pouches.[3] With the Axis defeat in 1945, Franco and his government became European pariahs, excluded from NATO and shunned by high-ranking officials who neither visited Spain nor invited leading Spanish officials to visit them. Successive U.S. governments lacked the same firm convictions and indeed welcomed the firmly anti-Communist Franco government as a partner in the containment of the Soviet Union. Despite the exclusion of Franco's Spain from NATO, the U.S. acquired air bases in Spain. Republican Presidents Eisenhower, Nixon, and Ford actually went to Madrid and met Generalíssimo Franco. Then Franco died, and King Juan Carlos—Franco's anointed successor—organized parliamentary elections. The structure of government in Spain would resemble that of the United Kingdom. The transition to democracy was peaceful and successful. Spain joined NATO in 1982 and the European Economic Community (now the European Union) in 1987. In 1975-1976, however, there was no guarantee of such happy developments. It is conceivable that Spaniards might have associated the U.S. with the repressive Franco régime and organized a less democratic and Western-friendly government of their own. Chapter Nine explains the way that President Ford responded to the transition.

In the case of Argentina, the trend went in the opposite direction. In 1976, that country's military rulers overthrew the constitutional president, Isabel Perón, and then tortured and killed political dissidents. The National Security Archive in Washington has found compelling evidence that Henry Kissinger was aware of these atrocities but decided that stability in Argentina must be a higher U.S. priority than human rights.[4]

President Ford, the 38th President of the United States, played some role in blazing the trail for President George H.W. Bush, the 41st President, and therefore, albeit unwittingly, for George W. Bush, the 43rd. In 1974 he appointed the elder Bush to represent U.S. interests in the People's Republic of China (PRC). From the Communist victory in 1949 until the Nixon administration (1969–1974), successive U.S. governments had maintained an adversarial relationship with the PRC. Indicative of that relationship were a trade embargo and a law which banned citizens of the United States from traveling there.[5] Then in 1972, President Nixon went to Beijing as a guest of PRC leader Mao Zedong and his government. Full diplomatic relations were not immediately possible because of U.S. commitments to the rival Chinese Nationalist government based in Taiwan, but it *was* possible to exchange diplomats whose *de facto* embassies in Washington and Beijing could handle most of the work usually managed by *de jure* embassies. From 1974 through 1975, George H.W. Bush was the quasi-U.S. ambassador at the quasi-U.S. embassy in Beijing.

In a conversation 25 October 1975 as Ford and Kissinger were discussing the forthcoming presidential visit to China, Ford asked Kissinger, "How is George Bush doing?"

Kissinger replied: "Magnificently. I am very, very impressed with him. I was not enthusiastic about his appointment, but he has grown into the job, and I think he will one day be a considerable national leader."

The President replied, "I agree with you about George. He is a fine man."[6]

Then, at the beginning of 1976, in the aftermath of the U.S. defeat in Vietnam and the scandals of the Nixon administration, the American public learned that in previous decades, the Central Intelligence Agency had tried to assassinate a series of foreign leaders. By 1976, many Americans had come to believe that assassination should not be a diplomatic tool and that unlike Mafia dons, U.S. presidents should not arrange the deaths of their opponents without a declaration of war. President Ford recalled the elder Bush from China and asked him to take command of the CIA. (See Chapter Eleven for an account of his performance in this role.) Before the Nixon administration, the elder Bush's public career had been brief and undistinguished—as a two-term Member of the House of Representatives who in 1964 had opposed President Lyndon Johnson's Civil Rights Bill. However, his father had been a Republican Senator from Connecticut, and during the Nixon years, George H.W. Bush served as Republican National Chairman and U.S. Ambassador to the United Nations. Ford kept Bush in the public eye with appointments as head of the U.S. mission in Beijing and then as Director of the CIA. The latter appointment was a risky one for someone with higher political ambitions, but in his case, it helped. It gave him a high profile, and this factor—along with his domicile in Texas (site of many votes in the Electoral College) and his success in the Republican primaries of 1980—rendered him a credible running mate for Ronald Reagan. Without the Ford appointments, it is inconceivable that Bush could have been a credible presidential candidate in 1980. It was from the vice-presidency that George H.W. Bush could launch his successful presidential bid in 1988. It is equally inconceivable that without the presidency of his father and namesake, George W. Bush could have become president in the aftermath of the election of 2000.

Two other prominent personalities involved in the U.S.-led war against Iraq which began in 2003 were Richard ("Dick") Cheney, by then Vice President of the United States, and Donald Rumsfeld, the Secretary of Defense. Both these men first became prominent under Gerald Ford. Rumsfeld served as President Ford's Chief of Staff; Cheney succeeded him in that position when Rumsfeld became Secretary of Defense, a position to which he would return during the presidency of George W. Bush (the junior Bush, 43rd President of the United States). In 2004, Ford honoured both men, saying "Dick and Don exemplify what public service is all about."[7] Many would disagree with this assessment, but for better or for worse, it was President Ford who made these men household names.

Finally, there were perennial controversies at the eastern end of the Mediterranean. During the final year of the Nixon administration, Henry Kissinger had served as an intermediary between the Egyptian and Israeli governments. The two protagonists agreed to talk to each other, and during the Ford presidency, there was progress which Jimmy Carter could build into the Camp David Accords. Additional significant developments, not always of a positive nature, occurred in Cyprus,[8] but the current crisis in Cyprus had begun late in the Nixon presidency and continues into the 21st century. As only a small part of an ongoing saga, Cypriot issues do not receive attention in these pages.

Several of President Ford's actions were and remain highly controversial. Without his pardon of President Nixon, he almost certainly would have avoided his narrow defeat in the presidential election of 1976. He undoubtedly bears some responsibility for the two Bush presidencies (the 41st and the 43rd), and many—particularly among those who live outside the United States—will not thank him for that. Arguably he prevented needed reforms in the CIA. On a more positive note, talks with Panama, which had begun following the riots of 9 January 1964 during Lyndon Johnson's term of office and continued during the Nixon presidency, scored a breakthrough when the Ford administration agreed that the U.S. would withdraw from the Canal Zone by the end of the century.[9] This cleared the way for the Carter-Torrijos Treaties, concluded in 1977 and ratified in 1978, which defused tensions on the Isthmus and provided for an orderly transition of the Panama Canal. It proved less than helpful in Ford's bid for re-election, but more than beneficial in the long run. On the other hand, especially as new documentation surfaces, Kissinger's record in Argentina is undoubtedly deplorable.

The initiatives in Portugal and Spain came from the Iberian peninsula, not from Washington. Without question, most of the credit for the successful transformation of Western Europe's last two authoritarian governments belongs to the Portuguese army officers who staged the 1974 coup against the Caetano régime and to King Juan Carlos of Spain. However, the Ford administration handled both situations with such aplomb that the U.S. managed to maintain both countries as allies and to keep the military bases on their territory. There are, nevertheless, strong grounds for criticizing the Ford administration's actions in the aftermath of the collapse of Portugal's overseas empire. East Timorese would pay a high price because of the determination of Ford and Kissinger to demonstrate to Indonesian leaders that the U.S. remained a worthy ally despite the defeat in Vietnam, and because of the U.S. desire for access to Indonesian oil. Congress, not the Ford administration, deserves any praise for avoidance of an even bloodier war in Angola, with U.S., South African and forces loyal to UNITA[10] leader Jonas Savimbi on one side, the MPLA[11] government of Angola and Cubans on the other.

In Rhodesia, which would become Zimbabwe in 1980 as the policies initiated by Kissinger at Cape Town in 1976 became reality, one tragedy has succeeded another. Ian Smith's willingness to accept a government led by black Africans came too late to prevent the election of one led by an insurgent leader, Robert Mugabe. First elected in 1980, Mugabe has remained in power through fair means and foul, intimidating his opponents and bribing his friends. As time passed, Mugabe has become increasingly arbitrary, and his policies have led to the economic collapse of his once prosperous nation. What had been the continent's bread basket became a famine zone, and highly skilled people—white and black—left the country in droves. One can hardly blame Ford and Kissinger for this. Until Mozambique achieved independence in 1975, Rhodesians had two outlets to the sea—through either Mozambique or South Africa. Smith did not become totally dependent on South Africa until then. Moreover, as long as Portugal controlled Mozambique, through which the mighty Zambezi River passes on its way to the Indian Ocean, forces loyal to Ian Smith's government could keep the insurgent forces of ZANU[12] and ZAPU[13] north of the Zambezi—inside Zambia and away from Rhodesia. Before 1976, it is unlikely that South African authorities would have heeded advice from North America to accept the inevitability of a black African government on their border and to engage in damage control.[14] Even if they had, as long as Mozambique remained Portuguese, Ian Smith and his ministers would probably have rejected such advice. Conceivably, Kissinger could have gone to Cape Town months earlier than he did, but it is doubtful whether any difference in what came later would have been more than marginal. In any event, Kissinger had other concerns in 1975, most of which arguably were higher U.S. priorities. Conceivably too, Kissinger might have continued to offer tacit support to Smith and his associates, but such continuity would have been short-lived. Jimmy Carter had already won the presidential election of 1976 and would certainly have switched course.

This book is the result of several years of teaching at Laurentian University in Sudbury, Ontario, Canada. Around the world, universities have a responsibility to create as well as to transmit knowledge, and professors engage in research. In 1993, I discovered the Gerald Ford Presidential Library (GFPL) while I was writing a book on U.S.–Canadian relations during the Cold War.[15] The GFPL offered a first class opportunity for fourth year undergraduates and graduate students at Laurentian. Located in Ann Arbor, Michigan, it was closer to Sudbury than any other presidential archive or the main U.S. Archives (the National Archives and Research Administration), situated in Washington, D.C. and College Park, Maryland. The GFPL offered a window on the world between 9 August 1974 and 20 January 1977, where students could examine the very documents produced by President Ford, members of his cabinet, and the White House staff. A great number of events which changed the world happened between those dates, and the process of declassification was ongoing. For various reasons, there have been more numerous studies of certain other presidents, and Laurentian students frequently found themselves using documents seen by no other historian. This gave them fresh information (and higher marks than those of students who repeated the findings of others). It also increased the level of excitement. Finally, the staff at the GFPL, especially Geir Gundersen, could not have been more helpful. Aware that trips—even from Sudbury to Ann Arbor —were costly, they extended the hours into evenings and Saturdays so that we could gather maximum material in minimum time. For this we are grateful.

Gerald Ford is the one President of the United States who established his archives and his museum in separate communities. The archives at Ann Arbor sit on the campus of the University of Michigan, President Ford's alma mater. The museum occupies grounds hours to the northwest in Grand Rapids, the community which sent Ford to the House of Representatives for decades before he became Vice-President of the United States in 1973. It was student Eric Hennigar who in 1998 suggested that rather than return directly to Sudbury, we should make a detour to Grand Rapids. The museum proved so fascinating and so informative about the way that the 38th president wants to be remembered that I have subsequently insisted that we must travel home that way.

By the time of my retirement 30 June 2005, ten Laurentian students had written strong essays about different aspects of Ford's presidency. (A eleventh had written a first class piece of work about Ford's role on the Warren Commission, which investigated President Kennedy's assassination, but he dealt with the period when the future president was still a member of the House of Representatives.) Collectively, the information from these ten essays seemed too significant to leave in the homes of the students and their friends, with a few copies on shelves at Laurentian University and the GFPL. One of the students who went to Ann Arbor in June 2001, Mark Gauthier, suggested that we collate, edit, and publish the essays—or at least their most important sections. In this way, the History Department could make a contribution to Laurentian's mandate to create knowledge and contribute it to the world. This book, with Mark's help, is the result.

Since Ford's inauguration as President 9 August 1974, there have been numerous books about his presidency. The first was that by J.F. terHorst, who served only one month as his press secretary and resigned in protest when President Ford pardoned his predecessor for any crimes which he might have committed while in office.[16] Once Ford was no longer President of the United States, significant books by other insiders appeared. Among these are the one by terHorst's successor, Ron Nessen, *It Sure Looks Different from the Inside*;[17] Ford's own *A Time to Heal*;[18] the mammoth tome by National Security Adviser/Secretary of State Henry Kissinger, *Years of Renewal*;[19] David Gergen's *Eyewitness to Power: The Essence of Leadership—Nixon to Clinton*.[20] While insiders' books are valuable as indicators of their authors' thoughts, they can be self-serving. Despite 1079 pages of text devoted almost exclusively to foreign relations, Kissinger says not a word about the horrors of East Timor. (See Chapter Seven.) Ford describes his visit to Indonesia as a complete success and does not mention that country's invasion of East Timor while he was flying between Jakarta and Hawaii.[21] Recently there have been some excellent monographs on the Ford presidency, most notably Jussi Hanhimäki's *The Flawed Architect: Henry Kissinger and American Foreign Policy*,[22] and Yanek Mieczkowski's *Gerald Ford and the Challenges of the 1970s*.[23] Unfortunately, the topic is so vast that no one author can cover everything that happened within a few hundred pages.

Nor is *895 Days* exhaustive. It omits discussions of the Ford administration's relations with Mexico, a neighbor whose multidimensional relationship affected U.S. trade, demographics, and water supply; and with Japan, despite the facts that Japan played a vital role as a U.S. trading partner and military ally. Australia, arguably the most loyal ally of the United States since 1945, appears only as a player in the East Timor story. Cyprus was a major concern to President Ford and Secretary Kissinger over the summer of 1974, but the crisis which the 38th President inherited—one of many since 1878, when Cyprus ceased to be part of the Ottoman Empire—had begun during the waning weeks of the Nixon administration and remained unresolved when Ford left office.[24] Quarrels between Christians and Muslims in Lebanon were another significant concern,[25] but the best efforts of the brightest people in Washington failed to prevent religious conflict in that country during the 1980s. The Vladivostok meeting of November 1974 between Ford and Kissinger on the one hand and their Soviet counterparts on the other set the stage for détente, a relaxation of tensions, but when Ronald Reagan challenged Ford for the Republican nomination in 1976 charging that he and Kissinger had been much too friendly to the Soviets, Ford himself soft-pedaled that aspect of his presidency.[26] These omissions are justifiable on the grounds that these cases represented continuity rather than change.

The thesis of this book is that developments which changed the world took place when President Ford led the United States. *895 Days* focuses on these. In some of these, he was an instigator. In some, he reacted to events precipitated by others. For better or worse, the world lives with the consequences of his administration, and it is appropriate that the world should understand what happened.

Graeme S. Mount, Sudbury, Ontario, July 2005

Notes

1. Henry Kissinger, *Years of Renewal* (New York: Simon and Schuster, 1999), pp. 626-634.
2. *World Almanac, 2005*, p. 227.3.
3. Provide full references from Graeme S. Mount, "Canada, Spain and Espionage during the Second World War," *Canadian Historical Review*, LXXIV, 4 (December 1993), pp. 566-575; Graeme S. Mount, *Canada's Enemies: Spies and Spying in the Peaceable Kingdom* (Toronto: Dundurn, 1993), pp. 94-105; and Graeme S. Mount, *Chile and the Nazis* (Montreal: Black Rose, 2002), pp. 92, 113, 146.
4. See articles from the *New York Times*, 27 Aug. 2004, p. A3, and 1 Oct. 2004, p. A9, as well as the books by Martin Edwin Andersen (*Dossier Secreto: Argentina's Desparacidos and the Myth of the Dirty War* [Boulder, Colorado: Westview Press, 1993]; and Dinges, *The Condor Years* (New York: New Press, 2004), pp. 202-205, 252.
5. Jeffrey A. Engel, "Of Fat and Thin Communists: Diplomacy and Philosophy in Western Economic Warfare Strategies toward China (and Tyrants Broadly)," *Diplomatic History*, XXIX, 3 (June 2005), pp. 445-474.
6. National Security Adviser: MEMORANDA OF CONVERSATIONS, 1973-1977, Box 16, Folder: October 25, 1975–Ford, Kissinger, Gerald Ford President Library, Ann Arbor, Michigan. Cited hereafter as GFPL.
7. *News from the Ford: The Newsletter of the Gerald Ford Foundation* (December 2004), p. 1.
8. John Robert Greene, *The Presidency of Gerald Ford* (Lawrence, Kansas: University Press of Kansas, 1995), pp. 117-129.
9. Stephen J. Randall and Graeme S. Mount, *The Caribbean Basin: An International History* (London and New York: Routledge, 1998), p. 128.
10. UNITA is the Portuguese acronym for National Union for the Total Independence of Angola.
11. MPLA is the Portuguese acronym for Popular Movement for the Liberation of Angola.
12. The acronym for Zimbabwe African National Union.
13. The acronym for Zimbabwe African People's Union.
14. The consensus among historians is that until 1975-1976, U.S. governments, like that of Ronald Reagan at a later date, identified with the anti-Communist Euro-African governments in the southern part of the continent. See Thomas Borstelmann, "Squeezing White Supremacy," *Diplomatic History*, XXIX, 3 (June 2005), pp. 569-572.
15. Edelgard E. Mahant and Graeme S. Mount, *Invisible and Inaudible in Washington* (Vancouver: UBC Press, 1999).
16. J.F. terHorst, *Gerald Ford and the Future of the Presidency* (New York: Third Press, 1974).
17. Ron Nessen, *It Sure Looks Different from the Inside* (New York: Playboy Press, 1978).
18. Gerald R. Ford, *A Time to Heal: The Autobiography of Gerald R. Ford* (New York: Harper and Row, 1979).
19. Henry Kissinger, *Years of Renewal* (New York: Simon and Schuster, 1999).
20. David Gergen, *Eyewitness to Power: The Essence of Leadership—Nixon to Clinton* (New York: Touchstone [Simon and Schuster]), 2000.
21. Ford, p. 337.
22. Jussi Hanhimäki, *The Flawed Architect: Henry Kissinger and American Foreign Policy* (New York: Oxford University Press, 2004).
23. Yanek Mieczkowski, *Gerald Ford and the Challenges of the 1970s* (Lexington: University of Kentucky Press, 2005).
24. Ford, pp. 137, 199, 244, 285, 288; Kissinger, *Years of Renewal*, pp. 192-237, and elsewhere.
25. Ford, p. 390; Kissinger, pp. 1020-1027, and elsewhere.
26. Mieczkowski, p. 288.

ACKNOWLEDGEMENTS

The authors wish to express their appreciation to the following Laurentian University students who visited the Gerald Ford Presidential Library and the Gerald Ford Presidential Museum, poured over documents, and drafted essays on important aspects of the Ford presidency. Without their assistance, this book could not have been ready in twice the time: Eric Hennigar (for Chapter Five); David Lefebvre (for Chapter Six); John Beech (for Chapter Eight); Sean Lougheed (for Chapter Nine); Constance Rossi (for Chapter Ten); Rebecca Vergunst (for Chapter Eleven); Trevor Mouhan (for Chapter Twelve); Chris Bartman and Tim Greenough (for Chapter Thirteen); and Matt Tessaro (for Chapter Fourteen).

Thanks also go to Laurentian University (especially Dieter Buse, Rose-May Démoré, and Pierre Simoni), the staff at the Gerald Ford Presidential Library (especially archivist Geir Gundersen), the Sudbury Catholic School Board (which provided release time so that Mark Gauthier could make a research trip to Michigan) and our wives, Joan and Cheryl. Thanks also go to Dimitri Roussopoulos and to Linda Barton of Black Rose Books for their confidence in us, their editing skills, and for their artistic sense which always make the finished product so pleasing to the eye.

Graeme S. Mount
Mark Gauthier
September 2005

Chapter One

THE FORD ADMINISTRATION
AND THE "SPECIAL" U.S.-UK RELATIONSHIP

Residents of several of the world's nations like to think that their country has a "special relationship" with the United States. Many Canadians hold that opinion, and to some extent it is a valid one. Canadians can travel to the United States more easily, with less red tape, than anyone else, and NAFTA allows for freer movement of goods and people. However, *Invisible and Inaudible in Washington* shows that U.S. authorities pay little attention to the opinions of their Canadian counterparts, especially when there is a difference of opinion.[1] Also, as any Canadian ten years old or more must now know, when President George W. Bush addressed a joint session of Congress 20 September 2001 to discuss the 11 September terrorist attacks, he ignored Canada completely—despite the hospitality which Canadians from Newfoundland to the Yukon had extended to thousands of stranded U.S.-bound passengers whose commercial flights had landed unexpectedly at Canadian airports, where they remained several days. With British Prime Minister Tony Blair watching from the gallery, Bush said, "America has no truer friend than Great Britain." Bush's listeners responded with a standing ovation.

There are other candidates for the "special relationship." Many Australians have regarded their country as the principal U.S. outpost in the Pacific, one with a "special relationship." In November 1996, when President Clinton paid a visit—the third president to do so (after Lyndon Johnson and George Bush)—he referred to the "unique partnership Australia and the U.S. have enjoyed."[2] In an op-ed column 29 November 1996, columnist Frank Moorehouse of *The Australian* discussed Australia's "special relationship," which dated from Australian-U.S. co-operation during World War II. Undoubtedly, Israelis, South Koreans, Japanese, Mexicans and others all can make the case that *they* have a special relationship with the United States. When President George W. Bush visited Poland in June 2001, a CBC commentator referred to the "special relationship" between Poland and the United States, where so many citizens of Polish extraction live.[3]

When Americans mention the words "special relationship," they invariably refer to the relationship between the United States and the United Kingdom. For his part, Henry Kissinger, National Security Adviser and Secretary of State to President Richard Nixon (1969-1974), spoke of the "special relationship" between the U.S. and the United Kingdom.[4] Another to hold that opinion was General Wesley Clark, NATO's commander-in-chief during the Kosovo War of 1999.[5] In a recent edition of the prestigious journal *Foreign Affairs*, commentator William Wallace referred to the United Kingdom as "traditionally America's most loyal European ally."[6] Almost simultaneously, in *Diplomatic History*, Warren F. Kimball saw World War II as the origin of the "special relationship" between the United States and the United Kingdom.[7] Then, in July 2001, as he made the first trip of his lifetime to the United Kingdom, President Bush himself referred to the "special relationship" between the United States and the United Kingdom.[8]

The U.S.-UK "special relationship" has nevertheless had its ups and downs. Whatever "special relationship" there has been began in 1941, as President Franklin Roosevelt and Prime Minister Winston Churchill held the first of several face-to-face meetings to plan the next stage of World War II. It also helped that while Americans and Britons co-operated militarily during World War II and the Cold War, Ireland—whose expatriates had had a powerful lobby within the United States—remained neutral. Such neutrality cost Irish-Americans dearly in terms of influence. The bilateral Anglo-American relationship hit a setback in 1956 when President Eisenhower and Secretary of State John Foster Dulles reneged on a promised Anglo-American loan to Egypt for building the Aswan Dam without consulting the British government, which then had to live with the consequences. Egyptian President Gamal Abdul Nasser responded with the nationalization of the Suez Canal, whose profits he could then use to finance the dam. Most of the Suez Canal Company's shareholders lived in Great Britain or France, and the British and French governments also feared the Nasser would jeopardize their countries' traffic through the Suez Canal, a transportation artery vital to their national economies. Without informing Eisenhower and Dulles, the UK and France joined Israel in an invasion of Egypt, and Eisenhower and Dulles, in turn, forced them to withdraw. British Prime Minister Sir Anthony Eden was bitter.[9]

The successors to Eisenhower and Eden, John Kennedy and Harold Macmillan, had a happier relationship. Kennedy even made time during the Cuban Missile Crisis for nightly telephone discussions with Macmillan[10]—at a time when he was not on speaking terms with Canada's John Diefenbaker.[11] The British refusal to send combat forces to Vietnam did not help the relationship,[12] which arguably did not fully recover until the era of Ronald Reagan and Margaret Thatcher in the 1980s.[13] Moreover, according to Kissinger, President Nixon and British Prime Minister Edward Heath, heartily disliked each other.[14] Reagan's successors —George H.W. Bush, Bill Clinton, and George W. Bush—have benefited from that "special relationship." Writing in 1999, Henry Kissinger noted that

> ...the British contingent in the 1991 Gulf War was the largest and most effective among the allies; similarly, Britain was the first NATO country to dispatch land forces to Bosnia in 1993.[15]

Others stress the "special relationship," which they would more appropriately label "complicity" between the United States and the United Kingdom, during the NATO bombing campaign of 1999 over Serbia and Kosovo.[16] The "special relationship" between British Prime Minister Tony Blair and the forty-third President of the United States, George W. Bush, was a major factor in making the United Kingdom Bush's most important ally when he invaded Iraq in 2003.

The "special relationship" worked in both directions. A British writer might have expressed appreciation for assistance rendered by the United States during the Falklands War of 1982, despite the Reagan administration's fond hopes for a close relationship with Argentina's military rulers and its support for the Monroe Doctrine. (British possession of the Falklands dates from 1833, ten years *after* proclamation of the Monroe Doctrine.)

This chapter demonstrates that Great Britain *did* enjoy a "special relationship" with the administration of Gerald Ford (9 August 1974 to 20 January 1977). The United Kingdom saw itself as a junior partner, a role the Ford administration was happy to acknowledge, but in certain areas, Gerald Ford's administration respected British opinions and policies and took political and diplomatic risks to help America's European ally. The British also took risks on behalf of the United States. Both parties benefited from this arrangement.

Appearances

Superficially, it would appear that Secretary of State Kissinger did not want to emphasize any "special relationship" with the United Kingdom. The first high level British visitor after President Ford's inauguration to go to the White House was Edward Heath, whom Kissinger considered guilty of a "passionate Eurocentrism." Kissinger later wrote of the man who had been British Prime Minister from June 1970 to March 1974:

> He was the only British leader I encountered who not only failed to cultivate the "special relationship" with the United States but actively sought to downgrade it and to give Europe pride of place in British policy. All of this made for an unprecedented period of strain in Anglo-American relations.[17]

Denis Clift of the National Security Council—headed by Kissinger until 3 November 1975—expressed concern about the timing of Kissinger's meeting with Heath in September 1974, shortly before the second British general election of that year. (No party had won a majority in the March 1974 election. Heath's Conservative government resigned, to be replaced by a Labour cabinet led by former Prime Minister Harold Wilson [1964-1970]. The Labour Party would win a majority in the election of 10 October 1974, but this was uncertain at the time of Heath's visit.) Accordingly, Clift prepared a hypothetical question along with a hypothetical answer for the White House press office:

> Q: Isn't it a bit strange for the President to be meeting with the Leader of the Opposition on the eve of the British General Elections?
>
> A: I would not relate this meeting in any way to domestic political events in Great Britain. It is an informal meeting on the occasion of Mr. Heath's private visit to the United States. (The UK Govt was informed of the meeting and had no objection.) As I believe you know, he came here to address the Council on Foreign Relations in New York on September 9.[18]

Later that same month (September 1974), British Foreign Secretary James Callaghan also visited President Ford at the White House, and the White House went out of its way to minimize any "special relationship." A statement prepared for White House Press Secretary Ron Nessen included the following hypothetical questions and possible answers:

Q: Should the President's meeting with Foreign Minister Callaghan be viewed as an expression of support for the Labor Party in the forth-coming British election?

A: I would not relate this meeting in any way to domestic politi-cal events in Great Britain. As the President's schedule suggests, he is meeting with a number of foreign leaders currently in the U.S. to at-tend the UN General Assembly session. The President's meeting with the Foreign Minister took place in that context and reflects the Presi-dent's commitment to close and continuing consultations with the leaders of Western Europe. Additionally, you may recall that the Presi-dent met with Mr. Edward Heath only two weeks ago.

Q: Whatever became of the "special relationship" between the United States and the United Kingdom?

A: As a result of many years of close ties and friendship, both countries are strong friends and allies. The importance of this relation-ship has not been diminished by efforts to promote a strong sense of cooperation and partnership among the Atlantic Alliance.[19]

The White House Press Secretary's Office was being cautious. A denial of the "special relationship" might have offended the British on the eve of their par-liamentary election, and it might have hurt the credibility of the White House, still reeling from the Watergate scandal, the resignation of Richard Nixon, and President Ford's pardon of his predecessor. Yet a confirmation could hardly have enhanced U.S. relations with other important European and Asian allies. In his memoirs, where he could be more candid, Henry Kissinger traced the origins of the "special relationship" to Anglo-American co-operation in the two world wars, then elaborated:

The special relationship could not have lasted so long…but for joint ef-forts to meld British and American interests. Had Britain passively ac-ceded to America's preferences, the special relationship would have soon degenerated into demoralizing dependence and fallen into disre-pair. A succession of British governments of both parties continued the close ties as American leaders, also of both parties, came to appreci-ate the combination of dignity and competence with which Britain contributed to the common enterprise, both in the sophistication of British diplomacy and the seriousness of the British military effort.[20]

Undoubtedly, said Kissinger, the changes of leadership, from Nixon to Ford and from Heath to Wilson, contributed to the restoration of that "special relationship."[21]

Queen Elizabeth's Bicentennial Visit to Washington

In 1976, Americans celebrated the bicentennial of their Declaration of Independence, the date of their nation's birth. That same Declaration of Independence tabulated a long list of wrongful actions of the British king, George III, who—according to the Declaration—had provoked the rebellion against his "misrule." George III was the great-great-great-great-grandfather of Queen Elizabeth II.

After confrontations with Hitler and Stalin, Americans concluded that George III was not really so bad after all. Moreover, any shortcomings on his part were hardly the fault of his direct descendant, the Queen. Not only would she be an honoured guest at the bicentennial celebrations; she would be central to the occasion. 4 July 1976, the anniversary of the signing of the Declaration of Independence, would be the climax of the bicentennial celebrations, and the Queen would arrive two days later and remain until the 11th. No other foreign head of state would have such a high profile.

Even as Americans celebrated a successful rebellion against British rule, the United States and the United Kingdom were consolidating a "special relationship!" To appreciate how unusual, perhaps unique, this was, consider possible parallels. As this book goes to press, the bicentennial of the Battle of Trafalgar (21 October 1805) is approaching. It does not appear likely that the British government will invite President Jacques Chirac of France to stand beneath Admiral Nelson's column in Trafalgar Square. Nor does it appear likely that the French President would attend even if invited to London for such a celebration. Also, how probable is participation of the German President in 2017, when the Canadian Armed Forces mark the centennial of the Battle of Vimy Ridge? The Queen's visit to Washington surely acknowledged the Anglo-American "special relationship."

Anglo-American Summit Meetings during the Ford Presidency

Early in 1975, after winning a majority in the second parliamentary elections of 1974, British Prime Minister Wilson visited the White House.[22] One background paper advised President Ford that Wilson would be going to Moscow in mid-February to discuss "the principles of non-proliferation." As loyal partners, said the memo writer, the British "wish to discuss the working of the text with us before giving it to the Russians." There were similar background papers on U.S. beef and grain exports to the European Community.[23] Evidently the Ford administration saw the UK as an intermediary between itself and other parts of the world. However, it does not appear that Ford and Wilson became particularly friendly during the White House visit. Two months later, when he decided to resign as British Prime Minister, Wilson notified the press before he advised President Ford of his intentions.[24]

Areas where the "Special Relationship" Really Made a Difference

Hong Kong and the United States:

In Hong Kong, British authorities took risks on behalf of the United States.

Hong Kong became a British colony in 1843 and remained one until its handover to the People's Republic of China (PRC) in 1997. After Mao Zedong's victory in 1949, it served as the U.S. window on the PRC,[25] which the United States treated as a moral pariah and with which the United States lacked even informal diplomatic relations until President Nixon's visit to Beijing in 1972. The Nixon administration arranged a liaison office in Beijing, but it maintained formal diplomatic relations with the Taiwan-based Republic of China (ROC). The U.S. embassy operated in Taipei, the ROC capital. This arrangement remained in place throughout the Ford presidency and until the Carter administration negotiated formal diplomatic relations with the PRC in 1979.

There was a certain element of risk in this for British interests. The U.S. consulate in Hong Kong was the largest consulate anywhere in the world,[26] and the Chinese must have noticed and had some suspicions. Indeed, some U.S. actions were sufficiently provocative that British authorities requested greater subtlety.[27] During China's "Cultural Revolution" of the mid-1960s, the behaviour of Mao's Red Guards was quite irrational and might easily have led to an invasion of Hong Kong. Mao, who had unleashed the Red Guards and the Cultural Revolution, was still head of state and head of government in the PRC. Yet, because of the "special relationship," U.S. intelligence officers co-operated effectively with their British hosts in Hong Kong.

Despite the presence of a U.S. Liaison Office in Beijing, headed for several months by a future U.S. president, George H.W. Bush, the U.S. consulate in Hong Kong continued to gather information on the People's Republic of China.[28] The Anglo-American "special relationship" also had an economic dimension. On 26 March 1975, L. William Seidman, Assistant to President Ford for Economic

Affairs, wrote a letter of appreciation to the British ambassador in Washington, Sir Peter Ramsbotham:

> Dear Mr. Ambassador:
>
> The importance which the British Embassy attaches to the inclusion of Hong Kong as a beneficiary of the United States Generalized System of Preferences is recognized and understood…[29]

Northern Ireland:

As British authorities accepted risks on behalf of the United States in Hong Kong, the Ford administration took risks on behalf of its British ally in Northern Ireland and British Honduras.

Irish hatred of Great Britain has been passionate for centuries, but it did not have much impact on U.S.-UK relations until the aftermath of the Civil War. For the next few years, refugees from the Irish famine and their children, many of whom had military experience in the Northern (Union or U.S.) forces, entered the Fenian Brotherhood and launched bloody, destructive attacks upon British North America.[30] There was a resurgence of such violence during the Boer War (1899-1902),[31] and for generations no president, especially a Democrat, could ignore the power of the Irish-American lobby. Angry that subject peoples of the Habsburg and Ottoman Empires could achieve independence after World War I while Ireland would remain part of the United Kingdom, Irish Americans lobbied against the Treaty of Versailles and the League of Nations, Article X of whose charter appeared to guarantee the inviolability of existing borders. It was to placate Irish-American voters that President Franklin Roosevelt sent Joseph Kennedy, whose advice to appease Adolf Hitler Roosevelt ignored or rejected, as U.S. Ambassador to the United Kingdom.[32] However, Irish neutrality during World War II discredited the Dublin government and its American supporters,[33] and even under presidents of Irish extraction such as John Kennedy and Ronald Reagan, Irish influence has subsequently been marginal. Such was clearly the case during Gerald Ford's presidency.

In 1969, violence between the "Green" Roman Catholic Irish and the "Orange" Protestant Irish resumed in Northern Ireland, six counties of Ulster which remained part of the United Kingdom after the partition of 1920. Members of the Ancient Order of Hibernians (AOH), a Green Irish association, wrote to President Ford from August 1974 until the eve of the presidential election campaign in 1976. They wrote from California, Michigan, Minnesota, and New York.[34] President Ford's correspondence gives no indication that Irish-Americans other than members of the AOH gave much thought to the problems of Northern Ireland, and there were other considerations. The UK belonged to NATO, and the Irish Republic did not. The Ford administration was Republican, and Roman Catholics traditionally supported Democrats. Above all, much of the AOH rhetoric was shrill and misleading, even inaccurate. For example, Sean Walsh from the AOH branch in St. Louis, Missouri attributed the victories of George Washington to his Irish combat forces. "His Army was composed of one-third Irishmen and, proportionately, their blood was spilled in torrents."[35] Presumably, some White House official with a knowledge of U.S. history would have known that Washington's victories preceded the Irish famine and the massive Irish Roman Catholic migration to America by more than half a century. Most Irish supporters of Washington were Protestants. John Bownes of New York summarized British alleged misrule in Northern Ireland:

> Men are still taken from their homes and murdered in cold blood by British soldiers while on the other hand, a policy of interment [sic] without trial is vigorously pursued. Thus, thousands of children have not seen their fathers in years. Meanwhile, unionist [pro-British] gangs are free to bomb and kill.[36]

Jim McGovern of St. Paul, Minnesota, approached culpability of treason when he warned President Ford against allowing the CIA to monitor activities of the Irish Republican Army or the even more violent Provisional IRA:

> God forbid, but frankly if there ever developed an altercation between CIA people and the Provisional IRA, there is no doubt where my sympathies would lie. They wouldn't be with the CIA.[37]

Few elected politicians seemed to approach the Ford White House to discuss Northern Ireland. McGovern sent letters to his states' two senators (Hubert Humphrey and Walter Mondale), Henry Kissinger, and four Representatives. Of these, only Representative Albert Quie bothered to reply.[38] New York Senator James Buckley, like Ford a Republican, wrote a much more restrained letter suggesting that the United States government use its "good offices" to mediate the conflict.[39]

There were a standard procedure and a standard reply for dealing with these letters from the Ancient Order of Hibernians. There is no evidence that anyone ever showed them to President Ford himself. Invariably, somebody on his staff would politely thank the letter writer for making the effort to write and then would say:

The situation in Northern Ireland distresses all men of good will every-where. The United States has avoided direct involvement, our position being that if the parties directly involved agreed there is anything the U.S. could usefully do, we would consider it, but that in the absence of such a request any involvement on our part would be inappropriate and counterproductive.

The problems of Northern Ireland affect two of the United States' closest friends, the British and the Irish. We are hopeful that their Governments will continue to consult with each other in their efforts to find a solution which will put Northern Ireland on the road to peace with justice.[40]

Official U.S. neutrality in the Northern Ireland conflict undoubtedly helped the British cause, as the British army and the British government were unquestionably more powerful than the IRA or any other terrorist organization. (They were also more powerful than the army or government of the Irish Republic, which did *not* support the IRA.) Brent Scowcroft, who replaced Kissinger as National Security Adviser to President Ford 3 November 1975, realized the danger to American interests which IRA activity could cause. In a memo written in January 1976, Scowcroft noted the death of ten Protestants in Northern Ireland by an IRA attack of 5 January 1976. "Highly publicized police reports," he said indicated that sympathizers within the United States had purchased those weapons for the IRA. Indeed, Scowcroft noted, Prime Minister Wilson had estimated that perhaps 85 per cent of all weapons reaching the IRA originated in the United States. Scowcroft called for an investigation by the Justice Department.[41]

Compare the concern of General Scowcroft and the professed neutrality of the Ford administration with U.S. actions elsewhere in comparable situations. The Eisenhower and Kennedy administrations failed to support France, like the UK a NATO ally, against the Front de Libération Nationale in Algeria, which until 1962 was at least as much a part of France as Northern Ireland was of the United Kingdom. Nor was there a serious suggestion to partition Algeria so that enclaves where French people were a majority could remain outside Algeria the way Protestant enclaves in Northern Ireland remain outside the Irish Republic or the Spanish North African enclaves of Ceuta and Melilla remain outside Morocco. The Kennedy administration was less than tolerant of another NATO ally, the Netherlands, which justified continuing Dutch sovereignty in Western New Guinea on the grounds that its people were not related to Indonesians. There are sound reasons as to why at least a part of Northern Ireland should remain out-side the Irish Republic, but President Ford might have won votes among New York State's Irish American community if he had shown more sympathy for the perspective of the Ancient Order of Hibernians. Those votes could have helped him to win New York in the 1976 presidential election, and a Ford victory in New York would have given him, not Jimmy Carter, the majority in the Elec-toral College. Official U.S. neutrality in Northern Ireland was an indication of the "special relationship" between the United Kingdom and the United States, in defiance of any efforts from the Ancient Order of Hibernians.

Central America:

British Honduras, like Northern Ireland, was a place where the Ford administra-tion soft-pedalled longstanding American principles for the sake of the An-glo-American "special relationship."

No longer as powerful as it had once been, in 1763 Spain ceded timber rights to British subjects near what would become the settlement of Belize. Spain did not cede sovereignty. After independence more than half a century later, Guatemala claimed that as heir of Spain, *it* had sovereignty over Belize. British authorities disputed that. As far as they were concerned, Guatemala could not claim authority which Spain had ceded before independence. The presence of British lumberjacks and their right to dispose of the area's most precious re-source meant that Great Britain had control, which evolved into sovereignty.

In 1859, Guatemalan and British diplomats negotiated a settlement. Great Britain would build a highway from the Caribbean coast to Guatemala City if Guatemala would recognize British sovereignty in the Belize area. (The British called their colony there "British Honduras.") However, when Guatemalan au-thorities took what seemed an unreasonably long period of time to approve the agreement, the British withdrew their offer. The dispute continued until 1981, more than four years after President Ford's departure from the White House. Most residents of British Honduras had as little desire to be part of Guatemala as Northern Ireland's Protestants had to be part of the Irish Republic, but the gov-ernment of Guatemala remained adamant. "Belice es de Guatemala!" ("Belize be-longs to Guatemala!") said signs throughout Guatemala, and the British army remained in British Honduras to protect the colonists from a Guatemalan mili-tary invasion. In an age when Great Britain was granting independence to her other Caribbean possessions, British Honduras remained a British colony out of fear of what Guatemala might do to a newly independent country.

The United States might well have sided with Guatemala in this dispute. The Annual Message of President James Monroe, delivered to Congress in December 1823, included what became known as "the Monroe Doctrine," a warning against the creation of new European colonies in the Western Hemisphere. British Honduras was not a "new" colony, created after 1823, although it did expand southward from the Sibún River to the Sarstoon. Although the status of the Monroe Doctrine was questionable under international law, by the end of the nineteenth century and throughout the twentieth, successive U.S. governments took it seriously. Understandably, the administration of Franklin Roosevelt did not want Hitler's Germany to annex Caribbean islands owned by such defeated nations as France or the Netherlands. Presidents from Eisenhower onward did not welcome a Soviet presence in Cuba. The Monroe Doctrine even provided an argument to exclude Canadian influences in Greenland and St. Pierre et Miquelon during World War II. Canadians might be British surrogates, and Dutch and French possessions should not become British ones. In British Honduras, however, the Monroe Doctrine did not seem to matter.

Also, when Guatemala raised the issue of British Honduras at the United Nations, its only consistent supporter was Israel. That in itself need not have been a deterrent. The United States is often Israel's only supporter in the United Nations General Assembly and on the Security Council. From Warren Harding, who repudiated the Treaty of Versailles in 1921, to George W. Bush, who repudiated the Treaty of Kyoto in 2001, U.S. governments have been willing to champion causes rejected by the rest of the world and to oppose those favoured by almost everybody else.

Gerald Ford's counterpart in Guatemala was Kjel Laugerud, and documents declassified in November 2000 indicate that President Laugerud (1974–1978) was willing to make concessions which his predecessors had refused. On 9 October 1975, the Guatemalan ambassador in Washington, Julio Asensio, delivered a note regarding Guatemala's claims to Belize, asking for U.S. support in the United Nations General Assembly on the matter, and indicating "that Guatemala would be willing to accept less than the whole territory of Belize [British Honduras] in a settlement agreement with the British." Guatemala, indicated Ambassador Asensio, might be willing to cede control of the area north of the Sibún, and he asked for Kissinger's assistance not as an arbitrator or a mediator but as an intermediary. Guatemalan authorities would be grateful if Kissinger would forward the proposal to the British government. Kissinger agreed to do so when he saw Foreign Secretary Callaghan in the near future.

Asensio explained to Kissinger that the situation was becoming desperate. British Honduras might declare its independence as "Belize," and this Guatemala could not accept without boundary changes. Guatemala's Caribbean coastline at the moment was simply too small. If Belize became independent, Guatemala would go to war. The Guatemalan army thought that it could deal with British forces, although it feared what might happen if Belizean authorities also invited the Cuban army to assist.[42]

One month later, U.S. Ambassador Francis E. Meloy in Guatemala City had a face to face meeting with President Laugerud. The President detailed the location of the Guatemalan army's troops and weapons. After the British reinforced their military presence in the colony, President Laugerud told Ambassador Meloy, he deliberately waited two weeks before reinforcing the adjacent Guatemalan province of Petén in order not to appear rash. Laugerud said that he had removed troops from the border area in order to lessen the possibility of conflict and promised "that he will not order an attack or any other military action against Belize as long as there remains the slightest possibility of a negotiated solution to the problem." According to Meloy, Laugerud faced a political problem at home. The United Nations General Assembly was almost certain to support Great Britain against Guatemala. Unless British authorities cushioned the blow with an offer to negotiate, he would face a serious challenge from Guatemalan public opinion and "hotheads" in the Guatemalan armed forces, who would demand action.[43]

Another "hothead," it would appear, was the Guatemalan Vice-President, Mario Sandoval, who resorted to damagoguery. On 8 December 1975, Laugerud told Meloy that Sandoval had a number of ideas, none of which he was keeping to himself. These included Guatemala's withdrawal from the United Nations and the seizure of any property owned by British subjects. Meloy commented that these ideas were what one might expect from Idi Amin, the notorious dictator of Uganda, and Laugerud agreed. Israel, added Laugerud, had received worse treatment in the United Nations General Assembly than had Guatemala, but it had not withdrawn.

For his part, Meloy thought that Laugerud too had made some rather irresponsible statements, including one that "anyone opposing Guatemala's claim to Belize is a traitor." Laugerud tried to explain the context of that remark. Again Laugerud warned that his public statements had to

...take into account the extremists. At the time a settlement is reached, "I will be accused of selling out and dismembering the national territory. But I will have to face that when the time comes."[44]

On 24 February 1976, Kissinger and Guatemalan Foreign Minister Adolfo Molina discussed Belize as they flew together from San Jose, Costa Rica, to the Guatemalan capital. Molina "stressed Guatemala's conviction that it was entitled to some compensation for UK failure to fulfil its obligations under the 1859 treaty." When Kissinger asked Molina to suggest a possible solution, the latter offered three options: (a) a Puerto Rican-type constitutional arrangement, whereby Guatemala would have sovereignty in Belize but Belize would have internal self-government; (b) cession of land from British Honduras to Guatemala in return for Belizean independence; (c) indefinite procrastination and postponement. Molina thought that his country's strongest asset was the British desire to withdraw from the area. Kissinger said that the United States would not act as a mediator but would "speak to the British and urge them to seek a solution that would be mutually acceptable."[45]

On the ground that same day, President Laugerud and Kissinger met in Guatemala City. Again Laugerud explained his views on Belize and forecast Guatemalan behaviour in the event that it achieved independence without an Anglo-Guatemalan accord. Talks on such an accord, he hoped, might begin in March. Kissinger warned Laugerud not to hurry. Negotiations were unlikely to succeed, he said, and postponement was preferable to failure. Kissinger also warned that he would "not try to force the UK to do anything" and that the U.S. would not "mediate the dispute." Laugerud admitted that he did not expect to win all the concessions he was demanding from the British but justified his position as "a good bargaining position."[46]

As in the case of Northern Ireland, U.S. neutrality favoured the British. Despite Ambassador Asensio's assertion that the Guatemalan army had no fear of the British, it is most unlikely that Guatemala could have won any military confrontation. Six years later the British armed forces defeated the armed forces of a much more powerful Latin American nation, Argentina, in the Falkland Islands.[47] Moreover, recovery of the Falklands in 1982 required offensive action, after an initially successful Argentine invasion of the islands. Holding British Honduras would have been a defensive operation, less difficult in every respect. In turn, the Anglo-Guatemalan dispute continued into the Reagan presidency, and when settlement came, it came largely on British terms. British Honduras transferred some territorial waters but no land to Guatemala.[48]

Other Issues of Empire

Two other legacies of the imperial era, Gibraltar and Rhodesia, offer examples of instances where U.S. and British interests coincided or where the Ford administration silently acquiesced in a reality of the British Empire. Since 1965, successive British governments had been coping with a rebellion in Rhodesia, whose Prime Minister, Ian Smith, had issued a Unilateral Declaration of Independence. Smith and his supporters favoured government dominated by competent Europeans to one dominated by the black African majority. Kissinger ignored the problem until 1976, by which time Angola and Mozambique had achieved independence from Portugal, Cuban forces had gone to fight in Angola, and the independence of Mozambique had altered the military balance of power in southern Africa. If black African government in Rhodesia was inevitable, thought Kissinger, it should come sooner rather than later. The longer the fighting between Rhodesian and African armies lasted, the greater the involvement of Cubans was likely to be. Kissinger persuaded South African Prime Minister Balthazar John Vorster to withdraw support from Smith, whose government resigned in 1979. This was a case where British and American interests coincided. Only when Rhodesia became a Cold War issue, when Fidel Castro sent combat forces to Southern Africa, did Henry Kissinger exhibit much interest.[49] Even then, Rhodesia became African-ruled Zimbabwe only after the newly elected British Prime Minister, Margaret Thatcher, took charge of negotiations in 1979.

Great Britain had occupied Gibraltar since the 1713 Treaty of Utrecht. During the Cold War, Spain's head of state, Francisco Franco, granted military bases to the United States. In order to pressure British withdrawal from Gibraltar, Franco sealed its border with Spain. Franco died in November, 1975, during the Ford presidency, and Spain began its transition, under the tutelage of King Juan Carlos, to democracy and into NATO. Documents at the Gerald Ford Library give no indication that anyone in the Ford administration gave any thought to the status of Gibraltar.

Francisco Franco of Spain, who desperately wanted to reclaim Gibraltar, died in November 1975, and despite the presence of U.S. military bases in Spain, in the absence of immediate pressure to do otherwise, the administration appears to have taken a "wait and see" attitude before discussing Gibraltar as a possible source of conflict between the longstanding British ally and Spain, excluded from NATO until 1982.

Reasons for Limitations on British Influence

The Anglo-American "special relationship" was, of course, not one between equals. The U.S. had more territory, more people, a larger Gross Domestic Product, and larger armed forces than the UK could ever hope to have. During the presidency of Gerald Ford, there was added concern about the state of the British economy. Small by U.S. standards, it nevertheless remained one of the world's largest. The prosperity of both the U.S. and the rest of the world depended to no small extent on the ability of the British people to purchase exports from other nations. Between 1974 and 1977, Washington's decision-makers were deeply concerned about the state of the British economy. They also realized that British and U.S.-based companies faced similar problems.

Alan Greenspan, then Chairman of the Council of Economic Advisers in Washington, joined National Security Adviser Brent Scowcroft in a telephone call to Prime Minister Callaghan 1 December 1976. The contents remain classified, and Box 7 of the Presidential Handwriting File contains only a notice of withdrawal. However, it is possible to guess the tone of the message from a despatch of Greenspan's dated 23 April 1975, when he sent President Ford a clipping from the *London Economist* entitled "Taxes rise, spending soars, wages blow through the roof." Greenspan commented:

> The enclosed article from the *London Economist* is a stark outline of the crumbling financial and fiscal condition of the United Kingdom. The budgeted level of total government expenditures approaches 60 percent of the GNP up from 57 percent in this fiscal year. (Recall that the comparable U.S. figure is one-third, but our transfer payments trend could eventually push us into the UK range.) Scheduled borrowing amounts to 9.8 percent of their GNP, the equivalent of approximately $150 billion of combined deficits for federal, state and local governments in the United States.
>
> Observe that the British economy appears to be at the point where they must accelerate the amount of governmental fiscal stimulus just to stand still. This is clearly a very dangerous situation. The frightening parallels, with a lag, between the financial policies of the U.S. and those of the UK should give us considerable pause.[50]

The role of the United Kingdom in the European Community (EC, now the European Union) was another consideration. British Ambassador Sir Peter Ramsbotham held discussions with Vice-President Nelson Rockefeller 5 June

1975, the very day when the UK was holding a referendum on continued membership in the EC. Polls correctly indicated that a majority of voters would approve continued membership, but the matter was on the Rockefeller-Ramsbotham agenda.[51] Sir Peter and Vice-President Rockefeller met again 16 June 1976, and once more economic matters were on the agenda. A briefing paper prepared for the vice-president noted:

Economic Recovery Underway

The crisis over the pound, a familiar predicament of Labor administrations in the days of fixed exchange rates, came perversely when the economic situation looks brighter than it has for some time. Retail sales, industrial production, and overall output are rising slowly. Unemployment is finally peaking and stands at about 6.2% in U.S. terms. Inflation has abated over 10 percentage points from its peak last summer and in April stood at 18.9% for the year...The second phase wage restraint agreement will be formalized at a special TUC meeting the day of your meeting with Ramsbotham. The new limit, which averages 4.5%, is a real achievement that should further reduce inflation.[52]

Unfortunately, problems remained. When Secretary of the Treasury William Simon and economic adviser L. William Seidman returned from a trip to London 2 December 1976, they felt sufficiently concerned about the state of the British economy that they reported to President Ford the same day.[53] There were problems involving Congress. Senator Gary Hart, a Democrat from Colorado, introduced a bill to force eighteen oil consortia to divest and become smaller, more specialized companies focusing on one aspect of the industry, such as extraction, refining, or marketing. Concerned about the impact of the Hart bill on British multinationals, the British government had approached the White House. The White House agreed with the British government, not with Congress. Similarly, the House of Representatives was considering a bill which would have allowed only U.S.-based companies to drill for oil and natural gas on the U.S.-owned portion of the Outer Continental Shelf. The British government wanted its multinationals to have access to those opportunities as well, and again the White House agreed. U.S. companies were sufficiently strong, it believed, that the bill—if it became law—would cost more American opportunities and jobs than it would save. American companies could compete with foreign-owned ones on Outer Continental Shelves anywhere in the world, and it would be a dangerous precedent to give a pretext so that other governments would resort to protectionism.[54] The White House and the British government had their way. Neither of these bills became law.

Economic considerations obviously inhibited the "special relationship." One government can hardly have full confidence in another if it questions its economic policies or the survival of its economy. Significantly, however, there were instances when the White House saw eye-to-eye with 10 Downing Street—even under a Labour government—and the conflicts were with Congress, controlled as it was by Democrats.

Conclusions

There was a "special relationship" between the United States and the United Kingdom during the presidency of Gerald Ford. At some risk, British authorities allowed U.S. intelligence to use Hong Kong as a window on the People's Republic of China. For its part, the U.S. remained neutral in two British controversies in which it could have become involved, Northern Ireland and Belize. Political pressure at home and the credibility of the Monroe Doctrine might have prompted some sort of intervention, but good relations with the UK overrode other considerations. The bicentennial visit of Queen Elizabeth II confirmed that the healing process was complete; Americans and Britons together could celebrate the events of 1776 together.

The Ford administration used the UK as a surrogate in dealings with the Soviet Union and the European Community. The Republican White House and the Labour governments of Harold Wilson and James Callaghan shared common outlooks with regard to energy and the role of giant corporations. However, it does not appear that the President became a personal friend of either prime minister.

Notes

1. Edelgard E. Mahant and Graeme S. Mount, *Invisible and Inaudible in Washington* (Vancouver: UBC Press, 1999).
2. *The Australian*, 20 Nov. 1996.
3. CBC News, 15 June 2001.
4. Kissinger, pp. 603, 606-7, 708, 914.
5. Wesley Clark, *Waging Modern War* (New York: Public Affairs, 2001), pp. 115 and 446.
6. William Wallace, "Europe, the Necessary Partner," *Foreign Affairs* (May/June 2001), p. 22.
7. Warren F. Kimball, "The Incredible Shrinking War: The Second World War, Not (Just) the Origins of the Cold War," *Diplomatic History*, XXV, 3 (Summer, 2001), pp. 358, 361-362.
8. BBC News, 19 July 2001.
9. Sir Anthony Eden, *Full Circle: The Memoirs of Sir Anthony Eden* (London: Cassell, 1960), pp. 419-584.

10. Ernest R. May and Philip D. Zelikow (editors), *The Kennedy Tapes: Inside the White House during the Cuban Missile Crisis* (Boston: Harvard University Press, 1998), pp. 283-287, 384-389, 427-430, 480-483.

11. Jocelyn Maynard Ghent, "Canada, the United States, and the Cuban Missile Crisis," *Pacific Historical Review*, XLVIII, 2 (May, 1979), pp. 159-184.

12. William Timmons, Assistant to the President for Legislative Affairs: Congressional Liaison Officer, to Alexander M. Haig Files (Haig was White House Chief of Staff), Box 2, Folder: Timmons, William, 8/10/74-8/31/74), GFPL.

13. Noted by Ford adviser X, who supported Fulbright's nomination as Ambassador to the UK. Regarding Reagan-Thatcher relations, see George Shultz, *Turmoil and Triumph: My Years as Secretary of State* (New York: Charles Scribner's Sons, 1993), pp. 11-154.

14. Kissinger, pp. 602-603.

15. Kissinger, p. 607.

16. Philip Hammond and Edward S. Herman (editors), *Degraded Capability: The Media and the Kosovo Crisis* (London:Pluto,2000).

17. Kissinger, p. 603.

18. Memo, A. Denis Clift to Kissinger, in White House Central Files, SUBJECT FILE, Box 56, Folder CO 160, 8/9/74-10/31/74, GFPL. Cited hereafter as WHCF.

19. Edward J. Savage Files (White House Press Secretary's Office), Box 3, Folder: Great Britain, President's meeting with Foreign Minister Callaghan, 1974/09/24, GFPL.

20. Kissinger, p. 607.

21. Kissinger, p. 607.

22. Edward J. Savage Files (White House Press Secretary's Office), Box 3: Folder: Great Britain, Visit of Prime Minister Wilson, 1975/01-l975/01, GFPL.

23. WHCF, Box 56, Anonymous, undated memo, "UK/USSR Statement on Non-Proliferation," Folder CO 160, 1/28/75-1/29/75, EXECUTIVE, GFPL.

24. Letter, Wilson, London, to Ford, Washington, 16 March 1976, WHCF, Box 57, Folder CO 160, 3/1/76-3/31/76, EXECUTIVE, GFPL.

25. Johannes R. Lombardo, "A Mission of Espionage, Intelligence and Psychological Operations: The American Consulate in Hong Kong, 1949-1964," in Richard J. Aldrich, Gary D. Rawnsley, and Ming-Yeh T. Rawnsley (editors), *The Clandestine Cold War in Asia, 1945-1965: Western Intelligence, Propaganda and Special Operations* (London: Frank Cass, 2000), pp. 64-81.

26. Lombardo, p. 64.

27. Lombardo, p. 65.

28. National Security Adviser: Presidential Country Files for Europe and Canada: Country File, Box 5, GFPL. The biggest file in this box, which deals mainly with the Republic of China (Taiwan), is the one from Hong Kong which deals with events inside the People's Republic of China.

29. Memo, Seidman, Washington, to Ramsbotham, Washington, 26 March 1975, WHCF, Box 56, Folder: CO 160, 2/1/75-4/30/75, GFPL.

30. Leon O'Broin, *Fenian Fever: An Anglo-American Dilemma* (New York: New York University Press, 1971); Hereward Senior, *The Fenians and Canada* (Toronto: Macmillan, 1978). See also Cecil Woodham-Smith, *The Great Hunger* (London: Hamish Hamilton, 1988).

31. Graeme S. Mount, *Canada's Enemies: Spies and Spying in the Peaceable Kingdom* (Toronto: Dundurn, 1993), pp. 12-24.

32. Michael Beschloss, *Kennedy and Roosevelt*, New York: Norton, 1980.

33. T. Ryle Dwyer, *Strained Relations: Ireland at Peace and the USA at War, 1941-1945* (Dublin: Gill and Macmillan, 1988), p. 172.

34. Letters, John Bownes, New York, to President Ford, 28 Aug. 1974, WHCF, ND 18/CO, Box 35, File: CO 160: Wars/Great Britain (Northern Ireland); George E. Foley, New York, to President Ford, 28 Oct. 1974, same box, same folder; Sean W. Walsh, St. Louis, Mo., to President Ford, 10 Dec. 1974, same box, same folder; Jim McGovern, St. Paul, Minn., to President Ford, 2 Nov. 1974, WHCF ND 18/CO, Box 36, Folder: CO 160: Wars—United Kingdom 12/26/74-10/1/77 (EXECUTIVE); Phillip C. Kelly, Jackson, Michigan, to President Ford, in WHCF, Box 58, Folder: CO 160, 8/9/74-12/31/75 EXECUTIVE; Clarence O'Day, Sacramento, California, to President Ford, 3 Aug. 1976, reply to which appears in Box 58, Folder: CO 160, 1/1/76- 1/20/77 EXECUTIVE; all at GFPL.

35. Walsh to President Ford, 10 Dec. 1974.

36. Bownes to President Ford, 28 Aug. 1974.

37. McGovern, St. Paul, to President Ford, 2 Nov. 1974.

38. See the McGovern-related correspondence in WHCF: ND 18/CO, Box 36, Folder: CO 160: Wars—United Kingdom, 12/26/74-20/1/77, GFPL.

39. Letter, Senator Buckley to President Ford, 29 Sept. 1976, WHCF, ND: 18/CO, Box 36, Folder: CO 160: Wars—United Kingdom, 12/26/74-20/1/77 (EXECUTIVE), GFPL.

40. See the correspondence in WHCF, ND 18/CO, Box 35, File: CO 160: Wars/Great Britain (Northern Ireland) and WHCF, Box 58, Folder: CO 160 12/1/76-1/20/77 (EXECUTIVE), GFPL.

41. Memorandum of Brent Scowcroft for the Attorney General: Foreign Policy Implications of Use of American-Supplied Weapons in Northern Ireland, January 1976, in WHCF, ND 18/CO, Box 36, Folder: CO 160: Wars—United Kingdom, 12/26/74-20/1/77 (EXECUTIVE), GFPL.

42. Memo of October 1975 from Secretary of State for distribution to U.S. embassies in Central America, London, and the United Nations, as well as to the U.S. consul in Belize, National Security Adviser: Presidential Country Files for Latin America, 1974-1977, Box 4, Folder: Guatemala—State Department Telegrams: from SECSTATE- EXDIS, GFPL. Cited hereafter as NSA.

43. Letter, Meloy, Guatemala, to Secretary of State (Kissinger), Washington, n.d., Nov. 1975, NSA, Folder: Guatemala—State Department Telegrams to SECSTATE, EXDIS, NSA-NODIS, GFPL.

44. Letter, Meloy, Guatemala City, to the Secretary of State (Kissinger), Washington, n.d. Dec. 1975, NSA-NODIS, GFPL.

45. Memo written by Meloy, Guatemala City, n.d. Feb. 1976, NSA-NODIS, GFPL.

46. Report written by Meloy, Guatemala City, who was present at the Kissinger- Laugerud meeting, n.d. Feb. 1976, NSA-NODIS. GFPL.

47. The *Sunday Times* of London: Insight Team, *War in the Falklands: The Full Story* (New York: Harper and Row, 1982).

48. For a concise summary of the Anglo-Guatemalan conflict over British Honduras, see Graeme S. Mount, *El Caribe* (Caracas: Historia de las Americas, XXIII, 1992), pp. 171-181.

49. Kissinger, pp. 903-957. The author interviewed Ian Smith in Harare, Zimbabwe, 2 June 1990.

50. Presidential Handwriting File, Box 7, File: United Kingdom, GFPL.

51. Memorandum from Brent Scowcroft (National Security Adviser) for Jon Howe (an assistant to Vice-President Rockefeller), "Vice President's Meeting with United Kingdom Ambassador Sir Peter Ramsbotham, 5 June 1975," in WHCF, Box 56, Folder: CO 160: CO 160 6/4/75-8/31/75, GFPL.

52. Memo from Jeanne W. Davis (of the National Security Council) for Jon Howe, "Background and Talking Points for Vice President's June 16 Meeting with UK Ambassador Ramsbotham," WHCF, Box 57, Folder: CO 160 4/1/76-4/30/76, GFPL. Cited hereafter as Davis-Howe report.

53. Memo, Simon and Seidman to Ford, 2 December 1976, WHCF, Box 58, Folder: CO 160 21/1/76-1/20/77 EXECUTIVE, GFPL.

54. Davis-Howe report.

Chapter Two

REVOLUTION IN PORTUGAL

T wentieth century Portugal gave Western Europe its longest lasting dictatorial regime, one which lasted 48 years, starting from 1926 when a military coup ripped power from Portugal's republican regime, until another military coup led by left-leaning soldiers declared a revolution against authoritarian rule in 1974. During this 48 year period the country became one of the most stagnant and backward places of the region. Its economy drained from a military fighting to keep its overseas colonies intact. Meanwhile, other nations were granting independence and relieving themselves of the economic burden of maintaining distant colonies.

Throughout most of that 48 year period, Portugal's leader was the conservative Antonio Salazar. Salazar assumed power in 1932 and remained Portugal's dictatorial figure until 1968 when he began to fall ill. His death came two years later. Salazar's successor was Marcelo Caetano, who continued the course Salazar had established. Not much changed with the new regime. Portugal was still spending about half its annual budget on the overseas wars being waged in Africa to keep Mozambique, Guinea, and Angola as Portuguese territories.[1] Portuguese men spilled their blood in the cause of imperialism.

Tired of fighting useless and costly wars led a group of young soldiers to take action against Caetano's regime. On 25 April 1974, they staged a bloodless coup and ousted Caetano as Prime Minister. It was a remarkable day for the Portuguese and the Portuguese military. The streets were full of cheerful people, and soldiers paraded the streets waving their guns. 25 April 1974 is known as the "Carnation Revolution," because soldiers hung colourful carnations from the ends of their guns.

Immediately following the Carnation Revolution, António Spínola became President, and a series of power struggles ensued between Spínola and the Armed Forces Movement (AFM), which had orchestrated the overthrow of the Caetano regime.[2] After some months, Spínola resigned from the presidency, as he grew tired of having the AFM monitor and scrutinize his decisions. The AFM evidently did not agree with all his proposed solutions.

The AFM was the real power behind Portuguese politics. It dominated the ruling provisional government established after the 1974 revolution. Its objective was to bring democracy to the people of Portugal, and to establish Portugal's *first* public election in half a century, scheduled for 25 April 1975; however, it was plagued with political infighting and differences. It was a movement which included members of many political parties, which had functioned underground during the Salazar and Caetano regimes. It included the Portuguese Communist Party (PCP), the Portuguese Socialist Party (PS), and the Social Democratic Movement (MDP). There was speculation that many of the soldiers among the AFM were members of the PCP. Even the New Prime Minister, General Vasco dos Santos Gonçálves, was suspected of having sympathy for the Communists. To maintain the balance of power, the provisional government relied on Socialists, such as Mario Soares, the leader of the PS and the provisional government's foreign minister. In the months following the revolution, it was not entirely clear whether the Communists or the Socialists would triumph.

The AFM, led by the new President, Francisco da Costa Gomes, and the new Prime Minister, General Vasco dos Santos Gonçalves, immediately began the decolonization process and withdrew Portuguese troops from the African territories. This created a huge problem within the colonies themselves. Upon receiving news of decolonization, the Portuguese territories began civil wars. Tribal insurgent groups fought for control and accepted help from every place possible, including the Soviet Union and China (PRC). In Angola a disastrous civil war raged throughout the country, as insurgent groups such as the MPLA, FNLA and UNITA fought for control. The MPLA received aid from Cuba and the Soviet Union, while the FNLA and UNITA received aid from the United States and China to defeat the Marxist MPLA. RENAMO fought FRELIMO in Mozambique.

Meanwhile, back in Portugal, the AFM was struggling to create a democracy. It had to deal with high employment rates and a struggling economy. To help ease the domestic crisis, Portugal looked to the United States and other NATO members for economic assistance.

The United States and Portugal

After Portugal's successful revolution, the Nixon administration immediately recognized the provisional government. On 18 October 1974, President Costa Gomes, accompanied by Foreign Minister Mario Soares, visited President Ford and Secretary of State Kissinger at the White House. This was the first visit of a Portuguese President to the United States. During the meeting President Costa Gomes attempted to clarify the situation in Portugal.

> There has been a profound and sudden transformation from a dictator to full freedom regained. We have not been able to avoid all kinds of disruption, but I am pleased to say we have managed to avoid violence. Many of the limits which should have been in place to handle continuity of rule—the laws, the framework for exchange—many were lacking. Nevertheless, all the various groups in the country have granted full freedom and have enjoyed that full freedom.[3]

In response, President Ford asked President Costa Gomes whether all the political parties in Portugal were allowed to participate in the government. Costa Gomes replied, "All parties are completely free to participate."[4]

Knowing that all parties were free to participate within the Portuguese government, President Ford and Kissinger expressed concern about strong Communist influence in Portugal, a charter member of NATO. In his memoirs, Kissinger says:

> The danger of Communist participation in the Portuguese government was serious indeed...Over the months that followed, the Communist influence increased in Portugal itself...[PCP] now emerged as the best organized political force in the country. Between May 1974 and July 1976, six provisional governments held what passed for power in Lisbon, and all of them moved progressively to the left. The President, Franciso da Costa Gomes, was later described by our extremely astute Ambassador Frank Carlucci as being "very far to the left."[5]

(For his part, Carlucci was sufficiently far to the right that in 1987 he became Secretary of Defense in the administration of Ronald Reagan.)

Deeply concerned about the prospect of a Communist controlled government and a leader with left-leaning sympathies, Ford did not beat around the bush, and told Costa Gomes, "We think it is important for NATO to be strengthened, and we are very worried about Communist influence in any member country. We just couldn't tolerate Communism in NATO itself." In response to Ford, Costa Gomes took a defensive stance, and stated that Ford and Kissinger were being influenced by unjustified media reports.

> This fear you express is unjustified. I am familiar with NATO—I have been with NATO since 1951...So I am certain that there is no doubt about our devotion to NATO...I am at a loss to know what to say except to invite you to Portugal...[to] see the trends in our country as they really are, to quiet your press, which I consider unjustified.[6]

Costa Gomes tried hard to assure Ford and Kissinger that the Communist influence in Portugal was not going to affect the goal of establishing democratic institutions. In an attempt to persuade the United States to provide economic aid, President Costa Gomes told Ford and Kissinger that Portugal would not fall into the hands of an undesirable government if its economy could recover. "As to the economic problem, as I see it, it is very serious to our country. If it is not solved it could lead to the extreme right or the extreme left prevailing."[7] Perhaps this was a tactic to influence Ford's decision about economic aid to Portugal.

After the meeting of Ford and Kissinger with Costa Gomes and Soares, Portugal remained a major issue. During meetings with other foreign leaders, Ford sought advice about the situation in Portugal and ways to handle or deal with the apparentCcommunist threat. This great concern is understandable, as a Communist government in Portugal would be disastrous for NATO and Europe, and would establish a precedent for other European nations. As Kissinger outlined in his memoirs, "No NATO country had faced the prospect of an internal Communist takeover since the early days of the Cold War. The danger in Portugal was magnified by the fact that simultaneously the Italian Christian Democrats under Aldo Moro were playing with the idea of forming a coalition with the Italian Communist Party."[8]

In order to curb what seemed to be the Communist threat in Portugal, the Ford administration had to find solutions to counter the possible outcome of a Communist victory in the upcoming April elections. This prompted Kissinger to state during a meeting at the Pentagon on 22 January 1975, "We should have a program in Portugal. There is a 50 percent chance of losing it."[9] The following sentences are erased from the conversation; therefore, there is no way of knowing what Kissinger meant by "a program." However, it is reasonable to suggest that he intended to plan a covert program to keep tabs on the Communists in Portugal.

Correspondence between Kissinger and Ambassador Carlucci shows that the U.S. Embassy and Kissinger expressed great interest in Portuguese internal affairs. In a State Department Telegram to the U.S. Embassy in Portugal, Carlucci received instructions to warn President Costa Gomes and Soares about a possible PCP coup against the moderate forces. During a thirty minute meeting with the president, Carlucci told Costa Gomes that the U.S. "intent was not to interfere in internal Portuguese affairs, but to share with him, as a friend, the reports [U.S. sources] were receiving." Carlucci emphasized that the U.S. government was watching Costa Gomes closely and supporting his work to bring democracy to Portugal. "We would not like to see anything happen that would divert Portugal from this path, particularly this week when Congress is debating [the] aid program."[10] Carlucci adds that Costa Gomes was aware of the proposed aid program that Congress was debating.

Costa Gomes tried to assure Carlucci that the U.S. was overreacting again to "rumors." He told Carlucci that Portugal was rampant with rumours, and that the rumours were spread to delay the Communist and Socialist rallies being held on 31 January 1975. Costa Gomes called for a joint rally between the Communists and Socialists. "After all, both the Socialists and the Communists were claiming that the purpose of their rallies was to support the AFM. In his judgment a joint rally might eliminate possible street clashes."[11] Although nation-wide coup attempts did not surface, on 11 March rightist elements of the Portuguese Armed Forces led by General António Spínola bombed an artillery regiment based near the Lisbon Airport. Spínola believed that leftist elements under the control of Communists controlled the site. However, the coup attempt proved short lived, and Spínola left the country.

In the remaining months before the Portuguese elections of 25 April, President Ford and Secretary Kissinger focused their attention on Portugal's status as a NATO member. Shortly after Costa Gomes' visit to Washington, Kissinger and Ford discussed Portugal's withdrawal from the NATO Nuclear Planning Group (NPG). It was their belief, along with that of NATO's Secretary General Joseph Luns (a Dutch citizen), that the highly sensitive information discussed within the NPG could not be shared with a government that might become Communist. In a letter to President Costa Gomes, Kissinger stated:

> As a military man, you will appreciate the highly classified nature of the issues discussed in the NATO's Nuclear Planning Group. Any compromise of that information could have adverse consequences for the

security of the entire Western Alliance. The introduction of communist elements into the Portuguese government, however, has brought
into serious question the ability of Portugal to protect the type of information discussed in the Nuclear Planning Group... I urge that you
personally consider the matter...and indicate to the allied representatives at NATO that Portugal will not participate in the activities of the
Nuclear Planning Group.[12]

Without hesitation, Costa Gomes gave instructions to his NATO ambassador to withdraw Portugal from the NPG. A Portuguese participant at the NPG
meeting would not have had much influence in the first place, since Portugal had
no role in NATO's offensive nuclear strategy. It would have been more of a "psychological" role.[13] As Costa Gomes gave his consent, he reassured the Americans
that he fully understood the nature of the matter; however, any information
that would be revealed at the meetings would not have jeopardized NATO even if
Portugal was to attend. His reasons were that there were no influential Communists in the Government of Portugal, and that PCP leader "Álvaro Cunhal [is] a
minister without portfolio and therefore without direct access to any GOP [Gov-
ernment of Portugal] secret files...Members with any access to NATO documents are carefully instructed to ensure that NATO matters are kept far from
Cunhal."[14]

some members of the Portuguese military and even the U.S. ambassador
disagreed with the exclusion from a NATO council. Frank Carlucci made his feelings known in a letter to Kissinger, telling him that Portugal's exclusion from
NATO matters "caused considerable resentment among military [personnel] and
contributed to leftward drift."[15] Carlucci reminded Kissinger that after a coup attempt from the far right had failed, many drifted to the left; therefore, any other
type of pressure from the United States and NATO might produce the same undesirable outcome.[16]

Ford and Kissinger tried to use economic aid as a tool to influence Portuguese politics. However, it was not enough to curb the other forces from moving
towards the Communists. Documents from the Gerald Ford Presidential Library
outline some of the U.S. efforts and strategies to influence Portuguese politics.
Outside of an economic program (to be discussed later in this chapter), the Ford
administration was:

- Urging Western European leaders to speak out in support of democratic
  elections in Portugal.

- Encouraging the press to give extensive coverage to the electoral campaign in an effort to minimize violence, intimidation and fraud.
- Continuing our plans to implement a $35 million economic assistance program.
- Consulting with NATO partners, the EC-9 and other friendly governments on ways to deal with the Portuguese problem.[17]

(The EC-9 referred to the nine NATO members which formed the European Community, now the European Union.)

Ford archival documents show that the U.S. *did* carry out all these programs. During successive visits with foreign leaders, Ford asked for advice. Some of those individuals were former Chancellor of the Federal Republic of Germany Willy Brandt; British Prime Minister Harold Wilson; Canadian Prime Minister Pierre Elliott Trudeau; Belgian Prime Minister Leo Tindemans; Spain's General Franco; and even Pope Paul VI. During Ford's European trip in the spring of 1975, President Ford, along with Secretary Kissinger, visited Vatican City. They discussed Portugal and NATO with the Pope. The conversation covers a couple of pages; however, everything the Pope had to say about Portugal was censored, and his views are unknown. Yet, the Pope must have been closely informed about the events within Portugal, as it is a Roman Catholic country.

In April 1975, reports indicated some NATO officials wanted more than simple Portuguese exclusion from the NPG. They were so concerned that they considered quarantining Portugal within NATO. According to a telegram to the Department of State, Defense Secretary James Schlesinger said, "It will be necessary to find a symbolic way to isolate Portugal without excluding it."[18] However, many Portuguese were already feeling excluded and ostracized. In response to NATO quarantines and isolation, Ambassador Carlucci added, "[The] Government of Portugal will react emotionally to every slap on [its] wrist it receives from NATO and communists will be right there to give condolences."[19] A NATO strategy of exclusion would only push the Government of Portugal and the members of the AFM further to the left. With an election scheduled the very same month, any movement to the left might have been disastrous for the Portuguese Socialist Party.

The Portuguese Elections of 1975 and 1976

Despite the coup attempts and political battles among Portugal's political parties, the Portuguese public *did* go to the polls. The Portuguese election on 25

April 1975, for creating a new Constituent Assembly and re-writing the 1933 Constitution, witnessed a victory by the Socialist Party. The Socialists received 37.9 percent of the vote gaining 116 seats out of a total of 249. The Communist Party was reportedly surprised with its finish behind the Social Democratic Party with only 12.5 percent of the vote and 30 seats in the house.[20]

For the next year the Constituent Assembly worked on a new constitution that reflected many democratic socialist ideas, and one year later the constitution was approved. In the 1976 legislative elections, a democratic government finally assumed office, and the Portuguese Socialist Party led by Mario Soares led a co-alition government. Soares would remain as prime minister until he offered his resignation two years later in 1978. However, Soares would return in 1983, and in 1985 he negotiated Portugal's entry into the European Economic Union (successor to the European Community and predecessor of the European Union).[21]

Portugal's Economic Crisis

After years of depleting the economy due to imperialist battles, Portugal was in an economic bind. Portugal's problems did not improve when the new ruling body announced Portugal's withdrawal from its African colonies. As the decolonization process began, Portugal's economy was overwhelmed with returning soldiers and settlers. Matters became worse when Portugal's PCP organized widespread labour strikes, which almost crippled the economy. Without adequate legislation, the new government was slow to introduce new labour laws to outlaw such strikes.[22] The new and inexperienced government was overwhelmed with such an economic problem that it looked elsewhere for help.

Portugal looked to the United States and other NATO nations for help. On their visit to Washington in October 1974, President Costa Gomes and Foreign Minister Mario Soares discussed economic aid. From Ford's point of view, the United States could not guarantee aid to Portugal because of the growing threat of Communist influence within the AFM (Portugal's Provisional Government). During the meeting, Ford told President Costa Gomes, "We want to help, but the Congress and I will have to have assurances that Portugal is a part of the same team as it has been…and is not going off in a different direction toward a different alliance. Then we will be willing to help, at least to do our share."[23] Costa Gomes and Soares then used the argument of gaining U.S. aid to battle the growing threat of Communism in Portugal. Costa Gomes argued, "American support for the [Portuguese] economy would enhance election prospects of [the] center."[24]

President Ford and Secretary Kissinger had to take the Portuguese President's fears seriously. If Portugal continued the course it was running, the PCP might take advantage of the situation. Another possibility was that Portugal could find new friends willing to help, such as the Soviets! Two months after the October meeting, the Ford administration grew increasingly concerned about this potential relationship. A National Security Council memorandum for Secretary Kissinger outlined a blossoming relationship between the Soviets and the Portuguese. Within the memo, A. Denis Clift, President Ford's head of NSC staff for the Soviet Union and Eastern and Western Europe, noted, "Moscow and Lisbon are beginning to implement the understandings reached during last month's visit to the USSR by Alvaro Cunhal, Minister without Portfolio in the government and head of the Portuguese Communist Party."[25] One of those understandings highlighted for Ford and Kissinger was an air agreement signed 11 December, which allowed regular air service from Lisbon to Moscow. Days later on 19 December, the two countries signed a trade agreement establishing trade missions in both capitals. At the end of the memo Clift wrote, "Meanwhile, the two sides have established visits by trade union delegations and friendship societies. In addition, the Portuguese are working on a long-term trade agreement with at least one of Moscow's East European allies."[26] Such consultations between these two countries might have appeared alarming for President Ford and the NATO alliance. Other countries had direct flights between their cities and Soviet destinations and had long exchanged delegations with the Soviets, but their political situation was more stable than Portugal's appeared to be. Therefore, what could President Ford do to ensure that the Soviet Union's influence would not jeopardize Portugal's standing in the NATO alliance?

Coincidentally or not, the United States announced an economic aid plan on 13 December 1974 to assist Portugal. As outlined in a State Department memo from Henry Kissinger, the plan called for immediate assistance, which included:

- 20 million dollars in private American loans for the construction of housing in Portugal.
- Mak[ing] U.S. government experts available to the Portuguese government, high priority fields of agriculture, transportation, public administration, education, and health. There would be no charge or services of experts sent to Portugal.
- If the Government of Portugal concurs, the U.S. will use the $200,000 remaining from the program previously devoted to education greatly to in-

crease the number of Portuguese brought to the U.S. for study visits or training in a variety of fields.

- The Export-Import bank will give sympathetic consideration to financing U.S. goods and services needed for Portuguese development projects.
- If Portugal's monetary reserves should fall to a dangerously low level, and if international facilities were not available, we would be willing to consider other means of remedying the situation.[27]

President Ford and Secretary Kissinger also introduced a bill that would authorize an additional $25 million to assist Portugal.

This economic aid would continue only if Portugal proceeded toward democracy. If Portugal did fall to the Communists or continue to move to the left, then the Ford administration would not be obligated to support a nation that might be a threat to NATO. Therefore, this economic aid plan was a gesture by the United States to show Portugal that it cared about its role in Europe. However, this economic aid plan was more of a gesture than a solution to Portugal's problems. With the growing crisis in Angola and the problem of resettling hundreds of thousands of Angolan refugees, the Portuguese government had been draining its financial assets. Also, the economy did not benefit from the country's continued political uncertainty. As a result of these unfortunate circumstances, Portugal was experiencing "a declining GNP; serious unemployment and underemployment; runaway inflation; and shortages of housing, health and educational facilities. In addition, depletion of foreign exchange holdings ha[d] resulted in a serious temporary shortage of internationally liquid assets."[28]

In 1975, after waiting for Portugal's internal politics to sort itself out, the Ford administration had hoped to find an ally in Portugal's sixth provisional government, that of Prime Minister José Batista Pinheiro de Azevedo and Ernesto de Melo Antunes. Antunes was Portugal's new Foreign Minister, and as Foreign Minister his objective was to ensure that Gerald Ford was on board with the new Portuguese government.

To guarantee a commitment from the U.S., Antunes arranged a meeting with President Ford. Again, the same standards that were set in 1974 remained in effect. In order to guarantee U.S. economic assistance and political support, the Portuguese government would have to be free of Communist influence. Also, Ford wanted Portugal's commitment and promise to ensure that a MPLA Communist government in Angola would not receive support. During this meeting President Ford told Foreign Minister Antunes that the U.S. would grant

Portugal increased aid in the area of $65 million for the fiscal year 1976, and that it would double its contribution to the Angolan airlift:

> I was pleased by the vote last spring and I was pleased to see that the most recent Cabinet was limited in Communist participation…Secretary Kissinger is meeting with you later today, but I want to say now that we are increasing our assistance to you, both for the refugees and to rebuild your economy…We are pleased to be able to help. We plan to help further with the evacuation of refugees, and I understand that this is on the basis that you will not leave military equipment in Angola, when you leave, for the MPLA.[29]

Along with the United States, European nations individually pledged approximately $326 million. For Portugal, many countries were willing to lend a helping hand; however, the economic situation was in such serious condition that this aid would not be enough.[30]

For the first time since the revolution, a provisional government was making a real effort to fix the economy. The previous five provisional governments, preoccupied with internal political fighting and power struggles, were capable only of applying band-aid solutions. Other than decolonization and labor strikes, the Portuguese economy had to battle a worldwide recession that every industrialized country had to face, and a rise in world oil prices, raw materials, and foodstuffs. Once again, the Portuguese would find themselves in an all too familiar situation. They would have to go to the United States again and ask for more help. In March 1976, months after the U.S. had pledged an economic aid plan, the Portuguese made an urgent request for $500 million gold-secured loan for the remainder of 1976.[31] This urgent request received serious consideration from President Ford and other European leaders, and in the fall of 1976, the Ford administration announced a three-year financial assistance program totaling $1.5 billion.[32]

With the United States and Europe pledging large amounts of economic aid, the Ford administration took another step to help Portugal develop more rapidly. In August 1976, President Ford approved a plan to designate "Portugal as a beneficiary of the Generalized System of Preferences (GSP)." The GSP was a system established to allow industrialized countries to grant duty free treatment to developing countries. This was not the first time President Ford granted GSP status to a less fortunate ally, as one year earlier Ford had approved GSP status to Israel on 24 November 1975.[33]

The Azores Base Negotiations

When Gerald Ford assumed the Presidency, the 1951 Azores base agreement had come to an end. The Azores are a Portuguese archipelago located in the Atlantic Ocean. In 1973, the Azores had proved to be a strategic refueling point for American aircraft when the U.S. helped defend Israel against an Egyptian-Syrian attack. Ford and Kissinger were interested in renegotiating a deal with the new Portuguese government; however, the Portuguese government had other concerns, such as decolonization and the economy. In order to maintain a friendly relationship with the United States, Portugal allowed the U.S. to continue military and NATO operations on the islands after the agreement had expired.

During his 1974 visit to the White House, Foreign Minister Soares was not ready to renegotiate a base agreement with the United States; however, he was willing to use the base negotiations as a bargaining chip to acquire United States economic aid. The United States, along with other NATO countries, needed the Azores base in order to maintain a strategic advantage point within Europe and Africa. Soares was not ready to jump into negotiations with Ford and Kissinger, but he was looking to use the Azores agreement as a "mechanism for providing aid to rescue Portugal from impending economic crisis."[34]

Throughout Ford's time in office, he was unable to conclude an agreement with the Portuguese government; however, he was not guilty of being passive or uninterested. If anything, it was the opposite. Ford's foreign policy with Portugal centred heavily around renegotiating a deal with the Portuguese government for the continuation of U.S. base rights at Lajes Base on Terceira Island. As indicated earlier, it was U.S. policy to defend Israel and maintain peace in the Middle East. Loss of the Lajes Base would put NATO in a tough position, as the base was a convenient and strategic refueling location for U.S. aircraft. According to documents from the Gerald Ford Presidential Library, Ford administration officials thought that no other viable or realistic option existed for the U.S.

> The most likely alternative airfields to Lajes for support of contingency operations in the Middle East or North Africa lie in mainland Portugal, the Madeira Islands, the Canary Islands, Morocco, and Senegal. *None* of these, however, could duplicate the capabilities of Lajes…without extensive augmentation and/or base development.[35]

During every discussion with Portuguese officials, Ford and Kissinger pushed for an agreement, but Portuguese officials were more concerned about securing U.S. aid than with reaching an agreement for Azores base rights.

Portugal's base agreement with the United States was essentially its most important contribution to the NATO alliance. The Lajes Base was Portugal's way to show NATO that it was committed to contributing to the defense of the West.

As Portugal and the United States tried to find solutions to the base agreement, the Ford administration was deeply concerned about possible armed uprisings from Portuguese exile groups and members of the Azorean independence movement. Looking to declare independence from the mainland, Azorean separatists sought U.S. support to launch an attack against the mainland government. The Azorean separatists planned to use such an attack to stimulate similar uprisings within mainland Portugal. In a National Security Council Memorandum, the U.S. position was stated clearly:

> The assumption…that [Azorean Separatists] will be able to stimulate a popular uprising in mainland Portugal…is a pipedream…and the government is in a strong position to resist coup attempts from the right, particularly since the abortive coup of March 11…Ambassador Carlucci adds that if the Portuguese find substance to support their already existing suspicions that the United States is backing right-wing dissident groups, our base rights could be in danger of immediate termination.[36]

Immediate action was required from Ford to inform the Government of Portugal that the U.S. would not become involved in internal matters and would remain neutral. Meanwhile, the U.S. would "inform the exile group…that the U.S. will not only *not* support them but might even be obliged to assist the Government of Portugal by providing transport and supplies should they try anything in the Azores."[37] If U.S. forces were to respond to an Azorean separatist attack on the Lajes base, the United States would almost certainly appear to be guilty to some of the Portuguese people, including some GOP officials.

In 1976 it seems U.S. fears of any right wing coup attempts were calmed, and Portugal granted the Azores partial autonomy. Gerald Ford was unsuccessful in reaching an agreement with Portugal, but he did lay the foundation for an agreement by his successor, Jimmy Carter. In 1979, the U.S. reached an agreement, and in 1983 under President Reagan the agreement was extended. The Azores proved to be a strategic location during the 1991 Gulf War, enabling the U.S. to deploy tens of thousands of troops.

During Ford's term, Portugal was a constant topic of discussion. Ford administration officials kept Portugal under a microscope, and President Ford did all he could to keep Portugal within NATO and free from Communist influence, by implementing huge economic aid programs and designating Portugal as a beneficiary of the Generalized System of Preferences. The assumption can be made that President Ford's foreign policy with Portugal was a complete success. Ford lobbied for Portugal within NATO and Europe to ensure that it would receive economic aid. All Gerald Ford wanted in return was the assurance that Portugal would keep struggling for democracy and remain free from Communist or dictatorial regimes. The efforts made by the Ford administration assisted Portugal in growing into the country it is today, a free, prosperous, and democratic society.

Notes

1. Felix Gilbert and David Clay Large, *The End of the European Era: 1890 to the Present* (New York: W.W. Norton & Company, 2002), p. 483.

2. Memo, 30 September 1974, Box 10, Folder: Portugal (1), NSA Presidential Country Files for Europe and Canada, GFPL.

3. Memorandum of Conversation, Ford, Kissinger and Portuguese President Costa Gomes, 18 October 1974, Box 6, Folder: Oct. 18/1974—Ford, Kissinger, Portuguese President Costa Gomes, Foreign Minister Mario Soares, NSA—Memorandum of Conversations 1973-77,GFPL.

4. Ibid.

5. Henry Kissinger, *Years of Renewal* (New York: Simon & Schuster, 1999), p. 629.

6. Memorandum of Conversation, Ford, Kissinger and Portuguese President Costa Gomes, 18 October 1974, Box 6, Folder: Oct. 18/1974—Ford, Kissinger, Portuguese President Costa Gomes, Foreign Minister Mario Soares, NSA—Memorandum of Conversations 1973-77,GFPL.

7. Ibid.

8. Kissinger, pp. 630–631.

9. Memorandum of Conversation, Secretary of State Henry Kissinger , Secretary of Defense James Schlesinger, Deputy Assistant to the President for National Security Affairs Brent Scowcroft and Major General John Wickham, 22 January 1975, Box 8, Folder: January 28, 1975—Ford, Kissinger, Rockefeller, Bipartisan Congressional Leadership, NSA Memoranda of Conversations, 1973-77,GFPL.

10. Department of State Telegram, Carlucci to Kissinger, 28 January 1975, Box 11, Folder: Portugal State Department Telegrams to Secretary of State NODIS (1), NSA Presidential Country File for Europe and Canada,GFPL.

11. Ibid.

12. Department of State Telegram, Secretary of State to the U.S. Embassy in Lisbon, October 1974, Box 11, Folder: Portuguese State Department Telegrams from Secretary of State—NODIS (2), NSA Presidential Country File for Europe and Canada,GFPL.

13. Department of State Telegram, Carlucci to Kissinger, November 1974, Box 11, Folder: Portugal State Department Telegrams to Secretary of State NODIS (1), NSA Presidential Country File for Europe and Canada,GFPL.

14. Ibid.

15. Department of State Telegram, Carlucci to Kissinger, April 1975, Box 11, Folder: Portugal State Department Telegrams to Secretary of State NODIS (1), NSA Presidential Country File for Europe and Canada,GFPL.

16. Ibid.

17. Memorandum, Clift to Scowcroft, March 1975, Box 10, Folder: Portugal (4), NSA Presidential Country File for Europe and Canada, GFPL.

18. Department of State Telegram, Carlucci to Kissinger, April 1975, Box 11, Folder: Portugal State Department Telegrams to Secretary of State NODIS (1), NSA Presidential Country File for Europe and Canada, GFPL.

19. Ibid.

20. Website: Wikipedia: http://en.wikipedia.org/wiki/Portuguese_legislative_election%2C_1975 15 July 2005.

21. Website: Wikipedia: http://en.wikipedia.org/wiki/M%C3%A1rio_Soares 15 July 2005

22. Briefing paper, The Secretary's briefing of the President on the Costa Gomes Visit, September 1974, Box 10, Folder: Portugal (2), NSA Presidential Country Files for Europe and Canada, GFPL.

23. Memorandum of Conversation, Ford, Kissinger and Portuguese President Costa Gomes, 18 October 1974, Box 6, Folder: Oct. 18/1974—Ford, Kissinger, Portuguese President Costa Gomes, Foreign Minister Mario Soares, NSA—Memorandum of Conversations 1973-77,GFPL.

24. Department of State Telegram, Sec. of State Kissinger to Lisbon Embassy, 22 October 1974, Box 11, Folder: Portugal State Department Telegrams from Secretary of State—NODIS (2), NSA Presidential Country File for Europe and Canada, GFPL.

25. National Security Council Memorandum, A Denis Clift to Secretary Kissinger, 27 December 1974, Box 10, Folder: Portugal (3), NSA Presidential Country Files for Europe and Canada, GFPL.

26. Ibid.

27. Department of State Telegram, Secretary Kissinger to Lisbon Emabassy, December 1974, Box 10, Folder: Portugal (3), NSA Presidential Country Files for Europe and Canada, Gerald R. Ford Library.

28. Memorandum, Brent Scowcroft to President Ford, 9 February 1976, Box 10, Folder: Portugal (8), NSA Presidential Country Files for Europe and Canada, GFPL.

29. Memorandum of Conversation, President Ford and Major General Ernesto de Melo Antunes, 10 October 1975, Box 16, Folder: November 28, 1975—Ford, Kissinger, Scowcroft, NSA Memorandum of Conversations 1973-1977, GFPL.

30. Memorandum for the President, Brent Scowcroft to President Ford, 9 February 1976,Box 10, Folder: Portugal (8), NSA Presidential Country Files for Europe and Canada, GFPL.

31. Memorandum, A. Denis Clift to Brent Scowcroft, 4 June 1976, Box 10, Folder: Portugal (10), NSA Presidential Country File for Europe and Canada, GFPL.

32. Memorandum, Arthur A. Hartman to Secretary Kissinger, 28 October 1976, Box 10, Folder: Portugal (11), NSA Presidential Country File for Europe and Canada, GFPL.

33. Memorandum for the President, L. William Seidman to President Ford, 13 August 1976, Box 7, Folder: Countries—Portugal, Presidential Handwriting File Countries—Korea, GFPL.

34. Department of State Telegram, Lisbon Embassy to Secretary Kissinger, September 1974, Box 11, Folder: Portugal State Department Telegrams to Secretary State EXDIS (1), NSA Presidential Country Files for Europe and Canada,GFPL.

35. National Security Study Memorandum, Box A1, Folder: Portugal 1975 (11) White House, Office of the Assistant to the President for National Security Affairs, GFPL.

36. National Security Council Memorandum, Clift to Kissinger, 3 April 1975, Box 1, Folder: Azores, NSA Presidential Country File for Europe and Canada, GFPL

37. Ibid.

Chapter Three

A FAILED DÉTENTE WITH CUBA[1]

Not until the Ford Administration did the U.S. begin efforts to ease tensions between the two enemies. President Ford was willing to undertake a series of negotiations to normalize relations with the Communist island, a bold move considering that Cuba was a Cold War enemy. However, the Ford administration was willing to normalize relations only if Cuba was ready to make changes. President Ford stated that the U.S. would lift some of the sanctions in place since the Kennedy Administration, but that it needed to witness some major changes on Castro's part before such a huge step to normalization.[2]

In 1947, the Truman Administration was looking for allies against communism in the Western Hemisphere. The Rio Treaty of 1947 established a military alliance of Central and South America countries with the United States. The treaty's purpose was to "prevent and repel threats and acts of aggression against any of the countries of America."[3] A year later in Bogotá, the ninth International Pan-American Conference resulted in the creation of the Organization of American States (OAS). The OAS was also to play the role of mediator among member states and to maintain the status quo within the Western Hemisphere:

> The High Contracting Parties, solemnly reaffirming their commitments made in earlier international conventions and declarations, as well as in the Charter of the United Nations, agree to refrain from the threat or the use of force, or from any other means of coercion for the settlement of their controversies, and to have recourse at all times to pacific procedures.[4]

Cuba was a charter member of the OAS, but after the Cuban Revolution, the OAS excluded the Cuban government from the inter-American system. Already the United States had imposed its own economic embargo against Cuba.

Successive administrations forbade subsidiaries of American companies located outside the United States from trading with Cuba. The U.S. also banned U.S. ships from visiting Cuban waters.

In 1964, after the Cuban government's exclusion from the OAS, Cuba faced sanctions from the OAS under a revision of the Rio Treaty of 1947. The OAS sanctions on Cuba extended to all but one of the members of the inter-American system. (Mexico alone continued to maintain diplomatic relations and trade with Cuba.) Throughout the 1960s, the Cuban issue dominated the OAS. The OAS, originally intended as protector of its members from foreign aggression, became an organization opposed to the government of one its former members.

At the inauguration of Gerald Ford, OAS sanctions remained in place against Cuba. However, as time passes, governments change. More and more Latin American countries sought to make their own decisions. After the Johnson and Nixon administrations (1963-1969 and 1969-1974 respectively), additional Latin American countries wanted to trade with Cuba. This sparked concern among members the Ford Administration. After years of trying to keep Cuba's influence away from Latin American countries, Castro was slowly gaining respectability. Faced with the possibility of the OAS lifting sanctions on Cuba, Ford was willing to normalize relations with Cuba, realizing that antagonistic feelings towards one another was not benefitting either country. Kissinger explained to Ford the current situation within the OAS:

> There are two aspects: bilateral and in the OAS. State is preparing a paper with these guidelines: we are being moved into relations with Cuba, but it should not appear to the American people as if it is being forced on us. So I would hold tough in the OAS, using the Brazilians. But we should start low-level talks with the Cubans to see what we can get for it. If we don't, we may be driven by majority votes from one position to the other.[5]

Ford was also feeling the pressure from such countries as Mexico, which had never cut its ties with Cuba, and with Panama, which had restored them in 1974. The growing feeling among an increasing number of Western Hemisphere nations was the primary reason why Ford began low-level diplomacy with Cuba to work towards a normalization of affairs. A secret U.S. government report dated 15 August 1974, commented on Fidel Castro's motives.

> Fidel Castro still perceives Latin American rejection of United States leadership as the ultimate guarantee of his revolution. Since 1968 he

has pursued that objective primarily through selective diplomacy directed at establishing state-to-state relations rather than by the promotion of continental revolution. His strategy now seeks relations and trade with "independent" governments as a means of legitimizing his revolution, while diminishing U.S. influence and weakening the OAS.

From our own standpoint maintenance of the sanctions has been increasingly complicated by their effect on the controls on the third-country operations of American corporations. Our controls on trade with Cuba involving U.S. subsidiaries is regarded in a number of Latin American countries as a direct challenge to national sovereignty. Opposition to the policy has also been growing in the Congress and among opinion makers in this country.[6]

The report said that Ford had no other option but to allow the OAS resolution to go through. Cuba was becoming less isolated. Therefore, to avoid any embarrassment, the U.S. government should no longer prevent members of the OAS from lifting the sanctions. The next move was to accept a resolution but maintain U.S. sanctions against Cuba.

Another indication of the U.S. failure to isolate Cuba was Canada's role as an active trading partner with Cuba. This was possible because Canada was not then a member of the OAS. The Kennedy administration had exerted some pressure on Canada to join a hemispheric boycott on Cuba, but Canada's Prime Minister, John Diefenbaker, had resisted. The Cuban policies of Diefenbaker's continued to diverge from what the White House wanted. In 1976, Pierre Elliot Trudeau and his wife Margaret actually went to Cuba and met Fidel Castro. The Prime Minister's actions there will be discussed in Chapter Four.

The Ford administration agreed to a special OAS meeting where members could debate relations with Cuba. In Quito, Ecuador, in November 1974, the members failed by two votes to reach a two-thirds majority required for the lifting of sanctions. Leaders of other countries blamed this failure on the United States. The U.S. was accused of not solving the problem by publicly announcing it would not end its own sanctions until Cuba convinced the U.S. it was willing to work on a reciprocal relationship for normalization. "Only Bolivia, Paraguay, Chile and perhaps Brazil continue[d] to resist any change in the status quo without pressure from the U.S.,"[7] said one official. However, this only delayed the inevitable. The Cuban issue remained a burning topic on the OAS agenda. For that reason, the OAS meeting of July 1975, this time in San José, Costa Rica, called for another debate on the issue. A resolution leaving each country free to deter-mine what it would like to do about the sanctions passed with a two-thirds ma-jority.

The OAS vote was a victory for Fidel Castro and a blow to the United States. Castro established diplomatic relations with a number of OAS members. Mem-bers of Congress debated the possibility of even the United States normalizing re-lations. After the lifting of the sanctions by the OAS, Ford had to repeat that his administration would not lift sanctions until the Cubans were willing to work towards a policy of détente.

Yet, even before the lifting of the OAS sanctions the U.S. had established a dialogue through intermediary Frank Mankiewicz, a freelance journalist at the time of the Ford administration but once a spokesman for Robert Kennedy, the assassinated presidential candidate of 1968. Kissinger had sent him to Cuba to establish a communication with Castro, but Castro offered nothing of substance concerning relaxation of tensions between the two countries. It was not until January 1975, when Ramón Sánchez-Parodi, a senior official in the Cuban Communist Party, approached Mankiewicz with an offer for a meeting with a senior American diplomat. Deputy Under-Secretary of State Lawrence Eagleburger was assigned to meet the Cuban delegates at La Guardia airport, New York, 11 January 1975. (Diplomats from countries which held member-ships in the United Nations could always go to New York.) The two Cuban dip-lomats were Sánchez-Parodi himself and Nestor Garcia, the First Secretary of Cuba's UN mission. For the first time since the Cuban revolution, Cuban dele-gates met American officials to negotiate. However, Eagleburger received a shocking statement from the Cuban diplomats. After Eagleburger established written talking points with the Cubans, Sánchez-Parodi said they lacked author-ity to begin negotiations and that the American statements would have to be re-ported back to Castro. "Castro would not authorize negotiations unless the United States first lifted the embargo. Such a move would create 'favorable' con-ditions for the solution of other issues which they would be graciously prepared to list in exploratory conversations but not to negotiate about," he said.[8]

After the Ford administration rejected the Cuban proposal, there were no further developments until mid-February when the White House offered to lift the embargo at the end of the negotiations, but not at the beginning. While wait-ing for a Cuban response, President Ford stated that the U.S. would contemplate a change in the policy only if Cuba reevaluated its policy towards the United

States.[9] This hard stance by Ford created a list of options for the Cubans to follow if they desired any progress toward normalization. If Castro was serious about improved relations with the United States, then he would have to adhere to a few U.S. demands for détente. However, the U.S. demands for normalization proved unacceptable. At the Pierre Hotel in New York on 9 July 1975, Cuban diplomats contacted the State Department, and this time the same Cuban delegation met with Eagleburger and Assistant Secretary of State for Latin America William D. Rogers. Rogers presented the Cubans with a list of steps drafted as a resolution introduced in the first session of the ninety-fourth Congress on 30 July 1975.

> Resolved, that it is the sense of the Senate of the United States that before bilateral economic or diplomatic relations be resumed with Cuba, the following issues must be resolved.
>
> • Acceptance of fundamental human rights through a liberalization of travel restrictions, free emigration of Cuban and American citizens still in Cuba, access by impartial observers to prisons and detention centers, and the extension of constitutional guarantees to those now unlawfully imprisoned.
> • Acceptance of the standards of international law in dealing with international criminals such as hijackers.
> • Acknowledgement of claims for compensation for confiscated American property and prompt, good-faith negotiations on a comprehensive settlement.
> • Cessation of illegal terrorist activities in Puerto Rico. They are totally unacceptable and must cease forth-with.
> • Acceptance of principles set down in the Charter of the Organization of American States, including the principle of non-intervention.[10]

The Cuban delegates immediately rejected the U.S. proposal for normalization. Politically, it might have been suicide for Fidel Castro to meet these U.S. demands. If Fidel Castro undertook actions to carry out such steps, his most important allies, the Soviets, might desert him. Any relaxation in tensions with the United States might prove detrimental to Soviet reliance on the Cubans, and might hurt relations between Cuba and the Soviets.[11] For that reason, it appears, Castro was unwilling to co-operate with the U.S. The best that Castro was willing to do was allow a few family visits. Thus, the meeting between Rogers and Eagleburger with the Cuban delegates made no progress. Sánchez-Parodi told the U.S. delegates: "We cannot negotiate under the blockade. We are willing to discuss issues related to easing the blocking but until the embargo is lifted, Cuba and the United States cannot deal with each other as equals and consequently cannot negotiate.[12] Hence, Cuba was telling the United States that negotiations were impossible. Fidel Castro was asking the Americans to lift the embargo, which was the only negotiable incentive the U.S. had, in order to make sure the Cubans would take reciprocal steps in the normalization process. If the Americans lifted the U.S. sanctions on Cuba, then what incentive would Castro have to ease tensions with the United States? How could the United States trust Fidel Castro? That Castro must have been thinking the same way helps to explain Castro's reluctance to follow U.S. demands. Once again, the U.S.-Cuban diplomatic talks remained deadlocked.

Ford, Cuba, and Puerto Rico

Castro further antagonized the Ford Administration by calling an international conference concerning the independence of Puerto Rico, despite earlier warnings not to do so. The timing could not have been worse. In July 1975, the U.S. State Department agreed to permit subsidiaries of U.S. companies in third countries (including Canada) to resume trade with Cuba. A confidential National Security Committee memorandum for the President expressed concern over Canada's growing hostility over the economic restrictions on trade with Cuba by subsidiaries of U.S. companies operating abroad. In other words, trade which was legal under Canadian law had been illegal under U.S. law, and Canadian authorities thought that Canadian law should apply to companies located in Canada:

> The governments of Canada and Mexico (among others) insist that the extraterritorial application of U.S. law and regulations to prevent trade with Cuba violates their sovereignty. The Canadian Government is considering legislation that would force U.S. subsidiaries in Canada to trade with Cuba irrespective of U.S. law and has announced that henceforth it will not act to bar re-export to third countries of U.S. components incorporated in Canadian manufactured goods.
>
> We believe the time has come to modify administrative regulations to permit local subsidiaries of U.S. corporations to conform to the national policies of host countries where those policies call for trade with Cuba.[13]

The decision received the necessary approval and was announced in August, the same day Cuba called for a conference on Puerto Rico. In the words of a biographer of Fidel Castro, Tad Szulc, Fidel Castro's "urging [of] Puerto Rican independence [was] calculated to provoke United States anger."[14] This was a costly Cuban mistake. Henry Kissinger would describe Castro's move as "rub[bing] salt into the wound."[15] This is the point when U.S.-Cuban détente effectively ended. For the remainder of Ford's presidency, the U.S. and Cuba were unable to agree on anything. Any attempt at détente between the two countries ended.

In early September 1975, Castro proceeded with his Puerto Rican Solidarity Conference. Castro believed that Puerto Rico was a country struggling for independence, similar to Cuba before the revolution of 1959. Both, after all, had been Spanish colonies until the Spanish-American War of 1898, after which the United States had annexed Puerto Rico but granted Cuba limited independence. However, the Puerto Rican experience after 1898 had been happier than the Cuban, and few Puerto Ricans wanted the kind of independence envisioned by Castro. According to Oscar Diaz de Villegas, Vice-President of the Republican National Party of Puerto Rico, Cubans were unaware of the general feeling in Puerto Rico, and most Puerto Ricans had little interest in Cuba:

> The great majority of the [Puerto Ricans] are unacquainted with the Cuban case and its far-reaching implications. It just simply does not exist for them. Informed persons are often astonished by questions made to them which reveal the utter lack of information and interest of the American people about communism in Cuba, right at the doorstep of their own country.[16]

Still, Cuban officials stressed their similarities with Puerto Ricans. In fact, during the U.S.-Cuban dialogue, the Cuban delegates told their American counterparts that their demand for normalization of negotiations, aside from the immediate lifting of the embargo, was that the United States admit to guilty actions concerning the meddling of affairs in the Dominican Republic and Chile.[17] (These were references to President Johnson's dispatch of marines to the Dominican Republic in 1965 and the CIA-assisted Pinochet coup of 1973 in Chile.) When Ford heard of Cuba's request for U.S. confessions on illegal revolutionary conduct, he was outraged. According to Kissinger, Ford was furious about the whole meeting, especially when he was briefed about Sánchez-Parodi's rejection of the U.S. request for Cuban restraint on Puerto Rico. Sánchez-Parodi said:

The history and the struggles of Cuba and Puerto Rico are very closely related. The essential difference is that we won our struggle for independence and the Puerto Ricans did not. It must be recognized that we believe Puerto Rico is a distinct and independent nationality. Puerto Rico is in fact a colonial matter. This explains our attitude in the U.N. We believe that Puerto Rico had a need for independence and self-determination...We do not believe that the current situation in Puerto Rico is a reflection of the will of the people of Puerto Rico.[18]

Clearly, such opinions on Puerto Rico could not have been more wrong. If Castro and Sánchez-Parodi believed the independence movement had the support of the people of Puerto Rico, then they must never have examined that island's election results and the poor showing of parties which favoured independence. On 2 November 1976, Puerto Rico's regularly scheduled quadrennial elections took place. As usual, the Puerto Rican Independence Party and the Puertico Riecan Socialist Party received barely 5% of the votes cast.[19]

Castro Accuses the United States of Sponsoring Terrorism

Nor was Puerto Rico the only bone of contention between the United States and revolutionary Cuba. On 6 October 1976, Castro joined Forbes Burnham, Guyana's head of government, in accusing the United States of sabotaging a Cubana airliner with seventy-three people aboard, all of whom died. The Ford administration denied any involvement in the incident. Its position was, "This government is committed both morally and by international law to the eradication of terrorism, and we take that commitment very seriously."[20] The Cubana airliner was heading to Cuba from Guyana and crashed near the coast of Venezuela. The Venezuelan Government arrested five terrorists, including Orlando Bosch.

On 9 June 2005, Washington's National Security Archive (NSA, despite the name a privately funded non-governmental organization) posted additional information on Bosch and the explosion. A CIA document obtained by the NSA revealed that a matter of days before the tragedy, a Cuban exile named Luis Posada had discussed his intention to destroy a Cuban airliner. At the time, Orlando Bosch headed what the FBI termed "an anti-Castro terrorist umbrella organization" with the acronym CORU. Between 22 September and 5 October, CORU hosted a $1000-a-plate fund-raising dinner. By 18 October 1976, almost two weeks after the explosion, Henry Kissinger received a report which included Posada's threat to attack the Cuban airliner and affirmed Bosch's knowledge of the plan. Three days later, an FBI document confirmed that CORU "was responsible for the bombing of the Cubana Airlines DC-8 on October 6, 1976." An FBI report of 29 June 1976 reported the founding of CORU earlier that month in Bonao, Dominican Republic. According to the CIA, the FBI's source cited CORU member Secundino Carrera, who justified the bombing "because CORU was at war with the Fidel Castro regime." CORU's leader, said the FBI, was Orlando Bosch. Posada had become a CIA agent in 1965, and although he became an officer of Venezuela's police force DISIP from 1967 to 1974, the CIA maintained contact with him. What Posada and the CIA actually did together during those years has been censored from the CIA document which the NSA obtained. According to the NSA, "The CIA also admitted that it had multiple contacts with Orlando Bosch in 1962 and 1963"[21]—that is, more than a decade before Ford became President. While the evidence appears to indicate that the Ford White House played no role in the seventy-three deaths, it does appear that with greater vigilance, the FBI and CIA could have given advance notice to some authority and perhaps prevented what happened. (Chapter Eleven will deal with the Ford administration's attitude toward reforms in the CIA.)

In the aftermath of the Cubana tragedy, Castro threatened to repudiate the U.S.-Cuban anti-hijacking agreement of 1973. The Cuban leader also stated that recent attacks on Cuban fishing vessels by exiles resident in the U.S. violated the U.S.-Cuban anti-hijacking agreement, and threatened that if the perpetrators were not punished Cuba would ignore the agreement. However, a Ford Administration official who commented on the Castro speech said:

> With regard to the incident to which the Cubans refer, the United States Government on April 16 informed the Cuban Government through the Swiss Embassy in Havana [which, in the absence of a U.S. Embassy in Cuba, acted as the protectors of U.S. interest there] that we are conducting an investigation of the incident and that appropriate actions will be taken if it is determined that persons subject to our jurisdiction have committed acts which appear to violate U.S. Federal law. The United States continues to honor the terms of the 1973 agreement on hijacking and the actions which we have taken and are taking are in accordance with the provisions of that agreement. The Cuban Government is well aware of our position on this, and we expect the Cuban Government also to honor the terms of the agreement.[22]

After this statement a journalist asked the official: "Are you saying the Cuban Government, prior to this Castro speech, was aware that U.S. officials are taking appropriate action regarding this incident?" The Ford Administration official then replied: "Yes, the Cuban Government had been assured that an investigation is underway."[23]

Fidel Castro was looking for any opportunity to portray the U.S. in the darkest terms. However, the false accusations made against the Ford administration were provocative attempts to antagonize the United States. On a more personal note, Fidel Castro referred to President Ford as a "vulgar liar" with regard to the Cuban involvement in Angola.[24]

Ford, Cuba, and Angola

For nearly 500 years, Portugal had African colonies. This changed 25 April 1974 when army officers from the Portuguese military staged a coup against Portuguese dictator Marcello Caetano. After the death of Antonio Salazar in 1970, Caetano had assumed the duties of the head of state. After the successful coup, the new rulers of Portugal wanted to free themselves from what they thought was a losing cause, the bloody civil war raging through Angola, which was depleting Portugal's national resources and claiming too many lives. Portugal's new leaders sought to free themselves from this burden, even if this meant leaving the Angola in utter chaos.

At the time of Portugal's withdrawal from Angola, there were three main anti-colonial groups competing for control of the country. All had support from elsewhere, principally Zaïre (the former Belgian Congo, now the Democratic Republic of the Congo), Cuba and South Africa. Each of the three significant Angolan factions sought to succeed the Portuguese in governing Angola. The first was the Movimento Popular de Libertação de Angola (MPLA), a Marxist group originating in 1957, supported primarily by Cuba. At the time of its anti-colonial struggle, the leader of the MPLA forces was Agostinho Neto, a doctor and poet. MPLA control of the capital, Luanda, made it a much stronger competitor than the other factions. However, its ties with Cuba created enemies, one of them the United States. The second contending faction was Holden Roberto's Frente Nacional de Libertação de Angola (FNLA). The FNLA received most of its support from the Bakongo people, and because Roberto was the brother-in-law of Zaïrian leader Mobutu Sese Seko, it enjoyed many privileges in neighboring Zaïre.[25] In reaction to the Cuban backed MPLA, the United States decided to offer aid to the FNLA. Another faction that received significant U.S. aid was the União Nacional para a Independência Total de Angola (UNITA), led by Dr. Jonas Savimbi. It was the youngest of the Angolan liberation groups, but had the support of the largest ethnic group in Angola, the Ovimbundu people. Along with the United States, China was an important supporter of UNITA. On 15 January 1975, Portugal and the three liberation movements agreed to a transitional government under the authority of a Portuguese High Commissioner until the date of independence, 11 November 1975.[26]

For years, historians who studied the events in Angola relied heavily on speculation or declassified American documents. However, now historians can confirm that the role the Soviets played in Angola was not as significant as once thought. During the Cold War, Conventional Wisdom was that the Soviets were the main supporters of the MPLA, and were pressuring Fidel Castro to send soldiers to Angola. Perhaps this was the price Castro had to pay for selling Cuban sugar to the Soviet Union at inflated prices and purchasing Soviet oil for less than the world price. However, historian Piero Gleijeses has shown that this was not the case. Gleijeses managed to gain rare access to Cuban documents with persuasive evidence that the Cubans usually provided the leadership in Angolan affairs, and the Soviets reluctantly felt obliged to follow.[27] Thus, the Soviets were not the main contributors to the MPLA. However, appearances can be more important than realities, and the supposed Cuban role as perceived Soviet surrogates raised the level of concern in the Ford White House.

Cuban importance to the MPLA dates from 1966-67, when a handful of Cubans briefly joined the MPLA in Cabinda, until the MPLA withdrew from that area to combat opponents on the eastern border of Zambia. The Cuban involvement halted during this transition, not because anyone wanted to withdraw, but because of growing Zambian opposition.[28] This prior involvement in Angola was a principal reason for renewed Cuban support in late December 1974, the period of Havana's first high-level contact with the MPLA. At that time, Agostinho Neto was not entirely certain what he wanted from Cuba, but he did tell Cuban officials that "he was confident that they would receive Soviet aid, but that it would not arrive for five months and that it was therefore imperative to move their material and equipment from Dar es-Salaam" (across the continent on the Indian Ocean in Tanzania) to Angola.[29] In order for the MPLA to do this, it would need $100,000. The puzzling piece to this story is that Cuba did not send the money to the MPLA. One reason why Cuban authorities might not have jumped on the idea might have been anticipated progress towards normalization with the U.S. (There will be further certainty when more Cuban documents become available.) Another reason might have been the fact that the OAS was beginning to lift sanctions on Cuba, and Cuba's leaders knew that an involvement in Angola thousands of miles away would jeopardize their country's status with the OAS. Another explanation was that the Soviet Union did not want the Cubans to become involved in Angola. However, Piero Gleijeses found none of these reasons persuasive. He asked rhetorically, "Can one seriously argue that Cuba needed Soviet permission to send $100,000 to Neto?"[30]

Nevertheless, eight months later, in August 1975, when the civil war in Angola was worsening, the MPLA requested aid once again. This time the MPLA received Cuban support; in fact, it received more than it had expected. On top of the $100,000, the Cubans would send 480 men who would help establish four training centers known as Centros de Instrucción Revolucionaria (CIRs). They would prepare to train recruits and arm them with Cuban weapons.[31] By August 1975, the Cubans were involved, but primarily with training and recruiting, not fighting. It would not be until mid-October when the instructors became involved at the battle of Morro do Cal on 23 October. Roberto's FNLA forces had invaded Morro do Cal, and the Cubans fought back. For the first time in the Angolan civil war, the Cubans, numbering around 40, participated in the fighting.[32]

Papers declassified in May 2001 at the Gerald Ford Presidential Library confirm that the Ford administration closely monitored events in Angola. In fact, the United States had been receiving many intelligence reports since the Kennedy administration, although it was not until the Ford presidency when the U.S. became directly involved in the shaping of Angolan events. President Ford wrote Carl Albert, Speaker of the House of Representatives, that the United States had provided no military aid to any group until the late summer of 1975, a few months after Communist forces captured Saigon. After this period, the United States "provided modest amounts of assistance to forces opposing the Soviet/Cuban-backed effort, solely to enable the indigenous majority to stabilize the military situation and to create conditions for a negotiated solution."[33]

The U.S. decision to help forces opposing the MPLA was influenced by many factors. Secretary of State Henry Kissinger, along with President Ford, received President Kenneth Kaunda of Zambia 19 April 1975. It was on this specific visit to the United States that Kaunda pleaded for U.S. help. President Kaunda expressed concern about the heavy influx of foreign aid from the Soviet Union and Cuba. He used this argument to persuade Ford and Kissinger to intervene for the sake of Angola's neighbors.[34] According to Henry Kissinger, the U.S. became involved for only those reasons. However, documents declassified 21 May 2001 indicate the extent of U.S. interests in Angola. As of Friday 27 June 1975, American private sector investment in Angola was worth over $400 million. $300 million of the total investment was situated with Gulf Oil, located in Cabinda. Protection of those investments was a consideration. Another reason the U.S. might have wanted to thwart Soviet/Cuban influence was the possibility of losing any access to port or airfield facilities along the coast of Angola.

One can only speculate upon the actual motives of President Ford and Henry Kissinger, but there are some really good explanations, which are not limited to the stated reasons. According to the officials of the Ford Administration, morality was a factor. They strongly believed the Soviets and Cubans had no right to exert their influence so far from home. On numerous occasions the Ford administration stated publicly it had no problem with an indigenous Marxist MPLA. The only problem was with the Soviet/Cuban influence on the MPLA. This is reinforced in the statement of Henry Kissinger to the Secretary General of the Organization of African Unity (OAU), William Eteki.

> For our part, the United States is pursuing no unilateral interests in Angola. As I have stated publicly, the United States has no other interests there but the territorial integrity and independence of Angola. We believe the people of Angola have a right to a government of their own choosing and to live in peaceful independence and well-being.[35]

According to Kissinger, Soviets and Cubans had no legitimate reason to intervene financially or militarily in Angola. Therefore, Angolans should have the right to establish a majority government through an African solution and not a foreign superpower solution.

Cold War factors offer at least a partial explanation as to why the Ford administration decided to become involved in the Angolan civil war. Cuba was and the Soviet Union appeared to be increasingly involved in Angola. The White House wanted to emphasize to both friend and foe that failure in Vietnam would not discourage the U.S. from fighting Communists elsewhere. It might be detrimental to the U.S. position in the Cold War if Americans allowed the Soviets and Cubans to intervene in peripheral Third World areas, especially areas where the U.S. had interests of its own. Nothing might stop Cubans and Soviets from going elsewhere after they had finished in Angola. Moreover, African friends of the United States might need reassurance that Vietnam was not going to weaken the global battle against Communism.

The Ford administration made its decision to intervene on the side of the FNLA and UNITA and to oppose the MPLA. Throughout the summer of 1975, Ford and Kissinger kept close tabs on the situation in Africa. Their primary goal was to stabilize the situation in Angola through a peaceful transition. In the meantime, Ford and Kissinger were trying to appropriate the desirable amount of funds for the FNLA/UNITA coalition. The funds would be presented to the 40 Committee, the CIA interagency committee supervising covert intelligence activities. In mid–July 1975, it studied Ford's request for $6 million and increased the amount to $20 million.[36] After pondering the problem for three months, the White House decided to send this money to Angola through Zaïre. In the meantime the U.S. would condemn the Soviets and Cubans publicly, thereby weakening their prestige among the member nations of the Organization of African Unity.

While the civil war in Angola was escalating, the FNLA/UNITA factions with U.S. aid were slowly marching towards Luanda, the Angolan capital controlled by the MPLA. Apart from the U.S. aid, the war was slowly turning in the favor of the FNLA/UNITA. The massive involvement by South African forces was another factor. In October 1975, U.S. intelligence reported that South Africans were staging battles in Angola against the MPLA. According to Henry Kissinger, "South Africa had opted for intervention without prior consultation with the United States. We learned of it no later than the CIA report of October 31…"[37] This statement is controversial and contradicts a statement in the memoirs of F. W. De Klerk, who would be South Africa's President from 1989 to 1994. A member of parliament during the Angolan Civil War but not a member of the cabinet until 1978, and without revealing his sources, De Klerk stated, "South Africa had been asked by the United States and several moderate African countries to come to the aid of UNITA and the FNLA, the anti-Communist movements in the country."[38] Documents at the Gerald Ford Presidential Library disagree. They indicate that Ford and Kissinger were deeply concerned about South Africa's involvement. They must have known that public collaboration between South Africa's white minority government in the era of *apartheid* could jeopardize U.S. prestige among black Africans. Ford and Kissinger said that they witnessed the "South African intervention as a political embarrassment…"[39]

Nevertheless, documents released by the National Security Archive Easter weekend 2002 confirm that South African forces preceded Cuban troops into Angola, and that the South Africans went there with full co-operation from the Ford Administration.[40] Fidel Castro's government was sending money and advisors as early as mid-1975, without consulting the Soviets. Revelations of Cuban involvement came as a complete surprise to Ford and Kissinger, who regarded Cubans in Angola as Soviet proxies, when they were there on Fidel Castro's initiative to fight South Africans.

In November, the Angolan situation became tense for the Ford Administration. The CIA was reporting a heavy influx of Cuban soldiers arriving in Angola aboard Soviet ships and planes. The MPLA was quickly turning the tables. The FNLA/UNITA forces were closing in on the capital and it looked as if they would be there by 11 November, the scheduled date of independence. Instead, the fresh Cuban troops were able to hold off the opposition, and the MPLA declared itself the government of Angola on 11 November 1975. Ford and Kissinger chose to counter the Cubans, and this meant that the U.S. would have to increase its funding of the FNLA/UNITA factions.

At this point, Ford and Kissinger hit a stumbling block. In order to halt the MPLA, the U.S. government needed more funds, and President Ford had three options. The first option was $28 million, the second option was $60 million and the final option was $100 million. Ford chose the smallest of the three. However, even this would require Congressional approval, and the Democrats controlled both houses of Congress, and this previously covert program became a controversial issue for Congress once it became a public issue. Throughout the whole ordeal, Ford and Kissinger briefed Congress. They also reported each escalation. When newspapers revealed U.S. involvement in Angola, Congress was quick to deny any knowledge of the incident. Kissinger's memoirs state, "[The] public outcry ended Congress's acquiescence in the covert program because few of those briefed were prepared to face the onslaught if they publicly endorsed what they had secretly approved."[41] Lack of support from Congress severely limited what Ford and Kissinger could do.

After the covert program became common knowledge, Congress ran for cover and tried to save itself from any involvement. Led by Senators John Tunney (Democrat- California) and Dick Clark (Democrat-Iowa), all funding for Angola, direct or indirect, was to be cut from the defense bill.[42] This became known as the Tunney/Clark Amendment. On 19 December 1975, U.S. involvement in Angola ended. When the Senate voted 54-22 to deny funding for military action in Angola, the immediate reaction of Ford and Kissinger was one of deep concern. A letter President Ford sent to the Speaker of the House, Carl Albert, depicts Ford's bitterness on the Senate decision:

> The Senate decision to cut off additional funds for Angola is a deep tragedy for all countries whose security depends on the United States. Ultimately, it will profoundly affect the security of our country as well.
>
> How can the United States, the greatest power in the world, take the position that the Soviet Union can operate with impunity many thousands of miles away with Cuban troops and massive amounts of military equipment, while we refuse any assistance to the majority of the local people who ask only for military equipment to defend themselves?
>
> The issue in Angola is not, never has been, and never will be, a question of the use of U.S. forces. The sole issue is the provision of modest amounts of assistance to oppose military intervention by two extra-continental powers, namely the Soviet Union and Cuba. This abdication of responsibility by a majority of the Senate will have the gravest consequences for the long term position of the United States and for international order in general. A great nation cannot escape its responsibilities. Responsibilities abandoned today will return as more acute crises tomorrow. I therefore call upon the Senate to reverse its position before it adjourns. Failure to do so will, in my judgment, seriously damage the national interest of the United States.[43]

Kissinger too was furious with the decision. On 27 January 1976, the house received the Defense Department Appropriations Bill, including the overt funding for anti–MPLA factions. The House also voted affirmatively (323:99) to another bill to stop any overt funding in Angola. Among members of the House of Representatives, the Republican vote was 72:69 and the Democratic vote was 251:30. Ford and Kissinger lacked support from a majority of even their own party's Representatives! This is not what President Ford expected from his own party. However, everybody in the House was reluctant to involve the U.S. in another Vietnam type war. The final blow to President Ford and Secretary Kissinger was the passing of the Clark Amendment in June 1976, which made the Tunney Amendment final. President Ford felt as though he had had the ground cut from under his feet, as he attempted to safeguard U.S. interests across the globe. To let the Soviets and the Cubans have a free hand would become a fatal scar for the U.S. image.

In the aftermath of these events, the Cuban forces doubled in size. They remained in Angola for another fifteen years and spread into Ethiopia, Somalia, and South Yemen. Even after the MPLA established itself as the Angolan government, twenty-two African nations refused to recognize it. Henry Kissinger says that diplomatic support could have easily been achieved if the Senate had not cut the funds. In the end the Angolan crises became a domestic fiasco for the Ford Administration. However, years later the Reagan administration countered the Cuban involvement by winning a reversal of the Clark Amendment and then re-introducing the covert program Gerald Ford had had to abandon.[44]

The next U.S.-Cuban diplomatic struggle over Angola resumed after the adoption of the Tunney/Clark amendments. Officials within the White House were debating whether the U.S. should vote in favor of Angolan recognition at the United Nations. President Ford's initial reaction was to veto any such membership, stating reasons as to why the U.S. felt this way. Ford believed that Angola's membership in the UN would be a violation of UN policy, which only recognized states considered peace loving. As long as Cuban troops were inside the country, Ford announced that the U.S. would never recognize the MPLA as the Angolan government. Ford had a strong case in presenting this stance within the U.S. It was clear that Angola lacked a peace loving government, as Cuban troops were militarily enforcing a minority regime upon the Angolans. In response to U.S. criticism, an Angolan representative in the UN stated, "Angola... would join the [UN] to fight the evils and injustices it struggled against within its own borders. It was fully prepared to shoulder the responsibilities of membership.[45] The Ford administration disagreed with this statement because it felt that the application of UN membership was not acceptable under Article 4 of the UN Charter. Article 4 states that only peace loving nations and governments which are willing to comply with the UN obligations within the charter can be eligible for consideration of UN membership.[46] In Ford's view, Angola did not meet those stipulations for membership because a nation was not independent if it depended on nations such as Cuba. Ford's first response was to veto the application, but as time passed, it appeared that a veto decision concerning Angola would be detrimental to U.S.-African relations. After a visit to Africa, Kissinger stated that the U.S. was willing to work towards normalizing relations with the MPLA. What might have been a UN Security Council veto on 1 December 1976 became an abstention. The General Assembly approved Angola's membership in the United Nations, even if led by an MPLA government, by a vote of 116:0, with one abstention. Ford's adviser's persuaded the President that an abstention was preferable to a veto:

An abstention would probably avoid a bitter debate which a veto could provoke and in which the Cubans and Soviets could gain propaganda advantage. Ambassador [William] Scranton…[can] point out our continuing non-recognition of the MPLA and our insistence on the Cuban withdrawal from Angola.[47]

Conclusions

Angola, like Puerto Rico, was a sore point which disrupted U.S.-Cuban relations during the Ford administration. The door had been open to reconciliation, but Fidel Castro regarded independence for Puerto Rico and the success of the MPLA as higher priorities than improved relations with the United States. The bombing of the Cubana airliner also proved detrimental to the cause of reconciliation. Revolutionary propaganda stressed the importance of international concerns,[48] and it seems to have meant what it said. Fidel Castro's values were not those of Ford and Kissinger, and differences of opinion over Puerto Rico and Angola kept them apart. Indeed, Castro's actions in connection with Puerto Rico and his rhetoric on such other U.S. misdeeds as Pinochet's coup in Chile indicate that he probably had little interest in an improved U.S.-Cuban relationship.

Notes

1. This chapter is an updated extract from Mark Gauthier's undergraduate Honours Essay (thesis), "Gerald Ford and Relations with Castro's Cuba," Laurentian University, 2002.
2. President Ford's prepared remarks for the press, Office of the Assistant Press Secretary for National Security Affairs, Box A2, GFPL.
3. "Inter-American Treaty of Reciprocal Assistance," Río de Janeiro, 2 September 1947, *United Nations Treaty Series*, Vol. XXI (1948), p. 93.
4. "American Treaty on Pacific Settlement (Pact of Bogotá)," Bogotá, 30 April 1948, *United Nations Treaty Series*, Vol. XXX (1949), p. 84.
5. Kissinger, p. 774.
6. National Security Adviser meeting, 15 April 1974, Presidential Country Files for Latin America, 1974, Box 2, GFPL.
7. National Security Advisor, Presidential Country Files for Latin America 1974-77, Box 2, GFPL.
8. Kissinger, p. 776.
9. *Public Papers of the Presidents: Gerald Ford*, Book II, 21 July to 31 December 1975 (Washington: United States Government Printing Office, 1977) 1987.
10. Senate Resolution, 30 July 1975, White House Central Files, Box 15, GFPL.
11. Kissinger, *Years of Renewal*, p. 786.
12. Kissinger, p. 780.
13. Memo, Ingersoll to the President, 25 February 1975, folder Cuba—Economic, Social—Sanctions (1), box A2, National Security Adviser. Temporary Parallel File of Documents from Otherwise Unprocessed Parts of the Collection, GFPL.
14. Tad Szulc, *A Critical Portrait: Fidel*, (New York: Avon, 1986), 712-13.

15. Kissinger, *Years of Renewal*, 782.
16. A letter from Diaz de Villegas to President Ford explaining Puerto Rico's concern of U.S.-Cuban normalization, WHCF, Box 15, Folder: Cuba, GFPL.
17. Kissinger, p. 781.
18. Statement made by Sánchez-Parodi, quoted in Kissinger's *Years of Renewal*, 781.
19. The *New York Times*, 3 November 1976.
20. Office of the Assistant to the President for the National Security Affairs, Box A2, 15 October 1976, GFPL, Ann Arbor, Michigan.
21. http://www.gwu.edu/~nsarchiv/NSAEBB/NSAEBB157/index.htm
22. Ibid.
23. Ibid.
24. Ibid.
25. Jeremy Harding, *The Fate of Africa: Trial by Fire* (New York: Simon & Schuster, 1993), p. 27.
26. Piero Gleijeses, "Havana's Policy in Africa, 1959-76: New Evidence from Cuban Archives," *Cold War International History Project* (1996-97): 8. Cited hereafter as *CWIHP*.
27. See Pierro Gleijeses, *Conflicting Missions: Havana, Washington and Africa* (Chapel Hill: University of North Carolina Press, 2002).
28. Gleijeses, "Havana's Policy,"p. 7, *CWIHP*.
29. Gleijeses: Letter from Neto to Cuban leadership, Dar-es-Salaam, 26 January 1975, p. 14, *CWIHP*.
30. Gleijeses, p., 9, *CWIHP*.
31. Gleijeses, p. 9, *CWIHP*..
32. Gleijeses, p. 11, *CWIHP*.
33. Letter, President Ford to Speaker of the House Carl Albert, 26 January 1976, Presidential Country Files, Box 1, Folder: Angola (2), GFPL.
34. Kissinger, p. 791.
35. Kissinger, p. 821.
36. Kissinger, p. 809.
37. Kissinger, p. 809.
38. F.W. De Klerk, *FW De Klerk: The Autobiography* (London: Macmillan, 1998), p. 58.
39. Kissinger, p. 821.
40. See also Gleijeses, *Conflicting Missions*. Gleijeses had access to the South African as well as the Cuban archives.
41. Kissinger, p. 827.
42. *Congressional Quarterly Inc.*, Vol. 33, no. 49 (Washington: GPO, 1975), p. 2833.
43. Letter, President Ford to Speaker of the House Carl Albert, 29 Dec. 1975, Presidential Country Files, Box 1, Folder: Angola (2), GFPL.
44. Kissinger, p. 832.
45. *United Nations Yearbook*, Consideration of applications for [Angolan] membership, 1976, p. 308.
46. Ibid., p. 305.
47. National Security Advisor Brent Scowcroft to President Ford, 10 May 1976, Presidential Country Files Box 6, Folder: Angola (2), GFPL.
48. Stephen J. Randall and Graeme S. Mount, *The Caribbean Basin: An International History* (London and New York: Routledge, 1998), centrepiece picture (#10) of a Cuban propaganda sign stating the importance of exporting the Cuban Revolution.

Chapter Four

CANADA JOINS THE ECONOMIC SUMMIT

W hat appeared as provocative behaviour on the part of Prime Minister Pierre Elliott Trudeau might easily have soured relations between the United States and Canada. In January 1976, Trudeau went to Cuba and shouted, "Viva Cuba y el Pueblo Cubano!," "Viva el Primer Ministro Comandante Fidel Castro!" and "Viva la amistad cubano-canadiense!"[1] ("Long live Cuba and the Cuban people!," "Long live Prime Minister Commander Fidel Castro!" and "Long live Cuban-Canadian friendship!")

Yet, clearly relations did not sour. Relations with the Ford administration were excellent, and in his memoirs, Trudeau indicated that of the five presidents whose terms coincided with his own (Lyndon Johnson, Richard Nixon, Gerald Ford, Jimmy Carter, Ronald Reagan), Ford was his favourite. "Of all the American presidents I had occasion to deal with, what set Ford apart was that he did nothing I can remember that rubbed Canada the wrong way."[2] So strong was the personal chemistry between the two men that they skied together over the New Year's holiday and continued to see each other after both had left public life.[3] Trudeau gives credit to the Ford administration for what he calls "one of the greatest achievements of Canadian foreign policy—Canada's admission to the Economic Summit."[4] Now known as the G-7, the Economic Summit was an annual series of conferences which began as the G-5 at Rambouillet in France during 1975 (with leaders from France, Japan, West Germany, the United Kingdom, and the United States in attendance), expanded to the G-7 at the Puerto Rican gathering of 1976 (with the addition of Canada and Italy), and became the G-8 (with Russian participation) after the Cold War. What Canada did in connection with the pricing of natural gas struck the White House as worse than what the Canadian Prime minister said or did in Cuba, but even that proved less than a barrier to membership in the G-7.

Early in January 1976, Ivan Head–Legislative Assistant to Prime Minister Trudeau–approached the U.S. Embassy in Ottawa to outline Trudeau's plans for the Cuban trip. It was Head's intention that Trudeau should reprimand Castro for sending troops to Angola, but he wanted information on the subject. Denis Clift of the National Security Council provided voluminous information[5] but also wanted to tell Head that the U.S. government preferred that the trip be cancelled or postponed. Castro would use Trudeau's visit to argue that what he was doing in Angola did not damage Cuban relations with other countries. Yet, if the trip *were* to take place, Trudeau could serve a useful purpose by protesting Cuban actions in Africa.[6]

It appears that Trudeau accepted Head's advice and thus played a role which the White House found useful, if not quite what Clift wanted. Trudeau's own account, without mentioning Ford or any other American, is that he forwarded the message that Fidel Castro should withdraw his army from Angola. When Head met Scowcroft for a working lunch 21 April, the briefing paper for Scowcroft which Clift had prepared said nothing about Trudeau's trip to Cuba except that Head had accompanied him there.[7] Evidently Trudeau's performance had not created consternation in Washington.

Certainly, from the standpoint of the White House, everything that Trudeau conveyed with regard to Angola was exactly what the Ford administration —or any other U.S. administration—would have wanted. Trudeau told Castro that the despatch of Cuban soldiers to Angola was "meddling in the internal affairs of a foreign country." Castro disagreed. There was no comparison in his eyes between what the U.S. had done in Vietnam and what Cuba was doing in Angola. Cuba was assisting Angola's legitimate government from attack by South African-backed guerrillas and "some NATO powers." In his memoirs, Trudeau accused Castro of dishonesty, telling him that a certain number of Cubans had gone to Angola when the actual figure was considerably higher. Trudeau responded firmly: "Until then," he wrote,

> [W]e had traded with Cuba and given the country economic aid in spite of constant pressure on us from the United States to do the contrary. But because of the Angolan war, we cut off all aid to Cuba, except humanitarian aid. I did not meet Castro again until many years later, so I don't know what his reaction was to our tough policy. But I'm sure he didn't like it.[8]

Ford could not have asked for more, and in the long run, even Fidel Castro could not have been too angry. Once Trudeau left public life, he visited Castro in Cuba, and when Trudeau died in 2000, Castro flew to Montreal to attend his funeral.

With regard to the G-7, the initiative came from West German Chancellor Helmut Schmidt. In his memoirs, Trudeau spoke fondly of Schmidt, a Social Democrat, as a kindred spirit, one whose "views seemed very close to my middle-of-the-road liberalism."[9] In 1975, Schmidt had been one of the five leaders in attendance at the G-5 gathering in Rambouillet, hosted by French President Valery Giscard d'Estaing. (The others in attendance were President Ford and the prime ministers of Japan and the United Kingdom.) The leaders of the five countries with the world's largest economies agreed that the gathering had proven so useful that it was worthy of repetition on an annual basis, perhaps with an additional member or two. Giscard wanted Italy as an additional partner, but he did not want Canada.

Until French archives become open to historians some twenty years from now, one must guess at Giscard's reasons. Two who have done so are Ivan Head and Trudeau himself. Together they discussed Canadian foreign relations during Trudeau's almost sixteen years as Prime minister, and suggested that Giscard might have been staying the course with his immediate predecessors, Charles de Gaulle (President of France from 1959 to 1969) and Georges Pompidou (1969-1974).[10] For the last two years of his presidency, de Gaulle openly supported the cause of Quebec independence, and Pompidou was a Gaullist, a members of de Gaulle's party. While this is a plausible explanation, it is far from certain. Mitchell Sharp, who served as Canada's Minister of External Affairs for the first six years of Trudeau's term of office (1968-1974) wrote that as early as 1970, French Foreign Minister Maurice Schumann told him that President Pompidou was trying to improve the relationship between Canada and France.[11] Historians J.L. Granatstein and Robert Bothwell say that Giscard's relations with Ottawa were better than they had been under de Gaulle and Pompidou.[12] (Granatstein and Bothwell seem unaware of Schmidt's role,[13] not surprisingly since the documents at the Gerald Ford Presidential Library were declassified only in 2004.) Another consideration is that from 1970 until the autumn of 1976, Quebec had a Liberal government favourable to Quebec's remaining in Canada, not one which was conspiring with Paris to detach the province from Canada.

Head and Trudeau note that in 1975-1976, Canada's economy was larger than Italy's, but that Giscard wrote "in very warm terms" to explain why Italy should be welcome and Canada should not. Italy was a neighbour, and an Italian chaired the European Community. According to their account, U.S. and Japanese authorities sought another non-European partner so that Economic Summits would not be overly Eurocentric. The British and the West Germans resented French dominance of such conferences and thought that Canadian participation would lessen the importance of France. So strongly did Schmidt—a professional economist—feel about this, say Head and Trudeau, that he threatened to avoid any subsequent Economic Summits unless Canadians could be there as well.[14] It is reasonable to assume that Giscard's thinking was the mirror image of Schmidt's. While Schmidt wanted Canada to offset French influence, Giscard feared that Canada *would* offset French influence. On a visit to the White House 3 October 1975, Schmidt suggested that if Italy was to be part of the group, Canada should also be there. President Ford and Secretary of State Henry Kissinger were supportive.[15]

One of the hallmarks of Gerald Ford's presidency, however, was an energy crisis in the United States. For various reasons, including an Arab refusal to sell unlimited quantities of oil to friends of Israel, Americans worried whether they could drive their cars, heat their buildings, and maintain full production at factories.[16] One solution was to use natural gas instead of oil for heating and other purposes, and Canada was an obvious source of natural gas. The Trudeau government was willing to sell but at a price which members of the Ford administration considered excessive. In order to forestall the increased costs, they considered reprisals. Perhaps after all they might not invite Canada to the second economic summit, scheduled for the summer of 1976 in Puerto Rico. "Why should U.S. ask Canada to RII [Rambouillet II, a second Economic Summit] if they act like this?" Ford wrote to Scowcroft.[17] At the very least, said Ford to Kissinger and Scowcroft on 18 May 1976, the White House need not argue forcibly when Giscard said that Canada did not belong in such a gathering.[18]

That meeting of 18 May, not Trudeau's trip to Cuba, appears to be the low point in U.S.-Canada relations during Ford's presidency. On 15 June, the newly elected leader of Canada's Progressive Conservative party, Joe Clark, visited the White House,[19] and while Kissinger rated him as "a new dynamic guy," he advised Ford not to "give him anything to use against Trudeau."[20] The following day, Ford and Kissinger met Trudeau and his Finance Minister, Donald Macdonald. Trudeau thanked the President "for getting us into the Puerto Rico summit," and the subject of natural gas never arose.[21]

In the end, Canada did receive an invitation, and since 1976 Canadian prime ministers have joined the other heads of government and participated as full members of the G-7 (now G-8), most of whom continue to regard the annual meetings as worthwhile. On 10 October 1975, Ford told the visiting Portuguese foreign minister, Major Ernesto Augusto de Melo Antunes, "Trudeau spoke highly [by phone] of our efforts for him at the economic summit."[22] There is a certain irony to the phenomenon of U.S. and West German support for Canadian participation and French opposition. In the long run, Canada proved a less than useful ally of the United States at G-7 meetings. During the 1980s, when Ronald Reagan occupied the White House, Trudeau says that he and French President François Mitterrand were usually minorities of two at such events, confronting Reagan, British Prime Minister Margaret Thatcher, West German Chancellor Helmut Kohl (Schmidt's conservative successor, a Christian Democrat), and whoever happened to be Prime Minister of Japan.[23]

In brief, President Ford appreciated Trudeau as a partner more than he deplored his Cuban and energy policies. In the wake of Chancellor Schmidt, he assisted Canadian entry into one of the world's foremost corridors of power.

Notes

1. James John Guy, "Trudeau's Foreign Policy and Latin America," *Revista/Review Interamericana*, VII, 1 (Spring 1977), p. 105.
2. Pierre Elliott Trudeau, *Memoirs* (Toronto: McClelland and Stewart, 1993), p. 219.
3. Trudeau, pp. 218-219.
4. Trudeau, p. 219.
5. Not all the information was accurate, although it was undoubtedly the best available at the time. As indicated in Chapter Three, the White House saw Castro as a Soviet surrogate in Angola; subsequently historian Piero Gleijeses gained access to the Cuban Archives and discovered that the Angola campaign resulted from a Cuban initiative. See Piero Gleijeses, *Conflicting Missions, Havana, Washington, and Africa, 1959-1976* (Chapel Hill: University of North Carolina Press, 2002).
6. Memo, Clift to Scowcroft, 10 Jan. 1976, National Security Adviser, Presidential Country Files for Europe and Canada, Box 3, Folder: Canada (8), GFPL.
7. Memo, Clift to Scowcroft, 20 April 1976, National Security Adviser, Presidential Country Files for Europe and Canada, Box 3 , Folder: Canada (8), GFPL.
8. Trudeau, p. 212.
9. Trudeau, p. 200.
10. Ivan Head and Pierre Trudeau, *The Canadian Way: Shaping Canada's Foreign Policy, 1968-1984* (Vancouver: UBC Press, 1995), p. 196.
11. Mitchell Sharp, *Which Reminds Me...A Memoir* (Toronto: University of Toronto Press, 1994), p. 191.

12. J.L. Granatstein and Robert Bothwell, *Pirouette: Pierre Trudeau and Canadian Foreign Policy* (Toronto: University of Toronto Press, 1990), pp. 145-146, 345.

13. Granatstein and Bothwell, p. 303.

14. Head and Trudeau, pp. 196-197.

15. National Security Adviser, MEMORANDA OF CONVERSATIONS, 1973-1977, Box 15, Folder: October 3, 1975—Ford, Kissinger, FRG Chancellor Helmut Schmidt, GFPL. Also, Folder: October 9, 1975—Ford, Kissinger, GFPL.

16. Mieczkowski, pp. 197-270.

17. Edelgard E. Mahant and Graeme S. Mount, *Invisible and Inaudible in Washington* , p. 122.

18. National Security Adviser, MEMORANDA OF CONVERSATIONS, 1973-1977, Box 18, File: May 18, 1976—Ford, Kissinger, Rumsfeld, GFPL.

19. National Security Adviser, MEMORANDA OF CONVERSATIONS, 1973-1977, Box 19, File: June 15, 1976—Ford, Canadian Opposition Leader Joe Clark, GFPL.

20. National Security Adviser, MEMORANDA OF CONVERSATIONS, 1973-1977, Box 19, File: June 15, 1976—Ford, Kisssinger, Scowcroft.

21. National Security Adviser, MEMORANDA OF CONVERSATIONS, 1973-1977, Box 19, File: June 16, 1976—Ford, Kissinger, Canadian Prime Minister Pierre-Elliott Trudeau, Minister of Finance Donald Macdonald, GFPL.

22. National Security Adviser: MEMORANDA OF CONVERSATIONS, 1973-1977, Box 16, File: October 10, 1975—Ford, Kissinger, Portuguese Foreign Minister Antunes, GFPL.

23. Trudeau, p. 222.

Chapter Five

THE COLLAPSE OF SOUTH VIETNAM[1]

P resident Ford's predecessors had bequeathed him a terrible inheritance in South Vietnam, and there was no easy escape from the mess. Given the political mood in the United States, any alternative to what actually happened there on his watch was probably unthinkable, but what happened shook confidence in the American shield on the part of some key Asian allies. President Ford and Secretary Kissinger had little choice but to engage in damage control, certainly to the dismay of the latter, who blamed Congress for betrayal of an ally.[2]

In 1858, the adventurous French government of the Emperor Napoleon III began to occupy Vietnam and to establish protectorates over neighboring Laos and Cambodia. The Vichy Régime, established to govern unoccupied France and France's overseas territories in the aftermath of France's defeat by Germany in June and July 1940, granted Imperial Japan permission to establish bases in Vietnam. The government of President Franklin Roosevelt (understandably) regarded those bases as a means whereby Japan would gain unrestricted access to oil in the Dutch East Indies (now Indonesia). The Roosevelt administration responded with reprisals which Japan's leaders regarded as a provocation, which in turn led to the Japanese attack on Pearl Harbor. Committed to the defeat of the Axis partners—Germany, Italy, and Japan—the Roosevelt administration provided assistance to Vietnamese nationalists led by Ho Chi Minh, who happened to be a Communist. Following Japan's defeat, French forces struggled with Ho's Viet Minh, and in the aftermath of the Communist triumph in China in 1949, the Truman administration financed much of the French war effort. It did not want the blame for the "loss" of two Asian countries. After a significant military defeat at Dien Bien Phu in 1954, French authorities wanted an end to the conflict. The government of Pierre Mendès-France, the Viet Minh, and other interested parties met at Geneva in July of that year and signed an accord. From Hanoi, Ho and his allies would control the area north of the 17th parallel, while from Saigon, a government friendly to France would govern the south. Nationwide elections scheduled for 1956 were supposed to reunite Vietnam, but they never took place. President Eisenhower's government thought that the French had made too many concessions, refused to sign the Geneva Accord and encouraged the government of South Vietnam not to hold the elections. The French army returned home, and the fate of South Vietnam became a U.S. responsibility.

It was the Eisenhower administration (1953-1961) which initiated the U.S. military commitment to South Vietnam, fearing that the alternative would be Soviet or Chinese domination not only of that country but of its neighbours, then its neighbours' neighbours, *ad infinitum*. The administrations of John Kennedy (1961-1963), and Lyndon Johnson (1963-1969) increased the commitment, to the point that by 1965, North Vietnam and the United States were engaged in a full scale war against the government of North Vietnam and its allies in the south, the Viet Cong. The war lasted throughout the first term of Richard Nixon (1969-1973), until during the first few days of his second term the belligerents concluded what President Nixon described as "peace with honor." By that time, an estimated 47,393 Americans had died in combat, and the war had become a political liability in the United States.[3] President Nixon extended the U.S. war effort into Cambodia, first secretly but in May 1970, openly. In April 1975, the brutal Khmer Rouge completed their conquest of Cambodia two weeks before the Communist victory in South Vietnam.

At the time of Nixon's "peace with honor," South Vietnamese President Nguyen Van Thieu[4] was reluctant to sign a peace agreement, as he anticipated that the North would not abandon its struggle for reunification. With specific military reassurances, Nixon managed to persuade Thieu to sign. On 14 November 1972, a few days after winning re-election, Nixon affirmed to Thieu:

> Far more important than what we say in the agreement…is what we
> do in the event the enemy renews its aggression. You have my abso-
> lute assurance that if Hanoi fails to abide by the terms of this agree-
> ment it is my intention to take swift and severe retaliatory action.[5]

Nixon's reference to "swift and retaliatory action" proved less than a commitment. Before the North Vietnamese launched their post-agreement military offensive, Nixon had resigned the presidency. Thieu corresponded with President Ford and reminded him of Nixon's promise to defend South Vietnam.[6] It was in vain. The South Vietnamese had to defend themselves.

Indeed, Press Secretary Ron Nessen emphatically dismissed any possibility of U.S. retaliation. On 7 January 1975, Nessen affirmed that the War Powers Resolution of 19 November 1973 prevented the president from retaliating militarily without prior approval from Congress.[7] The need for prior approval from Congress was a direct result of the Watergate scandal and the Vietnam War. Americans had lost faith in their president and deemed it advisable to impose restrictions on presidential war powers. Congress withheld funds for combat purposes in Vietnam and Cambodia, and prohibited the sending of troops there. Moreover, the Foreign Assistance Act of 1973 clearly stated that financial expenditures in Indochina would be strictly limited. The War Powers Act required

> ...that the President consult with Congress, in every possible instance ...before introducing United States Armed Forces into hostilities or into situations where imminent involvement in hostilities is clearly indicated by the circumstances, section 4 (a) requires the President to report within 48 hours to the Congress.[8]

Since the Democrats dominated the House of Representatives and the Senate, Congress exercised what appeared to be its right to refuse to cooperate with Ford's demands concerning aid for South Vietnam. (Subsequent Presidents have challenged the constitutionality of the War Powers Act on the grounds that it impinged on the President's role as commander-in-chief and the person ultimately responsible for U.S. foreign policy.)

The situation worsened as the North Vietnamese army launched its final offensive 10 March 1975, moving 100,000 troops down the newly paved Ho Chi Minh Trail. By then there was actually a pipeline beside the trail so that vehicular traffic could be refueled![9] President Thieu ordered a redeployment of troops in the central highlands; when fighting began, those troops fled in despair, abandoning most of their U.S.-supplied military equipment.[10]

Danang fell 29 March while President Ford was golfing in Palm Springs. Both images were broadcast simultaneously, revealing an apparent light-heartedness toward events in Vietnam. Ron Nessen attempted to explain the president's apparent insensitivity, but to no avail as footage of President Ford running away from journalists was also released. A reporter joked that Ford "ran almost as fast as the South Vietnamese Army."[11] On the other side of the Pacific, people fled south toward Saigon, while others boarded ships which would take them to the Philippines. Yet others fled to Guam, which quickly became a refugee community for South Vietnamese.

The Ford administration desperately needed to show the world that America was aware that it had a moral obligation to the people of South Vietnam. On 4 April 1975, President Ford ordered U.S. naval vessels, 12 helicopters, and some 700 Marines to assist in the evacuation of refugees. In a letter to Congress, Ford justified this action with reference to the Foreign Assistance Act (1961), which authorized humanitarian assistance to refugees.[12]

Still Congress opposed military assistance, on the grounds that the chances of success were slim and that only the North Vietnamese army would benefit from any equipment donated and then abandoned by America's erstwhile allies.[13] In order to demonstrate to Congress that South Vietnam deserved American help, a frustrated President Ford sent General Frederick C. Weyand, to compile an assessment of the military and social conditions within South Vietnam. Weyand went to Vietnam early in April and concluded that the probability of South Vietnam's survival was marginal at best. He affirmed that Congress should provide $722 million while the U.S. planned for a massive evacuation of Saigon and all southern regions of Vietnam. Weyand also expressed concern about the future credibility of the United States as a trustworthy ally.[14]

Despite the Weyand report, Congress remained intransigent, as did public opinion. Both regarded South Vietnam as a lost cause, unworthy of further U.S. assistance. Tens of thousands of American war dead, combined with energy and economic crises at home, seemed convincing arguments against revival of the war.[15] Thirty-six members of the House of Representatives sent letters to President Ford expressing opposition to aid for Vietnam and Cambodia.[16] Congress opposed even Ford's plan to rescue Cambodian and South Vietnamese refugees. Senator Joseph Biden (Democrat-Delaware) firmly stated that he would vote for virtually any amount for the evacuation of U.S. citizens but nothing for the evacuation of South Vietnamese.[17] The American public appeared to agree.[18]

Nor was there anything approaching unanimity among those who had already risked their lives for the cause. *Time* reprinted statements from veterans:

I don't want to see any more kids go back over there…[The South Vietnamese] have been wasting our supply…I get the overwhelming feeling of waste, waste, waste of everything…I served, I did my job. Now I don't care…If I could go back now, I'd fight with the North Vietnamese…I don't care if [the South Vietnamese] make it or not.[19]

While the debate intensified, the situation in South Vietnam worsened. On 8 April, a high powered jet bombed the Presidential Palace in Saigon. A Vietnamese soldier, flying in a stolen U.S. fighter, dropped the bomb, clearly demonstrating dissatisfaction with President Thieu's leadership.[20] Almost a week later, 14 April, an American C-5A transport crashed while carrying 243 Vietnamese orphans and 62 adults.[21] This incident proved a devastating blow to the reputation of the Ford administration. The White House received blame for the failed, and arguably unnecessary, rescue effort.

Tensions accelerated when Khmer Rouge forces occupied Phnom Penh, capital of Cambodia. By 17 April 1975, the last Americans had fled that doomed city.[22]

As the situation in South Vietnam deteriorated, President Thieu asserted that it was the Americans whom his fellow Vietnamese should blame for recent events. Thieu publicly accused the United States of abandoning the people of Vietnam by withholding military support. These statements infuriated many Americans,[23] but on 21 April, President Thieu resigned.

Immediately following his resignation, Thieu allegedly attempted to transport more than sixteen tons of gold onto an international Swiss aircraft. Some in the United States wondered why this gold could not have been invested in South Vietnam's war effort rather than become a pension fund for the former president.[24] Thieu's immediate successor, Tran Van Huong, lasted only until 28 April, but departed when the Viet Cong demanded that he do so. Huong's successor, Duong Van Minh, known colloquially as "Big Minh," was himself not a Communist, but he had a reputation which might have made him somewhat acceptable to the Viet Cong and the government of North Viet Nam.[25] While others blamed President Thieu for what had happened, Secretary of State Henry Kissinger thought that Congress could not escape responsibility. He suggested that President Ford should affirm that Congress had refused to co-operate with the administration during the Communist offensive of 1975.[26] President Ford exonerated himself with a reaffirmation that he had a long record of support for military action in Vietnam.[27]

Some blamed the performance of the South Vietnamese Army during the final months of the North Vietnamese attack. Given the equipment and other assistance which the United States had provided, why were the South Vietnamese retreating? At best, the Nixon administration's policy of "vietnamization"—allowing Vietnamese to play the major role in their own defense—had been less than a total success. President Thieu ordered the South Vietnamese Army to withdraw into a region which might be more easily defended, [28] but many South Vietnamese—military and civilian—fled further south. Many South Vietnamese cleared their bank accounts as plane tickets doubled in price, and banks ran out of cash.

The diplomatic situation reflected the worsening military horror. Indonesian leader Suharto affirmed that the fall of South Vietnam eroded any trust between the United States Government and authorities in Southeast Asia.[29] A former Argentine ambassador to the United States remarked: "As far as we're concerned, Kissinger and Ford are already lame ducks."[30] A headline in the Paris newspaper, Le Monde, stated: "What peace? What honor?" An editorial in Le Point, a Paris news magazine, warned: "This is what has become of the American giant. Let Europe beware. His paralysis is contagious."[31] Chapters 6 and 8 will deal further with diplomatic consequences of the fall of Vietnam.

Graham Martin, the United States Ambassador in Saigon, had personal reasons for his genuine sympathy toward the people of South Vietnam. His own son had died in the Vietnam War, and the ambassador did not want America's war effort to appear meaningless. With this in mind, Ambassador Martin envisioned the evacuation of 1,000,000 people.[32] Martin had a long history of involvement in Southeast Asia. As a diplomat, he had served as a U.S. envoy to the Southeast Asia Treaty Organization, SEATO, a military alliance which included the United States, Pakistan, the Philippines, Thailand, Australia, and New Zealand. From 1963 until 1967, he had been the U.S. Ambassador in Thailand, where he had worked with the Thai government to establish U.S. B-52 bases. He had some credibility for successful resistance against Communism, without a war.[33]

Martin's tour of duty in Saigon had begun 24 June 1973, after Nixon's "Peace with honor" had taken effect but while Nixon remained president. His behaviour indicated a greater commitment to the people of South Vietnam than to orders from the Ford White House. By 15 April 1975, Martin was expressing increasing concern with regard to the impact of an evacuation on the people of Saigon. Residents of the capital demonstrated their discontent with the lack of U.S. support.[34] Kissinger asserted that the political situation at home could not permit the gradual extraction of American evacuees; Martin had to accelerate the process. On 16 April, President Ford ordered the evacuation of all non-essential Americans still in Vietnam.[35]

That same day, in a cable to General Brent Scowcroft—at the time, Kissinger's subordinate on the National Security Council but who, six months later, would become President Ford's National Security Adviser—Ambassador Martin assured Washington that all Americans were out of immediate danger.[36] By 17 April, Kissinger asserted that the evacuation plan would eventually leak to the press, thus creating a potentially dangerous situation in Saigon. Kissinger affirmed that Martin must proceed quickly with the evacuation process as President Ford might be blamed for indifference concerning the protection of American citizens in Saigon.[37]

On 18 April, Kissinger underlined the importance of assuring that all U.S. citizens in Vietnam were safe. Kissinger said that all Vietnamese closely associated with Americans, including their employees, relatives of U.S. citizens, and resident aliens, would be protected and evacuated. The Secretary of State suggested that the American population in Saigon be reduced to 2,000 by 22 April.[38] Also on 18 April, the press released allegations that the United States Government was planning to negotiate for the release of Vietnamese nationals with the Government of North Vietnam following the occupation of Saigon. Martin was understandably concerned, as this press release created a sense of urgency throughout that city. Martin stated, "Another mistake like this in Washington could be enormously costly to us here."[39]

Shortly thereafter, Kissinger broke with his usual practice of dealing exclusively with heads of government and briefed Ambassador Martin regarding confidential negotiations which he had already had with Soviet leader Leonid Brezhnev. Brezhnev had tried to assure Kissinger that the North Vietnamese Army did not intend to damage the prestige of the United States. An orderly evacuation, claimed Brezhnev, would be in everyone's interest.[40] Martin's only deadline was the Kissinger-Brezhnev agreement that all Americans must be out of South Vietnam by 3 May.[41] Nevertheless, Martin refused to plan for an evacuation, as he feared that such an evacuation would create panic or worse (South Vietnamese taking reprisals against Americans).

On 21 April following Thieu's resignation, Ambassador Martin expressed displeasure regarding Washington's failure to keep him fully informed. The United States Ambassador, perhaps the single most important American remaining in South Vietnam, felt blindfolded.[42] Meanwhile at the White House, tension increased as Henry Kissinger asked privately, "Why don't these people die fast? The worst thing that could happen would be for [South Vietnam] to linger on."[43]

With tension rising, tempers peaked inside the White House. Many of the White House staff disliked Kissinger, who remained in the two roles which President Nixon had assigned him: Secretary of State and National Security Adviser. Kissinger clashed with, among others, Press Secretary Ron Nessen, whom he blamed for leaking rumors that he would lose his job over his involvement in Vietnam.[44] The situation peaked 23 April when President Ford announced at Tulane University, without advance notice to Kissinger: "Today, America can regain the sense of pride that existed before Vietnam. But it cannot be achieved by re-fighting a war that is finished as far as America is concerned."[45]

The Tulane speech effectively ended Martin's vision of a democratic South Vietnam. Martin had been ill for some months, and his utter exhaustion became evident. On 26 April, Martin wrote to Kissinger:

> Somehow my present situation reminds me of the chap who had all his staff progressively removed. Yet his national headquarters supervisor demanded more and more. Then he got a cable saying his supervisor had been informed the office was dirty. The local man called back, outlined all he was doing, and asked how the hell he could do all that and keep the office clean too. Back came a cable suggesting he stick a broom up his ass so he could sweep up the office as he went about the rest of his duties.[46]

Martin was tired of the numerous cables, most of which had little relevance to the security of Saigon.

On 28 April, Kissinger became concerned that Americans might be taken hostage by *South* Vietnamese. He warned Martin that a complete evacuation was fast approaching, but to appease Martin, Kissinger affirmed that consultation would precede any final decision.[47]

Early in the morning of 29 April, the North Vietnamese Army shelled Saigon's Tan Son Nhut airport, leaving the runway beyond repair. Two American Marines died in the attack, the last military casualties of the war.[48] Even then, Martin hesitated. Not wanting to launch Operation Frequent Wind (the evacuation plan), Martin—accompanied by bodyguards—went personally to the airport to see whether repairs were feasible. Even he had to admit that they were not. Further delays were impossible.[49]

Receiving directives to execute the evacuation as quickly as possible, Ambassador Martin questioned the moral implications of forcing Americans to abandon their half-Vietnamese children and the way this would reflect on the President of the United States. However, reality set in and obliged Martin to abandon Saigon. Still, Martin did what he could to exert a maximum of pressure on the Ford White House. A few Americans, including one Father McVeigh, refused to leave. McVeigh claimed that he would not abandon his Vietnamese friends, who would surely face persecution. Martin challenged President Ford to explain to leaders of the Church why the United States would abandon priests. Martin also ordered an additional thirty CH53 helicopter sorties, but Washington did not reply. The Ambassador's patience was wearing then, as was the composure of the North Vietnamese Army which waited nearly two days at the city limits so that the Americans might leave.[50]

In accord with the War Powers Act, the White House and Congress communicated once the evacuation was officially under way 29 April. Bing Crosby's "I'm Dreaming of a White Christmas" aired throughout Saigon in accord with a prearranged signal to all Americans and their Vietnamese associates that the time to evacuate had arrived. The Ford Administration believed that since the evacuation was announced publicly, serious criticism from Congress would be minimal.[51]

For eighteen hours, 865 Marine pilots flew 630 sorties with only 70 choppers. In total, 1,373 Americans, 5,595 South Vietnamese, and 85 third country nationals were evacuated during Operation Frequent Wind. These were the last of 120,000 South Vietnamese who left their homeland during March and April for a new life in the United States. On 30 April, President Ford announced publicly that the evacuation had been a success. Thus appeared to end the U.S. commitment of more than twenty years to South Vietnam.

Contrary to appearances, there remained one commitment in Saigon. After he had spoken, President Ford learned that 129 Marine security guards whom the Pentagon had forgotten were still inside the U.S. Embassy. Infuriated, Kissinger stormed out of the Oval Office screaming that this was "the most botched-up, incompetent operation [he had] ever seen!"[52] Two hours later, choppers removed all the remaining Americans from harm's way. Nevertheless, U.S. authorities abandoned 420 authorized evacuees who included fire fighters and members of the CIA at the South Korean Embassy, whom the Viet Cong later executed.[53] Former President Nixon commented that the United States had "won the war but lost the peace."[54]

Congress and public opinion prevented the Ford White House from doing more to defend South Vietnam. The President had asked Congress for $1,400 million in military assistance but received only half that amount. By April 1975, those funds had been spent.[55] It appeared that the time had come to cut American losses, human and financial.

Unfortunately, what appeared to be the end proved not to be the end. The Khmer Rouge, who assumed power in Cambodia, had a justifiable reputation as much more bloody than the Viet Cong or the North Vietnamese. On 12 May, the Cambodian Coast Guard seized an American merchant vessel, the *Mayagüez*, in the Gulf of Thailand. At the time of the seizure, the *Mayagüez* was sailing from Hong Kong to Satahip in Thailand. The Cambodians stopped and boarded her at 12:21

a.m. EDT,[56] about ten kilometers (six and one-half miles) off the disputed island of Poulo Wai, where both Cambodia and South Vietnam had claims.[57]

It was imperative for President Ford to let the world know that withdrawal from Saigon did not mean abandonment of U.S. interests elsewhere, particularly on the high seas, where the United States had a long tradition of freedom of navigation. The absence of diplomatic relations with the Khmer Rouge posed a serious but not insurmountable problem. U.S. authorities sent notes demanding the release of the *Mayagüez* through the Chinese liaison office in Washington. (After President Nixon's historic visit to Beijing in 1972, the People's Republic of China and the United States established "liaison offices" in each other's capitals. These served as quasi-embassies until the formal establishment of diplomatic relations during the presidency of Ford's successor, Jimmy Carter.) The Ford White House estimated that it made statements and released messages for sixty hours without any response from the Cambodians.[58]

Anticipating the failure of diplomacy, President Ford ordered a military build-up in the Gulf of Thailand. In his memoirs, he wrote that he recalled North Korea's seizure of the U.S. Navy spy ship the *Pueblo* in 1968, when captain and crew remained prisoners under abominable conditions for almost a year. He did not want the people from the *Mayagüez* to experience such a fate.[59] For the Ford White House, the *Mayagüez* also became a symbol of U.S. determination and military might. The President said to Brent Scowcroft, "I think we should just give it to them."[60]

On 13 May—the day after the seizure—units of the United States Air Force began to attack Cambodian patrol boats. In an effort to prevent the Cambodians from taking the *Mayagüez* to the Cambodian mainland, Ford ordered the Air Force and Navy to maintain a fighter/gunship cover over the vessel until further reinforcements could arrive from U Taphao in Thailand. Moreover, when crews on reconnaissance aircraft sighted a ship which appeared to have some Caucasians on board heading toward the Cambodian port of Kompong Som, the U.S. Air Force attempted to divert the vessel from the mainland. Ford received additional intelligence which suggested that the crew's destination might be nearby Koh Tang Island, which 100 U.S. Marines bombarded 14 May. The battle of Koh Tang began at 7:20 p.m. and lasted approximately six hours. U.S. helicopters assisted the ground troops, who encountered fierce resistance. The effort proved redundant, other than as an exhibit of the ongoing American will to protect U.S. interests, as the crew of the *Mayagüez* was nowhere to be seen.[61]

On 15 May at 6 a.m., a Cambodian radio broadcast announced the Khmer Rouge's decision to release the ship, but the statement failed to mention the fate of the crew. Accordingly, Ford, Kissinger, and Scowcroft pursued plans to bomb the mainland. They wanted Cambodians and the rest of the world to know that the U.S. was serious.[62] Moments later, a fishing vessel appeared with the crew on board, and the helicopters airlifted the crew to safety. Later that evening, in a televised address from the White House Briefing Room, President Ford announced the rescue of the *Mayagüez* and her entire crew. However, in the process, forty-one rescuers died and another fifty suffered injuries.[63]

Critics could and did criticize the operation. Was it necessary? Was it an over-reaction? Was it legal? Did the rescue of thirty-nine crew members justify forty-one military fatalities? Among those with doubts was Secretary of Defense, James Schlesinger. According to Ford, Schlesinger "agreed that our first priority should be to rescue the ship and her crew, but he was far less eager to use *Mayagüez* as an example for Asia and the world. He was concerned that our bombing plans were too extensive."[64] According to Kissinger, Ford lost a measure of confidence in Schlesinger which he never regained and which led to his replacement five months later by Donald Rumsfeld.[65] Definitive answers enter the realm of counter-factual history. Given the nature of the Khmer Rouge regime, it is certainly possible that the thirty-nine might have experienced a terrible fate without the deaths of the forty-one. Given the impression that the U.S. commitments to Asian countries might be less than firm, a less forceful response to the *Mayagüez* seizure might have encouraged other rogue states to challenge serious U.S. interests, even to destabilize the world. One of those rogue states was North Korea, which acted as though it were less than intimidated by the U.S. response to the *Mayagüez* affair.

Notes

1. This chapter is an updated version of the undergraduate Honours Essay (thesis) of Eric Hennigar, accepted by Laurentian University's History Department in 1999. Another excellent source on the topics covered in this chapter is Ralph Wetterhahn, *The Last Battle: The* Mayagüez *Incident and the End of the Vietnam War* (New York: Carroll and Graf, 2001).

2. Kissinger, pp.463–495, 520–529.

3. Vietnamese (both North and South) plus military allies of the United States also died in combat, but the American deaths would have the greatest political impact in the United States. The U.S. figure comes from the *World Almanac*, 2005, p. 227.

4. English-language publications usually place the surnames of North Vietnamese leaders, such as Ho Chi Minh, *ahead of* their given names, but the surnames of South Vietnamese leaders *after* the given names. Following convention, this manuscript does likewise.

5. *Keesing's Contemporary Archives, 1975* (Essex, England: Keesing's Publications, 1975), p. 27201A.

6. Memo, Thieu to Ford, 26 March 1975, Folder 012700153, Box 5, National Security Committee (NSC) Convenience Files, GFPL.

7. Ron Nessen, *It Sure Looks Different from the Inside* (Chicago: Playboy Press, 1978), p. 92.

8. Memorandum, Gerald Ford, 18 March 1975l, Box 65, Folder 7505423 [declassified 12/7/89], Philip W. Buchen Files, GFPL.

9. Michael Maclear, *The Ten Thousand Day War: Vietnam (1945-1975)* (Toronto: Methuen, 1981), p. 318.

10. Larry Engelmann, *Tears before the Rain: An Oral History of the Fall of South Vietnam* (New York: Da Capo Press, 1997), p. x.

11. Nessen, pp. 97-100.

12. Memo, John Marsh to President Ford, 4 April 1975, Box 122, War Powers Notification Folder [declassified 1/28/98], John Marsh Files, GFPL.

13. Memo, Roy Ash to Ford, 14 January 1975, Folder FO 3-2 [declassified 9/25/92], Box 22, Presidential Handwriting File, GFPL.

14. Memo, Weyand to Ford, 4 April 1975, Saigon Folder [declassified 7/29/92]. Bpx 7, NSC Convenience Files, GFPL.

15. Letter, Congress to Ford, 7 March 1975, Folder 3-2, Box 22, White House Central Files (WHCF), GFPL.

16. Letters, Congress to Ford, 11 March 1975, Folder 3-2, Box 22, WHCF, GFPL.

17. Ford, p. 255.

18. Memo, Kendall to Max Friedersdorf, 7 April 1975, National Security Folder, Box 33, Handwriting File, GFPL.

19. *Time*, 31 March 1975, p. 39.

20. *Vietnam: The Soldier's Story, Last Chopper Out: The Fall of Saigon* (New York: ABC News Productions, 1998).

21. *Time Magazine*, 14 April 1975, p. 8.

22. Ford, p. 255.

23. Memo, Loen to Friedersdorf, 7 April 1975, National Security folder, Box 33, Handwriting File, GFPL.

24. The *New York Times*, 21 April, 1975.

25. Engelmann, p. xi.

26. Memo, John Marsh to Richard Cheney, 3 April 1975, Box 122, War Powers Notification Folder [declassified 1/28/98], John Marsh Files, GFPL.

27. Memo, Assessing the Blame, 2 April 1975, Box 122, General Subject File [declassified 1/18/98], John Marsh Files, GFPL.

28. Ford, p. 250; Memo, Vietnam: concerns, undated, Box 33, General Subject File, Handwriting File, National Security: Vietnam War, GFPL.

29. Report, Indonesia's reaction to the fall of South Vietnam, 7 May 1975, Country File No. 67, Indonesia, CO 67, WHCF, GFPL.

30. *Time Magazine*, 28 April 1975, p. 22.

31. *Time Magazine*, 14 April 1975, p. 7.

32. A.J.C. Lavalle, *Last Flight from Saigon* (Washington: U.S. Government Printing Office, 1978), p. 40.

33. Maclear, p. 316.

34. Memo, Martin to Kissinger, 15 April 1975, folder 012700153 [declassified 1/17/97], Box 5, NSC Convenience Files, GFPL.

35. Telegram, Kissinger to Martin, 16 April 1975, U.S. Embassy: Saigon folder [declassified 9/30/94], Box 7, NSC Convenience Files, GFPL.
36. Memo, Martin to Scowcroft, 16 April 1975, folder 012700153 [declassified 2/3/95], Box 5, NSC Convenience Files, GFPL.
37. Telegram, Kissinger to Martin, 17 April 1975, U.S. Embassy, Saigon folder [declassified 9/30/94], Box 7, NSC Convenience Files, GFPL.
38. Telegram, Kissinger to Martin, 18 April 1975, U.S. Embassy: Saigon folder [declassified 11/8/94], Box 7, NSC Convenience Files, GFPL.
39. Memo, Martin to Washington, 18 April 1975, U.S. Embassy: Saigon folder [declassified 2/11/94]. Box 7, NSC Convenience Files, GFPL.
40. Telegram, Kissinger to Martin, undated, U.S. Embassy: Saigon folder [declassified 1/17/97], Box 7, NSC Convenience Files, GFPL.
41. Engelmann, pp. 53-54.
42. Memo, Martin to Kissinger, 21 March 1975, folder 012700153 [declassified 1/17/97], Box 5, NSC Convenience Files, GFPL.
43. Nessen, p. 98.
44. John F. Casserly, *The Ford White House: The Diary of a Speechwriter* (Boulder: Colorado Associated University Press, 1977), pp. 73-74.
45. *Public Papers of the Presidents of the United States: Gerald Ford* (Washington: United States Government Printing Office, 1975), p. 560.
46. Memo, Martin to Kissinger, 26 April 1975, folder 012700153, Box 5, NSC Convenience Files, GFPL.
47. Telegram, Kissinger to Martin, 28 April 1975, U.S. Embassy: Saigon folder , Box 7, NSC Convenience Files, GFPL.
48. Nessen, pp. 105-109.
49. *Vietnam: The Soldier's Story*.
50. Memorandum, Martin to Scowcroft, 29 April 1975, U.S. Embassy: Saigon folder, Box 7, NSC Convenience Files, GFPL.
51. Memorandum, John Marsh to President Ford, 29 April 1975, General Subject File, Box 64, Philip Buchen Files, GFPL.
52. Nessen, p. 112.
53. Lavalle, p. 111.
54. Richard Nixon, *No More Vietnams* (New York: Arbor House, 1985), p. 165.
55. Ford, p. 250.
56. All times in the text will be Eastern Daylight Time, the hour on which the White House operated. Add eleven hours to convert to Gulf of Thailand time.
57. *Keesing's Contemporary Archives*, 1975, p. 27239.
58. Briefing Paper, Possible Question With Regard to the *Mayagüez* Incident, Undated, General Subject File, Box 14, Ron Nessen Papers, GFPL.
59. Ford, p. 277. For information on the *Pueblo*, see Mitchell B. Lerner, *The Pueblo Incident: A Spy Ship and the Failure of American Foreign Policy* (Lawrence: University Press of Kansas, 2002).
60. Memcon, Scowcroft to Ford, 13 May 1975, Parallel File, Box 1, Henry Kissinger and Brent Scowcroft Parallel File, GFPL.
61. Briefing Paper, *S.S. Mayagüez*/Koh Tang Island Operation, undated, *Mayagüez* Folder, Philip Buchen Files, GFPL.
62. President Ford discusses the *Mayagüez* affair in his memoirs, pp. 275-284.
63. Ford, p. 284.
64. Ford, p. 279.
65. Kissinger, p. 573.

Chapter Six

CONSEQUENCES OF THE COLLAPSE OF SOUTH VIETNAM: KOREA[1]

Again, President Ford inherited a problem which was not of his making. The Kingdom of Korea had lost its independence during the Russo-Japanese War of 1904-1905, and Japan annexed it outright in 1910. In the autumn of 1943, President Franklin Delano Roosevelt of the United States, British Prime Minister Winston Churchill, and Chinese President Chiang Kai Shek[2] met in Cairo. There they agreed that when the Allied nations defeated Japan, Japan would lose its non-Japanese territories, including Korea. The fourth major ally, Soviet leader Joseph Stalin, subsequently agreed. In mid-August 1945, as World War II was ending, U.S. and Soviet officials agreed that north of the 38th parallel, Japanese forces would surrender to the Soviet Army. South of that line, they would surrender to the U.S. Army. Unable to agree on terms for Korean unification, both occupiers established rival governments in their respective zones of occupation. In 1950, North Korea—formally known as the Democratic People's Republic of Korea (DPRK)—invaded South Korea—formally the Republic of Korea (ROK)—and came close to overrunning it within the next two months. With assistance from fourteen other members of the United Nations,[3] the United States and South Korea then came close to annihilating North Korea. Forces from the recently triumphant People's Republic of China assisted the North Koreans, and in July 1953, both sides signed an Armistice Agreement at Panmunjom on the inter-Korean border. No longer would that border be the true 38th parallel. Rather, it would follow geographical contours, with North Korea gaining territory south of the 38th parallel in the west—including the former imperial city of Kaesong—and South Korea extending north of the 38th parallel in the east.[4]

Unlike World War II, the Korean War ended in a stalemate. Neither side could drive the other to unconditional surrender at a tolerable price. South Korea's war leader, Syngman Rhee, was overthrown in 1960. When the dust settled in May 1961, a military government led by Major General Park Chung Hee assumed office. During the Japanese occupation, Park had been a second lieutenant in the Japanese Imperial Army.[5] Park would be South Korea's leader until his assassination by the leader of the (South) Korean Central Intelligence Agency 26 October 1979, more than two years after Jimmy Carter had succeeded Gerald Ford. It would be President Park with whom President Ford would be dealing.

America's Adversary: Kim Il Sung

Kim Il Sung, who had lived in the USSR during the Japanese occupation of his homeland and who had instigated the attack on South Korea, was Chief of State and Head of Government in North Korea from his installation in 1948 until his death in 1994. Perhaps Kim mellowed with age, but this was far from certain. In 1968 Kim's navy had seized the U.S. Navy spy ship *Pueblo* in international waters and held her captain and crew in captivity under the most brutal conditions for eleven months.[6] On 15 August 1974, less than one week after Ford had replaced Nixon as President of the United States, North Korean agents tried and failed to assassinate South Korean President Park Chung Hee, but they did manage to kill his wife.[7] Also in 1974 and 1975, U.S. and South Korean forces discovered tunnels under the Demilitarized Zone—a belt four kilometers in width, two kilometers either side of the inter-Korean border.[8] Meanwhile, the United States Army reportedly had been sending soldiers and equipment from the inter-Korean border to Vietnam.[9]

Documents released after the Cold War indicate that officials of North Korea's Communist allies, East Germany and Hungary, regarded Kim Il Sung's government as bizarre and unpredictable. In 1960, the Hungarian Ambassador to North Korea, Károly Práth, reported to the Foreign Office in Budapest that he and his Czechoslovak counterpart found that North Korean authorities kept them under constant surveillance.[10] In 1964, just as the United States stopped fingerprinting Soviet citizens, North Korea began to do so.[11] Deputy Premier Nam Il, according to Práth's successor, József Kovács, told workers who were constructing an electrical dam that they should complete the final 80% within three months although it had taken them eighteen months to build the first 20%. Nobody dared to disagree with him. The workers, dressed in linen suits despite the late December cold, had to run around to warm themselves and lost working time.[12]

With the use of Russian and East German sources, historian Charles K. Armstrong was able to determine that from Khruschev's era onward, North Korean authorities made no effort to co-ordinate their economic policies with those of other Communist countries.[13] East Germans played a major role in the reconstruction of North Korea's second largest city, Hamhung, but once Khrushchev denounced Stalin in his famous speech of 1956, Kim Il Sung curtailed the contact that North Koreans and East Germans could have with each other—to the point that the East German workers began to "feel as if they resided in enemy territory."[14] After 1960, North Korean authorities claimed that North Koreans alone had rebuilt North Korea after the Korean War. Workers and diplomats from the Soviet Union, East Germany, other Soviet-bloc countries, and China—all of which had rendered assistance—knew better. In 1962, the last East German workers returned home.[15]

Nor did Kim's government become more pacific despite the horrors of the costly Korean War. On 29 March 1962, Ambassador Kovács reported that one Comrade Pak of the North Korean Foreign Office had told him that the East German decision to co-exist peacefully with West Germany was no precedent or model for North Korea. It wanted to absorb South Korea as quickly as possible.[16] This attitude evidently continued through Gerald Ford's presidency. Months after the inauguration of Jimmy Carter in 1977, East Germany's leader, Erich Honecker, visited Pyongyang—North Korea's capital—where Kim Il Sung told him that North Korea's governing Communist party "considers unification of the fatherland to be its primary mission."[17]

Relations with North Korea's erstwhile Korean War ally were little better than those with Soviet-bloc countries. In 1961, China's Ambassador to North Korea told Práth that Chinese diplomats stayed away from meetings which North Korean authorities organized for accredited diplomats. Práth added that according to the Czechoslovak Ambassador, whose country served on the Neutral Nations Supervisory Commission (NNSC) and had representatives in Panmunjom, the North Koreans treated the Chinese officials there in a most insulting manner. The North Koreans consistently voiced their opinions at meetings where Chinese and North Korean envoys stared across the table at Americans and South Koreans, while the Chinese were supposed to sit in silence. (Czechoslovakia and Poland were supposed to represent North Korean interests on the NNSC, Sweden and Switzerland those of South Korea.) Kovács said that newly arrived heads of the Swedish and Swiss NNSC contingents had paid courtesy calls on the Chinese and North Koreans and invited them to return the visit. The Chinese wanted to do so, but the North Koreans refused and pressured the

Chinese to do likewise. When a newly arrived Chinese officer visited the Czecho-slovaks and Poles, his North Korean counterpart refused to accompany him.[18] During China's "cultural revolution" later in the 1960s, China and North Korea reportedly "massed troops along their Yalu River border and even fought some minor clashes."[19] On his 1977 trip to North Korea, Erich Honecker said that during the cultural revolution, Chinese authorities placed loudspeakers along the 1500 kilometer common border with North Korea and yelled insults at the "revisionists" on the other side of the Yalu River. Since then, said Honecker, Kim's government had tried to improve its relations with China, not because it admired the Chinese government but because North Korea "cannot concentrate troops in the north and in the south [opposite South Korea] simultaneously."[20] Presidents Park and Ford thus had good reason to regard North Korea as an untrustworthy enemy, and even if they had known of that country's erratic relations with other Communist countries, it is unlikely that they would have relaxed their vigilance. In many respects Kim's foreign policy was irrational and therefore dangerous. He was ready to challenge everyone at once.

U.S.-South Korean Relations in the 1970s

By all accounts, South Korea's Park Chung Hee was a highly competent individual but hardly a committed liberal democrat. As responsible as any single person for his country's transformation from an impoverished Third World country to one of the world's economic powerhouses, Park had reason to distrust the United States. In order to placate a U.S. electorate weary of military commitments in Asia—and ignoring the fact that South Koreans were fighting as allies in Vietnam —President Richard Nixon had withdrawn an infantry division from Korea in 1971.[21] Reversing decades of adversarial relations between the People's Republic of China and the United States, President Richard Nixon had gone to Beijing in 1972 and authorized an exchange of "liaison offices" or quasi-embassies. South Korean combat forces had fought effectively in Vietnam, but in April 1975, President Ford had occupied the Oval Office while Communist forces overran Saigon. Unpersuaded by the Ford administration's response to the seizure of the *Mayagüez*, President Park decided that South Korea must fend for itself. The memoirs of Major-General John K. Singlaub, appointed Chief of Staff of the United Nations Command and U.S. Forces in Korea in the spring of 1976, provide strong evidence of a military build-up in North Korea during Ford's presidency; U.S. and South Korean soldiers actually discovered tunnels which North Koreans had dug under the De-militarized Zone so that large numbers North Korean soldiers could launch a surprise invasion of South Korea.[22] Of all the United Nations members who had assisted in the defence of South Korea between 1950 and 1953, only the United States retained combat forces in that country. (Shortly after the Korean War, the Chinese withdrew their soldiers from *North* Korea.) Under pressure of public and Congressional opinion, might the Ford administration or some successor withdraw them as Presidents Nixon and Ford had withdrawn their counterparts from Vietnam? After all, President Nixon had already cut in half the number of American troops based in South Korea[23]—a step in the wrong direction as far as Park Chung Hee was concerned.

The evidence indicates that even before the 1975 Communist offensive in Vietnam, President Ford was determined to support the government of South Korea. Between September and December 1974, U.S. and South Korean Marines staged an amphibious landing exercise, while U.S. soldiers stationed in South Korea held maneuvers with their South Korean counterparts.[24] In November, President Ford included Seoul, South Korea's capital, among the Asian cities (Tokyo, Kyoto, Vladivostok) which he was visiting and said that not to have gone "would have been misunderstood by North Korea and questioned by our allies." Kissinger, who was also there agreed. It was "very important," he said that President Ford visit South Korea. Otherwise, "the North Koreans might have underestimated our determination to support our friends." Of the economy and the reception which he received, Kissinger said,

> Seoul looks like a modern American city, with skyscrapers, cars, and an obviously thriving economy. My welcome was amazing—there must have been two million people lining the streets between the airport and the hotel.[25]

President Park, noted Kissinger, said that the discovery of the tunnels confirmed that North Korea remained a threat to South Korea. Understandably, what happened in Saigon in April 1975 was hardly reassuring to President Park.

The Nuclear Weapons Issue

One obvious solution was to acquire nuclear weapons so that South Korea could meet any challenge from North Korea and its Soviet and Chinese allies, but the Department of State was less than enthusiastic. In December 1974, the Lockheed Propulsion Company signed a contract with President Park's government to sell advanced missile technology. The State Department disapproved. South Korea had nuclear ambition, and South Korea's neighbors, including Japan, might feel uneasy.[26]

Unable to obtain the weapons which he wanted from the United States, President Park negotiated the purchase of nuclear technology from France and Canada. Fearful of nuclear proliferation, the Ford administration spoke to the French and Canadian governments and stressed the U.S. commitment to the Non-Proliferation Treaty (NPT) of 1968.[27] That treaty, signed by the United States, the United Kingdom, the Soviet Union, and fifty-nine other countries, had taken effect in March 1970. It committed signatories with nuclear weapons not to provide them to nor to share nuclear weapons technology with any country which did not already have nuclear weapons. Signatories without nuclear weapons pledged not to acquire or develop them. Park suggested that he wanted the technology only for peaceful purposes, but the Ford administration had its doubts.

On 3 March 1975, the Staff Secretary of the National Security Council, Jeanne W. Davis, wrote to George S. Springsteen, an Executive Secretary at the State Department. It was clear, she said, that the South Korean government was "proceeding with [the] initial phases of a nuclear weapons development program," and this could lead to several complications. South Korea's neighbors—Japan, the Soviet Union, China—would be within target range, and their responses could destabilize the neighborhood. The Soviets or Chinese might respond by providing nuclear weapons to North Korea. South Korea's acquisition of nuclear weapons would also affect relations between that country and the United States. President Park wanted those weapons because it was losing confidence in the United States, and a South Korea which no longer had to depend on the United States for defense might be a loose cannon in an inflammatory part of the world. The United States Government opposed "the further spread of nuclear explosives" and was proposing "a confidential conference" of those countries capable of spreading those weapons: the United States, the United Kingdom, France, West Germany, China, Japan, and the Soviet Union.[28]

The Ford administration did more than attempt to persuade President Park. Quietly it exerted pressure. In return for abandonment of a South Korean nuclear weapons program, it offered support to South Korean endeavors to use nuclear energy for peaceful purposes. It prepared to threaten a reduction in U.S. military commitments to South Korea if Park persevered with his nuclear weapons program. The ideas was to convince Park that he had more to gain from cooperation with the United States than from striking out on his own.[29] Thus, the Ford administration managed to extract promises that South Korea "would not reprocess fuel from U.S. and Canadian reactors" and pressure Park not to buy a reprocessing plant from France.[30] Indeed, the Canadian government of Pierre Elliott Trudeau–undoubtedly on its own initiative and without pressure from Washington–insisted that if South Korea wanted to purchase a Candu reactor from Canada, it must first ratify the NPT, and the Park government obliged. Under pressure, Park accepted a U.S. veto on the use of reprocessed fuel from reactors provided from the United States. The National Security Council considered threats that if South Korea were to purchase a reprocessing plant from France, the U.S. might try to block a loan from the Export-Import bank so that South Korea could purchase its second U.S.-built reactor, the KORI-II. What would be tolerable would be South Korean participation in "an eventual multinational regional reprocessing plant in East Asia."[31]

In the end, successful diplomacy with Canada and France rather than pressure upon President Park blocked the reprocessing of nuclear fuel in South Korea. The Trudeau government had "serious reservations" about any reprocessing to be done in South Korea and agreed to co-ordinate Canada's nuclear efforts in that country with U.S. authorities. The French government of Valéry Giscard d'Estaing decided that profits from the sale of a nuclear reprocessing plant would not compensate for all the ensuing problems. The French offered to cancel the sale provided that U.S. authorities compensate the manufacturer for "termination costs."[32]

Other Consequences of the Collapse of South Vietnam

Another way to dissuade South Korea from adopting nuclear weapons was to maintain a credible level of conventional warfare on the Korean peninsula. After the fall of Saigon, Ford agreed to delay the withdrawal of obsolete U.S. military equipment and the downsizing of U.S. forces in South Korea, lest North Korea draw the wrong conclusions.[33] The equipment and the troops would remain in South Korea even if technology had rendered them superfluous. Within days of the fall of Saigon, President Ford received the Speaker of South Korea's National Asembly, Chung Il-Kwon, in the Oval Office. Kissinger prepared a briefing paper for the president which said that the purpose of the meeting was "To reassure South Korea of the solidity of our security commitment in the wake of Indochina." Kissinger continued:

> The fall of Indochina [Vietnam, Cambodia, and neighboring Laos] has
> had a serious impact on South Korea. Even before that development,
> South Korea had been troubled in the past year or so by concerns over

the dependability of our security commitment. The impact of Indochina events on South Korea was aggravated when...Kim Il-sung promptly left for Peking [Beijing], his first visit there since 1961, as if to concentrate new pressures against the South.[34]

In that same briefing paper, Kissinger told Ford that there were no plans to reduce the number of U.S. military personnel in South Korea. Under the circumstances, North Korea might have a rather dangerous interpretation of any such reductions, he wrote. On 25 June 1975, President Ford received six members of the South Korean National Assembly. Again Kissinger emphasized the importance of reassuring them that the United States would not abandon South Korea. He wrote:

> Since the fall of Indochina and North Korean President Kim Il-sung's visit to Peking, there has been a sharp interest in the Republic of Korea's concern [i.e., South Korea's concern] over the intentions of North Korea. This concern has been manifest in a tendency to question the reliability of the United States as an ally...[35]

Secretary of Defense James Schlesinger also sought to reassure the South Koreans, but there was a limit to what he could do. In August 1975 he went to Seoul for talks with South Korean Defense Minister Suh in August 1975. He could and did promise President Park, "as a special favor," to leave in Korea for another year the two U.S. generals currently there, Richard Stilwell and James Hollingsworth,[36] but there was a limit to what he would commit the United States in the event of North Korean attack. He tried to be optimistic and suggested to Defence Minister Suh that neither the Soviet Union nor China wanted North Korea to attack the South. In fact, he said, when Kim Il Sung visited Beijing, Chinese leaders actively discouraged such a venture. Both men agreed that North Korea was the wild card, but Suh noted a few unpleasant realities. In the event of another North Korean attack on South Korea, U.S. constitutional realities might require Congressional approval before U.S. forces could defend those areas where U.S. soldiers were not themselves physically present. Congress could debate, said Suh, but Seoul was "only one hour's drive from the DMZ [and] would be endangered by a lightning war." (The DMZ was the Demilitarized Zone, two kilometers either side of the inter-Korean border.) Schlesinger dismissed Suh's concern's as hypothetical, and Suh's response to that was whited out in the document available to researchers 11 June 2002.[37]

Nevertheless, Schlesinger probably said too much. When he returned to Washington, members of the National Security Council expressed concern than in his attempts to placate Park and Suh, Schlesinger misled them. On 29 September 1975, Thomas J. Barnes of the National Security Council prepared a memorandum for General Scowcroft. Regarding a possible North Korean attack, Barnes feared that "Secretary Schlesinger's commitment of automatic involvement by U.S. forces…went beyond any previous comment that I am aware of by high U.S. officials." Regarding islands near the inter-Korean border identified as "the Northwest Islands," Schlesinger had promised U.S. involvement in the event of a North Korean attack. Without authorization—especially if President Ford were to lose the election of 1976—Schlesinger had indicated that there would be no U.S. troop reduction for at least five years. In the same spirit, General Stilwell had developed a war plan on his own, without consultation with Washington. It appeared, said Barnes, "that Secretary Schlesinger came close to committing the U.S. to defend the Northwest Islands." Scowcroft approved the Barnes letter, and Colonel Granger of the National Security Council wrote that he "strongly concur[red]."[38]

Stilwell had what he called a "short-war strategy." It envisioned the use of such fire-power to defend Seoul that the war would end within nine days. South Korean and U.S. forces had been conducting maneuvers so that they could implement the short-war strategy should North Korea attack. However, the Department of Defense had not approved the plan, and both the Joint Chiefs of Staff and the Commander in Chief of the Pacific Command had reservations about it. According to General Hollingsworth, Schlesinger liked it.

As already indicated, Suh repeatedly raised the question of the Northwest Islands. Suh insisted that there were constitutional problems. If the North Koreans should attack Americans in or near the DMZ, there would be no question of a U.S. response, but there were no Americans on the Northwest Islands. Schlesinger indicated that Suh need not be "unduly concerned" for

> This is not a problem that would be referred to Congress. U.S. action would be firm and speedy, and the issue would not be submitted to Congress for debate.[39]

Members of the National Security Council had their doubts about this on Constitutional grounds.

The problem became more than hypothetical in May 1976, by which time Rumsfeld had replaced Schlesinger as Secretary of Defense. Once again, North Korea launched an offensive of words and actions. After a pledge of "faith with absolutely loyalty to…Comrade Kim Il-song [sic]," a statement of 10 May from

Pyongyang, the North Korean capital, referred to "the U.S. imperialists and their stooges" and said:

> We must not forget the compatriots in the south even for a single moment but actively encourage and support their revolutionary struggle with might and main, produce, build, and save many more with the warm compatriot feelings of rescuing them.[40]

A State Department official identified as "the North Korean watcher" interpreted the language of that statement as "a few degrees more threatening than normal."[41] Thomas J. Barnes of the National Security Council, who cited the State Department official, summarized subsequent North Korean provocations. On 25 May, North Korea accused a South Korean stationed in the DMZ of shooting at a North Korean guard and threatened retaliation if such actions were to continue. Two days later, two North Korean gunboats approached one of the aforementioned Northwest Islands. The South Korean commander stationed there "requested permission to fire a warning shot," which his superior, a U.S. naval officer, denied. The North Korean government also protested a U.S. military reconnaissance flight of 6 May over a North Korean commercial vessel and accused the U.S. of "provoking a new war in Korea."

Throughout June and July, strategists in Washington worked feverishly to prepare contingency plans for a North Korean attack on the Northwest Islands.[42] However, when trouble came, it came not there—in the ambivalent zone—but right at Panmunjom in the DMZ.

President Ford faced his most formidable challenge with North Korea as the Republican Convention met in August 1976 to decide whether he or California Governor Ronald Reagan should be the party's candidate in the presidential election of 1976. On 18 August 1976, two American soldiers—Captain Arthur Bonifas and Lieutenant Mark Barrett—went to the South Korean end of the Bridge of No Return at Panmunjom. That bridge—so named because hardly anyone made a return trip—spanned the Imjim River which separated North and South Korea; the *Pueblo*'s crew had crossed it in December 1968 on the way home from captivity. South Korean workers under the command of Bonifas were pruning a tree so that U.S. and South Korean observers could have a better view of the bridge from the observation tower located on the South Korean side of the Demilitarized Zone at Panmunjom. North Korean soldiers crossed the bridge and hacked Bonifas and Barrett to death with knives. Ford had to teach the North Koreans a lesson which they would not forget, hopefully without starting a war. Under the circumstances, he launched Operation Paul Bunyan, named for the legendary lumberjack. This involved the highest "alert" status since the end of the Korean War in 1953, the despatch to South Korea of F-4 fighters from Okinawa, F-111 fighter-bombers from Idaho, B-52 bombers from Guam, and the aircraft carrier *Midway* from Japan. Kissinger sent a warning to the North Koreans via the Chinese liaison office in Washington. Some advisers recommended an attack on North Korea itself, but President Ford accepted the advice of the Joint Chiefs of Staff not to do so for fear of the consequences.

On 21 August, American and South Korean forces swarmed the southern side of the DMZ near the Bridge of No Return—twenty-three vehicles in all. They removed more than the tree in question, and while they worked, twenty-seven helicopters flew overhead. Within sight were the B-52 bombers, accompanied by F-4 fighters from the United States and F-5 fighters from South Korea. F-111 fighter-bombers waited nearby in case they were needed, and the *Midway* sailed offshore. Other South Korean and U.S. forces guarded the southern approaches to the DMZ. North Korean soldiers watched from the other side of the Imjin River but took no action.[43] Historian Bruce Cumings claims that U.S. authorities had permission to use nuclear weapons if necessary and were planning to do so, but the North Koreans would not have known that, and it was not necessary.[44]

Operation Paul Bunyan evidently reassured President Park, but whether it sent the right message to North Korea is somewhat uncertain. On 15 September, Brent Scowcroft met Richard Sneider, the U.S. Ambassador to South Korea. Scowcroft noted that in the aftermath of 18 August, "Park's toughness seemed to grow" until he became more belligerent than ever toward North Korea. Sneider suggested that Operation Paul Bunyan offered him such reassurance that he had developed an "Israeli complex"—an attitude that no matter what he did, he could rely on the United States for support.[45] Nevertheless, Kim Il Sung might not have absorbed the message. In 1978, by which time Jimmy Carter was President of the United States, U.S. and South Korean forces discovered yet another tunnel.[46] On 9 October 1983, North Korean agents detonated a bomb while the South Korean cabinet was visiting the Burmese capital and killed eighteen South Korean officials, including the deputy-premier and three cabinet ministers.[47] Two comparable fatalities at Sarajevo had triggered the outbreak of World War I in 1914, but U.S. President Ronald Reagan and South Korean President Chun Doo Hwan demonstrated greater restraint than had the Habsburgs. Undeterred, on 29 November 1987, North Korean agents destroyed Korean Air

Lines flight 858, killing all 115 people on board.[48] In any event, another legacy of the Ford administration was the annual Operation Team Spirit, a joint South Korean–US military exercise, staged for the first time in 1976 and organized by General Stilwell. From a distance, North Korean officials watched these manoeuvres with concern.[49]

Human Rights in South Korea

Another problem was human rights,[50] although President Ford appears to have been somewhat ambivalent on the subject. Kissinger advised him that after the fall of Saigon, President Park became even less tolerant of dissenters than ever, and that he had always been one for "repressive measures." Park's apparent brutality was creating problems in Congress and among members of the public at large, where many were regarding South Korea in a negative way. When Ford met Park five months later, he raised the matter, and on his return to Washington, he told the National Security Council:

> I was forthright in talking to Park and indicated that we don't agree with some of his oppressive domestic tactics. But on the other hand, it doesn't hurt to have a strong leader in that part of the country, with all the problems there…[51]

Some Christian missionaries stationed in South Korea found such ambivalence disgusting and did not hesitate to express their feelings. One member of the National Security Council who had accompanied Ford and Kissinger to South Korea wrote a lengthy brief to Kissinger. Park's critics, they told W.R. Smyser, were non-Communist patriots. What they wanted was liberty, and the Ford's visit might have been a setback "President Park," they said, "may become even tougher with the opposition now that he has been bolstered by the visit of the American President."[52]

President Park was not the only ally intolerant of dissent; witness U.S. relations with the Argentine military government which seized power in 1976. (See Chapter Fourteen.) The Ford administration feared that human rights abuses would complicate efforts to persuade Congress to assist South Korea, and although President Ford received the Speaker of the South Korean House of Deputies and other deputies, he discouraged a 1976 visit by President Park. Given his record of human rights abuses, a visit by Park would attract dissenters to Washington and hinder the Ford administration's efforts to win support in Congress for sending military support to South Korea.[53] The human rights abuses in themselves appear not to have bothered President Ford or Secretary of State Kissinger. The problem was their possible impact on sensitive members of Congress. The Ford administration was willing to work with authoritarians elsewhere and could do so in Korea as well. (See Chapters Seven and Fourteen.) At a National Security Council Meeting of 15 December 1976, during the interval between his defeat in the 1976 presidential election and the inauguration of President-elect Jimmy Carter, Ford spoke defiantly. "We are going to stay in Korea… If Carter cuts Korea, he is cutting off from what I would do. I favor keeping forces in Korea."[54] Ford's relative indifference to the human rights issue seems to have had few consequences for U.S. interests at the time, but there is evidence that such an attitude on the part of the next Republican administration (Ronald Reagan's) provoked anti-US demonstrations in South Korea. Recent commentators report that during Reagan's second term, students invaded South Korean offices of the Chamber of Commerce and the United States Information Service.[55]

Aftermath and Conclusions

Excluded by the Cold War from the United Nations until 1991, South Korean officials considered the possibility of eliminating the United Nations Command, which retained residual authority, and assuming its responsibilities. Given the withdrawal of forces from fourteen Korean War allies, combined with the Soviet and Chinese vetoes on the Security Council, the United Nations seemed too unreliable a body. In the interests of Northeast Asian stability, the Ford administration saw little merit to this suggestion.

Even Middle Eastern problems intruded on the U.S.-South Korean relationship. The Shah of Iran, a firm U.S. ally, still occupied his country's throne, but North Korea nevertheless managed to negotiate an arms deal with the Shah. (Arms were one of North Korea's few profitable exports.) Park's government tried to forestall conclusion of the deal and offered to sell Iran anything which the North Koreans were offering. South Korea's post-Cold War policy of "Sunshine Diplomacy" toward North Korea lay in the future. Roughly a decade after the end of the Cold War, South Korean authorities would encourage investors to spend money in North Korea so that if, sooner or later, South Korea had to absorb North Korea as West Germany had absorbed Communist East Germany, South Korea would not have to assume responsibility for a hopelessly impoverished asset. That was definitely not the policy of Park Chung Hee.[56]

Notes

1. Laurentian University student David Lefebvre wrote his Honours Essay (undergraduate thesis) on this topic during academic year 2004–2005. Mount and Gauthier thank him for the opportunities to discuss the issues raised in this chapter.

2. The most recent system of transcribing Chinese characters into the Latin alphabet identifies Chiang Kai Shek as Jiang Jie Shi. However, in his time, the former name was the one used in English-language publications and documents.

3. Australia, Belgium, Canada, Colombia, Ethiopia, France, Greece, Luxembourg, New Zealand, the Philippines, South Africa, Thailand, Turkey, the United Kingdom.

4. For a history of the partition of Korea and the Korean War, see Graeme S. Mount, *The Diplomacy of War: The Case of Korea* (Montreal: Black Rose Press, 2003).

5. Shin Jiho, "'386 Generation' Has No Right to Reexamine History," *Korea Focus*, XII, 5 (Sept.-Oct. 2004), p. 12; Lee Jong-Chan, "Prudence Needed to 'Right Korea's History'," *ibid.*, pp. 17–18.

6. Michael Lerner, *The Pueblo Incident: A Spy Ship and the Failure of American Foreign Policy* (Lawrence: University Press of Kansas, 2002).

7. Andrew C. Nahm, Introduction to Korean History and Cuture (Seoul: Hollym, 1993), p. 297.

8. Nahm, p. 299.

9. Gordon Cucullu (a Korean specialist with the United States Army), *Separated at Birth* (Guildford, Conn.: Lyons Press, 2004), pp. 119–123.

10. Práth, Pyongyang, to Hungarian Foreign Ministry, Budapest, 8 Dec. 1960, *Cold War International History Project*, XIV/XV (Spring 2004), Document 23, p. 119. Cited hereafter as *CWIHP*.

11. József Kovács, Hungarian Ambassador in Pyongyang, to Hungarian Foreign Ministry, Budapest, 11 Jan. 1964, Document 35, *CWIHP*, p. 133.

12. Kovács to Hungarian Foreign Ministry, 11 Jan. 1964, Document 36, *CWIHP*, p. 134.

13. Charles K. Armstrong, "'Fraternal Socialism': The International Reconstruction of North Korea, 1953-62," *Cold War History*, V, 2 (May 2005), p. 168.

14. Armstrong, p. 179.

15. Armstrong, p. 180.

16. Kovács to Hungarian Foreign Ministry, 29 March 1962, Document 26, *CWIHP*, p. 123.

18. Report on the official friendship visit to the DPRK by the party and state delegation of the G[erman] D[emocratic] R[epublic], led by Comrade Erich Honecker, 8-11 December, 1977, Document 6, *CWIHP*, p. 50. Cited hereafter as Honecker report.

19. Práth, Pyongyang, to Hungarian Foreign Ministry, 16 March 1961, Document 24, *CWIHP*, p. 121.

20. Bernd Schäfer, "Weathering the Sino-Soviet Conflict: The GDR and North Korea, 1949-1989," *CWIHP*, p. 31.

21. Honecker report, p. 51. Singlaub, pp. 358-364.

22. James V. Young, *Eye on Korea: An Insider Account of Korean-American Relations* (College Station, Texas: Texas A&M University Press, 2004), p. 39. Young (p. 26) was among the admirers of Park's economic achievements. See also John K. Singlaub, *Hazardous Duty: An American Soldier in the Twentieth Century* (New York: Summit, 1991), p. 359.

23. Rhee Sang-woo, "Korea's Strategic Options in the 21st Century," *Korea Focus*, X, 2 (March-April 2002), p. 55.

24. Joint Chiefs of Staff, Washington, Memorandum for the Secretary of Defense, 21 Sept. 1974, National Security Adviser: Presidential Country Files for East Asia and the Pacific, Country File: Korea-(1), Box 9, GFPL. Cited hereafter as NSA.

25. N[ational] S[ecurity] C[ouncil] Meeting, Washington, 2Dec. 1974, National Security Adviser, NSC Meeting File, 1974–1977, Box 1, GPFL. Cited hereafter as NSC Meeting File.

26. George S. Springsteen, Executive Secretary, Dept. Of State, to Scowcroft, 4 Feb. 1975, Box 9, NSA.

27. Emphasized by Secretary of Defense James Schlesinger when he visited Seoul in August 1975; Memorandum of Conversation, n.d., Folder: Korea (11), Box 9, NSA, GFPL.

28. Davis to Springsteen, 3 March 1975, File: (Korea 4), Box 9, NSA, GFPL.

29. Young, pp. 18–19.

30. John Marcum, NSC, to Brent Scowcroft, 24 July 1975, Folder: Korea (9), Box 9, NSA, GFPL.

31. Jan. M. Lodal and Dave Elliott, NSC, to Kissinger, 24 July 1975, Folder: Korea (9), Box 9, NSA, GFPL.

32. Memorandum to the Assistant to the President for National Security Affairs, written by Acting Secretary of State Robert S. Ingersoll, 2 July 1975, Folder: Korea 9, Box 9, NSA, GFPL.

33. Suggested plans for the troops reductions, on the grounds that South Koreans were more capable than ever of handling their own defense, appear in Deputy Secretary of Defense Clements: Memorandum for Assistant to the President for National Security Affairs, 19 Sept. 1974, Folder: Korea (1), Box 9, NSA, GFPL.

34. Kissinger to Ford, 8 May 1975, Folder: Korea (6), Box 9, NSA, GFPL.

35. Kissinger to Ford, 25 June 1975, Folder: Korea (7), Box 9, NSA, GFPL.

36. Memorandum of Conversation, n.d. indicated but August 1975, Folder: Korea (11), Box 9, NSA, GFPL.

37. Memorandum of Conversation, 26 Aug. 1975, Folder: Korea (11), Box 9, NSA, GFPL.

38. Barnes to Scowcroft, 29 Sept. 1975, Folder Korea (14), Box 9, NSF, GFPL.

39. "Comments on Secretary Schlesinger's Discussions in Seoul," n.d., Folder: Korea (12), Box 9, NSA, GFPL.

40. Someone from the State Department marked the paragraph quoted here for special attention. In connection with the name of the North Korean leader, there are various ways of writing Korean names in the Latin script. The document at hand uses this format, but Kim Il Sung is more common. The translation of the North Korean statement appears in File: Korea (16), Box 10, NSA, GFPL.

41. Barnes to Scowcroft, 28 May 1976, File: Korea (16), Box 10, NSA, GFPL. All the quotations in this paragraph come from the Barnes letter.

42. There are at least ten documents on that subject from those two months in Folder: Korea (17), Box 10, NSA, GFPL.

43. Bruce Cumings, *Korea's Place in the Sun: A Modern History* (New York: Norton, 1997), p. 481; *Don Oberdorfer, The Two Koreas: A Contemporary History* (Reading, Mass.: Addison-Wesley, 1997), pp. 74–83.

44. Cumings, p. 481. Singlaub provides a detailed account of the tree incident and Operation Paul Bunyan from the perspective of a field commander on the spot; see pp 365–379.

45. Memorandum of Conversation, 15 Sept. 1976, Folder: Korea (20), Box 10, NSA, GFPL.

46. Nahm, p. 299.

47. Nahm, p. 305.

48. Oberdorfer, pp. 183–186.

49. Young, p. 151.

50. For a recent South Korean account of human rights during the Park era, see Paik Nak-chung, "How to Think About the Park Chung Hee Era," *Korea Focus*, XIII,3 (May–June 2005), 116–124.

51. NSC Meeting, 2 Dec. 1974. Box 2, GFPL.

52. Smyser to Kissinger, 29 Nov. 1974, NSC Meeting File, Box 1, GFPL.

53. Smyser to Kissinger, 26 Feb. 1975, Folder: Korea (3), Box 9, NSA, GFPL. A briefing paper for Defense Secretary Schlesinger prepared for his August 1975 visit to Seoul made the same point; Folder: (Korea 11), Box 9, NSA, GFPL.

54. NSC Meeting, 15 Dec. 1976, NSC Meeting File, Box 2, GFPL.

55. Ted Galen Carpenter and Doug Bandow, *The Korean Conundrum: America's Troubled Relations with North and South Korea* (New York: Palgrave Macmillan, 2004), p. 11.

56. For a recent update on inter-Korean relations, see Roland Bleiker's newly released book, Divided Korea: *Toward a Culture of Reconciliation* (Minneapolis: University of Minnesota Press, 2005).

Chapter Seven

CONSEQUENCES OF THE COLLAPSE OF SOUTH VIETNAM: INDONESIA AND EAST TIMOR

In early December 1975, the Indonesian army invaded the former Portuguese colony of East Timor, and the government of Indonesian President Suharto annexed East Timor to Indonesia. It remained part of its gigantic neighbour until 1999, when Suharto's successor relented and granted East Timor its independence. During the decades of Indonesian occupation, violence would claim the lives of an estimated 200,000 of East Timor's 1,000,000 people.[1] The Ford administration bears considerable responsibility for the Indonesian invasion and occupation, even if it was not prescient and could not foresee the horrors which would result. It deliberately shut its collective eyes to the high handedness and illegal acts of the Suharto government because the U.S. had significant interests in Indonesia—a Cold War ally, a producer of oil, a strategically located country with its own interests in the Law of the Sea, a country with a vote at the United Nations (formulator of international law)—and none in East Timor.

East Timor was more than a victim of Portugal's rapid decolonization. It was also a victim of the Vietnam War. Like President Park Chung Hee in South Korea (See Chapter Six), President Suharto of Indonesia sought assurances that his country was not as expendable to the United States as South Vietnam evidently had been. Ford and Kissinger liked Suharto, a pleasant contrast (from their standpoint) from his predecessor, Sukarno, whom the Central Intelligence Agency had tried to assassinate and whom Suharto managed to oust in 1967. (See Chapter Twelve.) Provoking Suharto within months of the fall of Saigon hardly seemed compatible with U.S. interests. Moreover, Indonesia was an oil producing nation, and East Timor was not. Indonesia was huge and influential; East Timor was small and insignificant. Indonesia had a presence near the Strait of Malacca;[2] East Timor did not. In the words of Robert S. Ingersoll of the National Security Council, Suharto was leader of a "strongly anti-communist government...deeply concerned with the problems of living with a communist Indochina."[3] East Timor's FRETILIN leaders (the effective government of briefly independent East Timor) seemed suspiciously like Communists. Also, as Indonesia was an archipelago, its co-operation in Law of the Sea talks was highly desirable. Whatever prevailed in the Indonesian archipelago could set a precedent for places much closer to the United States, including the Bahamas.[4] David Newsom, the U.S. Ambassador to Indonesia, said., " We have many interests in Indonesia, none in Timor."[5] After Indonesia's invasion of East Timor, Brent Scowcroft—who by then had succeeded Henry Kissinger as National Security Adviser—wrote to White House Press Secretary Ron Nessen, "We have no real national interest in Portuguese Timor."[6]

Indonesia was the successor state to the Dutch East Indies, a heterogeneous archipelago stretching from the Indian to the Pacific Ocean. In 1965, two years after the United Kingdom had created the Federation of Malaysia and granted independence to *its* former southeast Asian colonies, Indonesia—then led by Suharto's predecessor, Sukarno—invaded North Borneo, previously British and currently Malaysian, which shared an island with Indonesian Borneo. Indonesian forces also invaded the Malaysian territories of Sabah and Sarawak. More than 90,000 Malaysian soldiers would die because Sukarno thought that Indonesia should include more than what had been Dutch territory.[7] On that point, Sukarno and his successor, Suharto, agreed. Indonesia and Portugal shared the small island of Timor in the eastern part of the archipelago. With the collapse of Portugal's empire in 1975 (See Chapter Three), Portuguese Timor became briefly the Democratic Republic of East Timor. Barely one week later, the Indonesian army invaded and extinguished East Timorese independence (until 1999).

Ongoing coverage in the *New York Times* confirms that conditions in East Timor were chaotic throughout the second half of 1975. The 1975 edition of the *Yearbook of the United Nations* confirms the less than peaceful conditions there.[8] On 12 July, Portuguese authorities suggested that Portugal would continue to govern Portuguese Timor until 1978, thereby allowing an orderly transition.[9] However, when challenged, they allowed law and order to collapse. Still, a reasonable person may wonder to what extent fewer than one million residents of tiny Portuguese Timor could possibly threaten the security of Indonesia, one of the world's largest countries in terms of both population and territory.

There is no doubt that Ford and Kissinger accepted, even encouraged, Indonesia's invasion of East Timor. There were two opportunities to do so. As part of a round-the-world trip, President Suharto visited President Ford at Camp David, Maryland 5 July 1975. That was the Indonesian president's first visit to the United States since 1970. Five months later, President Ford included a visit to Jakarta, Indonesia's capital, as part of a visit to Southeast Asia. Briefing papers prepared for both occasions reveal the thinking of the moment. Those briefing papers, along with information provided by Suharto himself, appear to have influenced President Ford's thinking on East Timor.

As Ford's National Security Adviser, Henry Kissinger prepared a brief which, for the benefit of historians, is marked "THE PRESIDENT HAS SEEN."[10] Vietnam's fate was a dominant factor. In the aftermath of what had happened there, Kissinger warned, President Ford must "reassure President Suharto on the constancy of U.S. intentions toward Southeast Asia...as well as toward Indonesia itself." Suharto had anticipated the survival of South Vietnam for a longer period, during which Indonesia could prepare itself for any aggression or subversion directed from Hanoi, the Communist capital in Vietnam. The speed of South Vietnam's disappearance had been a shock and a threat to U.S. credibility in the region. To compensate, at least partially, the government of the United States ought to offer Suharto military equipment which it had managed to remove from South Vietnam and offer to assist Indonesia economically as well as militarily. Kissinger praised Suharto's economic development programme, but noted that Indonesia, a member of the Organization of Petroleum Exporting Countries (OPEC), was still far from developed. The situation would improve, Kissinger predicted, but for the moment Indonesia produced only four per cent of OPEC's oil. Kissinger advised Ford to tell Suharto that as OPEC raised the price of crude oil, Congress would become less and less supportive of aid to an OPEC member.

Kissinger had a highly positive interpretation of Indonesia's international role. The Suharto government was useful as a mediator in a territorial dispute between Malaysia and the Philippines as well as in a conflict between Muslim insurgents in the southern Philippines and the Manila-based government of that country. Indonesian soldiers had participated in the International Commission of Control and Supervision, established in January 1973 to oversee the cease-fire agreement between the United States and North Vietnam. The Suharto government had also sent troops to the United Nations Emergency Force in the Middle East and helped to train anti-Communist Cambodians.

On the negative side, Kissinger noted that Indonesian authorities had collaborated with their counterparts from the Philippines, Fiji, and the Bahamas to "claim national jurisdiction over waters enclosed by baselines connecting their outermost islands." While the United States was willing to allow the archipelagic countries some authority over the waters of their respective neighbourhoods, it could not endorse the kind of Law of the Sea (LOS) treaty which Suharto wanted. Indonesia's demand that ships and aircraft entering the waters around or the space above the archipelago must provide advance notification to the archipelagic state conflicted with "U.S. navigation objectives." The United States was often willing, said Kissinger, "as a matter of courtesy," to offer such notification, but it could not accept a legal obligation to do so.

At Camp David 5 July 1975, Ford and Suharto discussed at length the events of the previous April in Vietnam. Ford said that despite what had happened there, the United States remained fully committed to Southeast Asia. Suharto expressed sorrow that after so much sacrifice, the U.S. effort in South Vietnam had proved futile. The events in Vietnam, he said, threw a new perspective onto the international situation in the region.

Ford and Suharto also discussed the other points raised by Kissinger. Ford said that Congress was reducing the funds provided for military assistance but hoped that he could increase the amount allotted to Indonesia. They discussed economic assistance, the Law of the Sea, and Indonesia's membership in OPEC. As OPEC raised the price of crude oil, warned the U.S. President, it became increasingly difficult to persuade members of Congress to vote funds for assistance to an oil exporting country. At Suharto's behest, they discussed the situation in Portuguese Timor, as it still was then.

According to Suharto, Indonesia would not commit aggression. To do so would violate its Constitution of 1945, which remained "our basic principle."[11] Instead he depicted Portuguese Timor as a Communist threat to Indonesia, against which Indonesians might have to defend themselves. The government of Indonesia, said Suharto, agreed that self-determination should be at the centre of Portugal's decolonization process. As he explained the situation, those making the decisions really had three options: independence; continuation of Portuguese rule; and union with Indonesia. Portuguese Timor was too small to be viable as an independent country, especially as it lacked resources. Portugal itself was so remote that caring for Portuguese Timor "would be a big burden."[12] Nor could Portuguese Timor become a semi-autonomous or largely autonomous region of

Indonesia, "because Indonesia is a unitary state. So the only way is to integrate into Indonesia."[13]

At that point, President Ford interrupted to ask whether the Portuguese had set a date for a referendum on the various options in their colony. Suharto replied that there was no date yet, but that there was agreement in principle,

> that the wishes of the people will be sought. The problem is that those who want independence are those who are Communist influenced. Those wanting Indonesian integration are subjected to heavy pressure by those who are almost Communist...I want to assert that Indonesia doesn't want to insert itself into Timor self-determination, but the problem is how to manage the self-determination process with a majority wanting unity with Indonesia...[14]

Historian Jussi Hanhimäki finds Suharto's interpretation of events highly simplistic. According to Hanhimäki, the two main political organizations in East Timor when Portugal abdicated responsibility for its governance were the Revolutionary Front for an Independent East Timor (with the Portuguese acronym FRETILIN) and The Timorese Democratic Union (UTD). What Hanhimäki calls "Timorese elites and senior Portuguese colonial administrators" supported the UTD, while FRETILIN was the favourite of young people and "lower level colonial officials." In the local elections of July 1975, FRETILIN won 55% of the votes after calling for the almost immediate independence of East Timor. Hanhimäki identifies FRETILIN as "a left-leaning nationalist movement...but...hardly communist inspired." The UTD, by contrast, "strengthened its ties with Indonesia."[15]

By the time of the December Ford-Suharto conversation, Brent Scowcroft had replaced Kissinger as National Security Adviser. Scowcroft advised President Ford that his visit to Jakarta would be "largely symbolic...to demonstrate the significance and importance [which] we attach to our relations with Indonesia [and] to reassure our friends in Southeast Asia that we remain fully committed to supporting them [and] to illustrate to less friendly powers that we are not abandoning Southeast Asia."[16] Regarding Portuguese Timor, Scowcroft recommended

> that we would view incorporation of this territory into Indonesia as a "reasonable solution." I recommend that you avoid any such direct endorsement of Indonesian action on Timor and limit yourself to an expression of self-determination and a peaceful solution of the situation.[17]

Scowcroft advised Ford that Indonesian authorities had publicly urged Portugal to oversee an orderly decolonization process which would include a government representative of all factions. Scowcroft also noted that the Indonesians had indicated a willingness "to incorporate Timor into Indonesia if that is what the Timorese desire."[18] Scowcroft informed Ford that "Indonesia is afraid Timor might become a base for Communist insurgents."[19]

At the time of the author's visit to the Gerald Ford Presidential Library in May 2005, the next six lines of the Scowcroft memo were whited out. When the commentary resumed, Scowcroft suggested that if Suharto were to raise the question of East Timor, Ford should say:

- We fully understand Indonesia's concern over developments in Portuguese Timor.
- We admire the restraint Indonesia has shown in dealing with the problem.
- We support Indonesia's call for an orderly decolonization of Portuguese Timor and self-determination for the people of that colony.[20]

Closer to the visit, Scowcroft prepared another briefing paper for the December talks. Indonesia deserved praise, said the briefing paper, for not raising the price of crude oil to the levels allowed by OPEC. However, Indonesia should finance its economic development by exporting larger quantities of oil rather than increasing the price per barrel. Scowcroft also dealt with the matter of human rights in Indonesia. If the subject arose, suggested Scowcroft, Ford might tell Suharto that Americans had become aware of the existence of political prisoners in Indonesia, and this was creating a negative impression of that country in Congress and in the public at large.[21] On 26 November, the *New York Times* estimated the number of political prisoners detained in Indonesia as close to 50,000, despite the release of some 1,300 within the previous year.

Then came the smoking gun. Late in November one of the factions contending to replace Portugal, the FRETILIN, had declared the independence of what it called the Democratic Republic of East Timor. Regarding East Timor, Scowcroft advised Ford not to raise the issue until and unless Suharto did. If that happened, advised Scowcroft, Ford should tell Suharto that the United States government agreed that East Timor was a "problem" for Indonesia, especially since FRETILIN's unilateral declaration of independence 28 November. The briefing paper suggested that Ford praise "the restraint that Indonesia has exercised to date." Then came the most critical words, which Ford might or might not have repeated in his conversation with Suharto:

The problem essentially is one for the parties most concerned—Indonesia, Portugal, Australia, and the Timorese people—to work out. If, with the assent of its people, the territory were merged with Indonesia, this would be a reasonable solution.

We understand that with the help of neighboring countries you [the Suharto government] are proposing a resolution at the United Nations which meets your needs and for which you sought our support. I have instructed our delegation in New York to support these efforts.[22]

Despite advance notice in his intelligence briefing of 1 December 1975 that Indonesia was about to invade East Timor, Ford proceeded with his visit to Jakarta. The invasion, according to the briefing, would not take place before Ford's visit.[23] While that was technically the case, the days before his arrival were lively in every respect. The White House Intelligence Summary of 3 December 1975 stated bluntly: "Ranking Indonesian and civilian government leaders have decided that the only solution to the Portuguese Timor situation is for Indonesia to launch an open offensive against Fretilin." The next line of the report remained whited in May 2005 but the following lines were clear:

- Suharto has approved the idea of full-scale intervention, but is skeptical about the tactical plans provided by the military and had not given the final approval as of December 2 for the invasion.
- The government is somewhat concerned about international reactions to timing such a move for soon after President Ford's visit, but considers this will not present a serious problem since "all the world knows that Indonesia has tried its best to solve the problem peacefully."[24]

After another line of whited information, the intelligence briefing said that according to the Reuters news agency, Foreign Minister Adam Malik had met pro-Indonesian elements from East Timor and subsequently declatred "that the Timor problem could now be solved only on the battlefield."[25]

The story becomes worse. A National Security Memorandum of December 4, which Ford probably did not see but which Brent Scowcroft undoubtedly did (for it was addressed to him), summarized developments of the previous days. Between 24 and 27 November, Indonesian forces blockaded the coast of Portuguese Timor "and stepped up military operations and air strikes inside Timor." On the 28th, the FRETILIN government proclaimed the Democratic Republic of East Timor. The following day, the four opposition parties publicly announced that they supported Timor's integration into Indonesia. (There was no mention of the fact that FRETILIN alone had won considerably more votes than those four parties combined.) The following day, the Portuguese government indicated that it did not recognize East Timorese independence and would take the matter to the United Nations. On 1 December, the government of Indonesia challenged both the Timorese declaration of independence and Portugal's decision to take the matter to the United Nations. The same day, Indonesian Foreign Minister Malik proclaimed his support for the integration of Portuguese Timor into Indonesia. Between 1 and 4 December, the four days preceding Ford's arrival in Jakarta, Indonesian forces "stepped up their operations inside Portuguese Timor." On 4 December, Suharto's government issued a statement which said that "recent events in Timor [had] threatened Indonesia's national security and stability and that the government [of Indonesia] would take steps necessary to safeguard its territory." Despite all this, the National Security Council official who tabulated these events, Kenneth Quinn, advised that President Ford should congratulate President Suharto "for the restraint Indonesia has shown to date."[26]

Actually, there were pressing domestic political reasons for Ford to go to Indonesia. On 25 October 1975, the very day when the President advised Kissinger that he would no longer serve as National Security Adviser (although he could continue as Secretary of State),[27] the two men discussed Ford's forthcoming trip to China at the end of November. Ford had initially agreed to the trip in order to placate the Chinese after his 1974 visit to Vladivostok in the Soviet Union. There were dangers, Kissinger warned. Ford's bargaining position could be weak. If nothing came of the trip, Americans would question why he had bothered to go. However, if he cancelled the trip, he would lose his "leverage" with the Soviet Union. Also, the Chinese might invite various candidates for the Democratic presidential nomination to go to Beijing and receive an earful about the way "you screwed up the Chinese policy." Nor should Ford compensate for a possible fruitless visit to Beijing by visiting another Chinese city. Nixon had visited two of them in 1972, and Americans were bound to make comparisons. Ford must separate himself from his disgraced predecessor's profile. Hence, in order to have something positive to show, Ford must visit some city or cities on the other side of the Pacific but outside China.

Where would Ford go? He suggested India, but Kissinger objected. "The Indians are such shits."[28] Information released 29 June 2005 by the National Security Archive in Washington indicates that during the Nixon administration,

Kissinger had regarded the government of India as such a "Soviet Stooge" that in 1971 when India and Pakistan went to war, he and President Nixon decided to ignore evidence of Pakistani genocide in what was then East Pakistan and is now Bangladesh. According to the National Security Archive, they "even suggested that China intervene militarily on Pakistan's side."[29]

Given the poor relations between India and China, it would not be diplomatic to visit one after the other, and it would be impossible to go to India without also going to Pakistan, a time consuming process. Kissinger suggested Manila and Jakarta, where a visit would "bolster our friends."[30] Ford nominated Australia and New Zealand as possible destinations, but it was fortunate that he did not go there. On 11 November 1975, Australia's Governor General, Sir John Kerr, dismissed the government of Labour Prime Minister Gough Whitlam among circumstances of dubious legality and invited Opposition Leader Malcolm Fraser to assume office. Fraser's Liberal-Country coalition won the parliamentary elections of 13 December, but had Ford gone to Australia in the days following his stay in China, he would have stepped into one of Australia's hottest political crises of the twentieth century. Of the places Ford could go in order to balance Beijing, Jakarta appeared one of the least controversial. That it would not be so should have been evident before President Ford went there.

Hanhimäki quotes Suharto as telling Ford and Kissinger 6 December, during their time in Jakarta, "We want your understanding if we deem it necessary to take rapid or drastic action." Suharto reportedly told Ford that four of East Timor's five political parties—all except FRETILIN—thought that East Timor should be part of Indonesia.

"We will understand," was Ford's response, according to Hanhimäki. Kissinger was not concerned about any invasion as such, only about political consequences in the United States if, contrary to U.S. law, Suharto's army used U.S.-supplied weapons during the invasion.[31]

The invasion took place 7 December, within hours of Ford's departure from Jakarta. Scowcroft urged U.S. silence and neutrality in the matter. Two close U.S. allies, Indonesia and Portugal, had taken incompatible positions. The U.S. should not side with either of them when it had no interests of its own in East Timor.[32] The State Department's position–that it would be reasonable for Portuguese Timor to merge with Indonesia but "with the assent of the Timorese people"[33]—had been overtaken by events. As early as 8 December, the CIA informed

Scowcroft that the Indonesians had used two destroyers and other military equipment supplied by the United States when staging their invasion.[34]

Indeed, it would appear that Scowcroft's recommended policy of strict U.S. neutrality was dead on arrival, ignored by President Ford and incredible to all concerned. The U.S. Embassy in Jakarta told the State Department that in a conversation with Dutch diplomats, Malik had reported that during his visit to the Indonesian capital, President Ford had said that he "understood Indonesia's problems and did not oppose its actions in Timor." The government of Portugal was suspicious that the invasion would occur while the U.S. President was airborne between Jakarta and Hawaii.[35] East Timor's President, Xavier do Amaral, sent a telegram to President Ford protesting Indonesian aggression against his country.[36] There appears to be no reply in the file. On 10 December, Ford's morning intelligence report included confirmation from the U.S. Embassy in Jakarta that Suharto's army had used military equipment supplied by the United States during the invasion.[37] That same day, speaking to leaders of the Republican party in Congress, Ford said: "[From China] we went next to Indonesia. It was important to go there in the aftermath of Vietnam to show we were still an Asian power. I was impressed with Suharto, who is trying to keep the country together and uphold the cause of anti-communism there."[38] There was no mention of East Timor. Then on 13 December, Staff Secretary Jeanne W. Davis of the National Security Council advised George S. Springsteen, Executive Secretary at the State Department, that President Ford was sending golf balls to President Suharto as well as to President Ferdinand Marcos of the Philippines, whom he had visited on the same trip. Davis advised Springsteen to let "the two Presidents know that the golf balls are a personal gift from President Ford."[39] (The underlining was Davis's). On 9 January 1976, Ford wrote "thank you" letters to various Indonesian dignitaries who had offered assistance during his December visit to the Indonesian capital. To Adam Malik, Indonesia's Foreign Minister, he wrote:

> It was a distinct pleasure to renew my acquaintance with you during my visit to Jakarta. I was grateful for the opportunity we had to spend some time together, and I welcome the extra dimension of understanding which these personal contacts provide.[40]

In a conversation at the White House with Malik 7 October 1976, Ford said, "We think we are on the right track and I think our relations with allies have never been better. I am glad the President [Suharto] is well and things are going well…"[41] Again, there was no hint of disapproval.

Recently declassified correspondence indicates White House thinking in the aftermath of President Ford's visit to Jakarta. On 12 December 1975, the CIA informed Thomas Barnes of the National Security Council, who in turn informed Scowcroft, that Indonesia had unchallenged control of East Timor. Its 15,000 soldiers there outnumbered the FRETILIN army by a margin of 3:1, and while FRETILIN would probably "make maxium international effort to publicize its cause," the rest of the world was likely to remain indifferent.[42] Vietnam and China had "voiced support for Fretilin's cause [but] obviously do not regard it as a viable contender for power."[43] China and the Soviet Union would not risk their relations with Indonesia for the sake of East Timor, said William Colby, Director of the Central Intelligence Agency.

Even the Vatican appears to have withheld any indication of disapproval of the Indonesian invasion. Documents accessible to historians at the Gerald Ford Presidential Library concerning U.S.-Vatican relations make no mention of East Timor, despite its overwhelmingly Roman Catholic population. One report mentions Vatican support for the Christians who were fighting Muslims in Lebanon.[44] On 4 January 1977, Henry Cabot Lodge—who was serving as Presidential Emissary to the Holy See—told President Ford about Vatican support for an international status for Jerusalem and concern at the Vatican about Communist influence in Italy,[45] but there was nothing about East Timor. Unless documents still declassified at the time of writing surface in either the United States or the Vatican, Vatican silence on East Timor may prove the papacy's worst sin of omission against Roman Catholics since the German invasion of Poland in September 1939. Hanhimäki estimates that the Indonesian army killed 60,000 East Timorese during the first year of occupation, 200,000 altogether.[46]

At this point, the Ford administration had no choice but to play diplomatic chess—immediately. The two countries other than Indonesia, East Timor itself, and the United States, which had interests in the situation, were Portugal (the former colonial power) and Australia (other than Indonesia, the closest neighbour). With its air base in the Azores, the U.S. government wanted good relations with Portugal, a NATO partner. For reasons already elaborated, it wanted good relations with Indonesia. Throughout the month of December 1975, Portugal and Indonesia held adversarial positions. How could President Ford simultaneously maintain his credibility with both of them? Ambassador David Newsom in Jakarta and Ambassador Frank Carlucci in Lisbon offered conflicting advice.

Australia was not as serious a challenge as Portugal and Indonesia. Relations between the U.S. and Australian governments had been compatible. Australian Prime Minister Gough Whitlam had visited the Oval Office twice, 4 October 1974 and 7 May 1975. Both times Ford and Whitlam discussed East Timor, and their views were similar. Both liked Suharto, and they both agreed that given the size of East Timor, absorption by Indonesia made sense.[47] Whitlam had said as much during a conversation in Jakarta with Suharto 6 September 1974. Too small to be viable, East Timor would have to look to a larger country for assistance, and that country could be a Communist one. Whitlam did not want a Chinese or Soviet client state so close to Australia. However, Whitlam told Suharto that for the sake of public opinion in Australia, the Indonesian takeover should "appear to be a natural process arising from the wishes of the people."[48] The essence of Whitlam's conversation with Suharto was known in Washington.[49] Then came the Australian constitutional crisis of 11 November 1975. (See page 97.) At the time of the Indonesian invasion (7 December), and the United Nations General Assembly (12 December), the government of Malcolm Fraser, Whitlam's replacement, lacked a mandate to govern and was operating in a caretaker capacity.

The government of Portugal acted to assist East Timor. After the invasion, it broke diplomatic relations with Indonesia and took the matter to the United Nations. On 12 December, the General Assembly approved by a margin of 72:10 a resolution which "strongly deplore[d] the military intervention of the armed forces of Indonesia in Portuguese Timor." Australia and Portugal, two countries with which the White House had hoped to co-operate, were among the seventy-two. The United States was one of 43 countries which abstained, presumably as an indication of its "neutrality" in the matter. The U.S. Embassy in Jakarta found the U.S. abstention tolerable. With Ambassador Newsom in Washington for consultations, an official wrote that the abstention "enabled us so far to preserve intact [the] U.S.-Indonesian relationship." He also recommended an abstention on the forthcoming resolution in the Security Council and indicated Indonesian disappointment that the Australian delegation had voted with the Portuguese. Perhaps, reasoned the Suharto government, once Prime Minister Fraser actually won an election, he would prove more supportive.[50]

From Lisbon, Ambassador Carlucci sent a different interpretation. American "lack of support for the GOP [Government of Portugal]," he warned, "will not go unnoticed here." First, there was "all too obvious" a contrast between the

U.S. position on Angola and that on East Timor, both former Portuguese colonies. Secondly, the U.S. had lectured the Portuguese on their obligation to maintain NATO solidarity and vote with other Western countries whenever the United Nations considered resolutions on Korea. NATO solidarity, reasoned the Portuguese, ought to be reciprocal. Why should they offer unconditional support to any U.S. position on Korea when the U.S. felt no obligation to support Portugal in a territory where it still had claims?[51]

On 22 December, the Security Council unanimously called "upon the Government of Indonesia to withdraw without delay all its forces from the Territory."[52] Once confirmed in office by the election of 13 December, the Fraser government instructed Australia's delegation to the United Nations to prepare the Security Council resolution, even though Australia was not then a member of the Security Council.[53] Thereafter, quite apart from any U.S. moral commitments to Portugal and Australia, Indonesian behaviour was making unconditional support for that country increasingly difficult. In the aftermath of the Security Council vote, the Suharto government refused to admit observers from the United Nations.[54] Indeed, President Ford's morning intelligence briefing of 1 February 1976 indicates that if the UN envoy who was supposed to go to East Timor decided to sail there from the Australian port of Darwin, Indonesian authorities would consider sinking the Portuguese frigate taking him there. (That was one of three options to prevent his arrival and one which the Suharto government rejected as too controversial. The other two depended upon Australian co-operation in denying either the UN envoy or the Portuguese frigate landing rights in Darwin.) Suharto's fear, said the intelligence briefing, was that if the UN official did manage to reach East Timor, he would "find confirmation of the presence of a large Indonesian military force, and evidence that Fretilin is stronger than admitted."[55]

There were also challenges on the home front, but these could be managed more easily. Kissinger was correct in thinking that Americans would be concerned about Indonesia's use of U.S.-supplied weapons to invade East Timor. On 12 December 1975, the White House received a detailed account of what U.S.-supplied weapons Suharto's forces had used in the battle for East Timor. From 21 November onward, a destroyer which had served in the U.S. Navy as the *Charles Berry* and which had become the Indonesian Navy's *Martadinata* had shelled the Timorese coastline. The *Charles Berry/ Martadinata* bombarded Dili, capital of East Timor, for two hours 7 December, the day of the actual invasion.

Two other destroyers—the *Monginsidi* (ex-*Claude Jones*) and the *Ngurahrai* (ex-*McMorris*)—had patrolled the Timorese coastline. In the air, continued the report, "Transportation throughout the operations has been provided by ex-U.S. 511 class LSTs…" Two C-47 transport aircraft supplied by the United States attacked Dili while another bombed Baucau, another Timorese community. Hercules aircraft of U.S. origin "participated in the paradrops on Dili and Baucau." U.S. officers trained the jumpmasters, and "Defense believes that both brigades are using their U.S.-supplied equipment."[56] The use of U.S.-supplied equipment for an attack on another country was clearly illegal, contrary to what Americans learned in school to be acceptable behaviour. (During the U.S. Civil War, British suppliers had provided ships to the Confederate Navy—the *Alabama*, the *Florida*, and the *Shenandoah*. Subsequent actions of those ships created such animosity that war between Great Britain and the United States appeared a distinct possibility until the British accepted responsibility for what they had done and paid compensation.[57])

While Americans outside the White House and the CIA could not have known the details of U.S. weaponry used in the attack on East Timor, there were suspicions. On 13 December, an editorial in the *New York Times* urged Congress to act cautiously before increasing the level of military aid to Indonesia.[58] Three days later, Senator Gary Hart (Democrat-Colorado) wrote to Defense Secretary Donald Rumsfeld to ask whether the U.S. had supplied the weapons and equipment which Indonesian forces used for the "naval bombardment" of East Timor prior to the invasion and whether U.S. authorities had advance knowledge of Indonesia's plan to invade.[59] Rumsfeld drafted an honest reply but sent it to the White House for approval with the understanding that unless he received instructions to the contrary, he would forward it to Senator Hart 31 December. Rumsfeld wrote:

> [W]e did become aware of impending military operations just before the actual landings took place…
>
> Since Timor is a remote locale having no U.S. observers on the scene, we must rely on reports of Indonesian operations from other foreign sources. Notwithstanding the gaps in information, it is clear that equipment supplied under U.S. programs was used.[60]

Despite the Ford administration's reputation for openness and integrity,[61] Thomas Barnes of the National Security Council and his boss, Brent Scowcroft, thought that Rumsfeld was telling Hart too much. On seeing the draft, Barnes wrote to Scowcroft, "You may wish to intervene to modify or cancel the letter." If the truth should become known, warned Barnes, Congress—controlled by Democrats—might reduce aid to Indonesia and U.S.-Indonesian relations would suffer. Scowcroft agreed to "modify" the sentence "it is clear that equipment supplied under U.S. programs was used" to "it is my understanding that the Indonesians probably used U.S. equipment." Handwriting in the file at the Gerald Ford Presidential Library indicates that the final draft stated "that at least some U.S. equipment was used."[62]

Early in the new year, Kissinger blocked further shipments of U.S. military equipment to Indonesia until the storm subsided. According to law, the State Department, which he headed, had to certify whatever the Defense Department was planning to supply to another country. Without publicity, Kissinger withheld certification and the shipments stopped—to the dismay of Ambassador Newsom and others at the U.S. Embassy in Jakarta.[63] This was only a tactical manoeuvre, as events would indicate.

In the spring of 1976, Senators Hubert Humphrey (Democrat-Minnesota) and Clifford Case (Republican-New Jersey), chair and ranking member of the Senate Subcommittee on Foreign Assistance of the Senate Foreign Relations Committee, expressed concern and threatened to deny assistance to Indonesia until "we are satisfied that we have had an opportunity to consider all facts relevant to Indonesia's use of American-supplied arms and equipment in East Timor."[64] In a memorandum to National Security Adviser Brent Scowcroft, Thomas J. Barnes and Les Janka of the National Security Council offered reassurance. Barnes and Janka admitted that the Indonesian forces had used U.S.-supplied weapons for the invasion but warned that it would be contrary to U.S. interests to make a serious issue of the matter.[65]

In a letter of 14 April 1976 to Secretary of State Kissinger, Senators Humphrey and Case expressed concern that if there was no U.S. reaction to Indonesia's use of U.S.-supplied weapons to invade another country, other recipients of U.S. weapons might note the precedent and decide that they too could invade their neighbours with impunity. Robert McCloskey, Assistant Secretary for Congressional Relations at the Ford White House, replied that East Timor was a special case. The Portuguese government had decided to decolonize in the spring of 1974, explained McCloskey, and bilateral Indonesian-Portuguese talks took place in order that the process of decolonization might be orderly. The talks were the idea of the Indonesian government. Factions within East Timor began to fight. "This left a political vacuum in East Timor, a situation which Indonesia considered a threat to stability and security in the area."[66] One of the Timorese factions was FRETILIN, whose soldiers captured weapons which the Portuguese troops simply "abandoned." Armed with those weapons, FRETILIN quickly became the dominant force in East Timor and some 40,000 people, whom McCloskey estimated as seven per cent of the population, fled to Indonesian West Timor as refugees. As the fighting continued, late in November 1975, FRETILIN issued a unilateral declaration of independence and proclaimed "the Democratic Republic of East Timor." Certain leftist governments and factions (mostly in former possessions of Portugal)—Guinea, Guinea-Bissau, Mozambique, Cape Verde, and Angola's MPLA—extended diplomatic recognition. FRETILIN's domestic opponents appealed to Indonesia for assistance. With the help of Indonesia's military, they managed to take control of much of East Timor, but, continued McCloskey, "we understand that there have also been incursions by Fretilin forces into Indonesian territory."[67] (In his telegram to President Ford, President do Amaral had indignantly denied Indonesian charges of East Timorese aggression.)

For its part, McCloskey said, the Indonesian government urged the government of Portugal to act. Jakarta wanted Lisbon to restore order in East Timor and persuade the various politicians to talk to each other. In October 1975, the Indonesian and Portuguese foreign ministers met for talks in Rome, but nothing happened. According to McCloskey, Indonesian authorities tried and failed to persuade Portugal and various Southeast Asian nations to create a peacekeeping force for East Timor. Regarding the U.S. role, McCloskey admitted that "the Indonesian forces in Timor used some U.S.-supplied equipment in their operations" but added that he lacked "a complete list of the equipment used."[68] While it seemed probable that Indonesia would take military action against East Timor, he said, the Indonesians did not share their plans with U.S. authorities who remained unaware of the specifics until immediately before Indonesia's December invasion.

Before "Fretilin's action and the subsequent Indonesian reaction," said McCloskey, U.S. policy had been that the situation in East Timor was one for "Portugal, Indonesia, such closer neighbors as Australia, and the people of East Timor" to resolve.[69] The Ford administration *did* advise Indonesian authorities that U.S. law prevented them from using weapons supplied by the United States to invade another country. At time of writing, McCloskey told Senators

Humphrey and Case, the White House hoped that the United Nations could handle the matter. Nevertheless, on 28 April, the two senators advised Kissinger that the U.S. should supply no more "arms or other items" to the Indonesian government.[70]

Notwithstanding the objection of Senators Hart, Humphrey and Case as well as Suharto's defiance of the United Nations, U.S. military aid to Indonesia resumed. McCloskey's arguments must have proved convincing. Congress dropped its opposition, and Philip Habib of the State Department found himself with a stronger hand to play at the United Nations, where he was courting Indonesia's vote on issues which appeared likely to arise. Fidel Castro was threatening a resolution on independence for Puerto Rico, and North Korea's friends might be considering one incompatible with the interests of South Korea.[71] Indonesia had a vote at the United Nations, but East Timor did not and would not until its admission in 1999. The Ford administration felt so strongly on the subject of Puerto Rico that it planned to boycott the remainder of the forthcoming session if the United Nations General Assembly approved the Cuban resolution.[72]

Nevertheless, the Ford administration did not *completely* capitulate to President Suharto. On 29 June 1976, Scowcroft was to have lunch with Secretary Kissinger and Foreign Minister Malik, who was visiting Washington. A briefing paper advised:

> Suharto is upset because we [the United States] have not sent Embassy representatives on two GOI [Government of Indonesia] fact-finding missions to observe the process of integration on East Timor. If Malik raises this subject, you may wish to explain that we have attempted to take a balanced approach in dealing with Timor, keeping the entire issue low-key, supporting Indonesia where we can but also observing other political pressures which we feel from other directions.
>
> The Indonesians have not brought up our suspense of military deliveries to them...Should they mention it, you could point out that our careful handling of this matter has enabled us to turn off Congressional critics such as Senator Humphrey and at the same time allow us to resume military assistance shipments to Jakarta.[73]

Someone provided advice which might have enabled the Ford administration to avoid some historical controversy. On 8 May 1975, Singapore's Prime Minister Lee Kuan Yew visited the Oval Office and warned President Ford not to provide weapons to President Suharto's government. "There is no danger from the outside," said Lee, presumably because Indonesia was so large that only a Great Power could successfully invade it and none was likely to do so. "Don't support building a big military machine because that could lead to his overthrow from within." Another danger, thought Lee, was that the Indonesian army might invade a neighboring country—albeit the example he gave was Malaysia.[74]

Unfortunately, President Ford accepted bad advice on East Timor. The reason was largely expediency—to offer the benefit of any doubt to the anti-Communist Suharto in the aftermath of the failure in Vietnam, especially when the U.S. had many other interests in Indonesia.[75] Another factor may have been economy—a reluctance to finance the CIA or anyone else to visit East Timor to see whether the heavily Roman Catholic residents of what had been a Portuguese colony since 1586 had much in common with Indonesians. (President Ford repeatedly called for fiscal restraint.) Historian Jussi Hanhimäki finds the Ford administration's actions in East Timor inexcusable, attributable to Kissinger's "limited world view [which] resulted in mistaken policies."[76] Polemicist Christropher Hitchens finds them criminal.[77] Either way, the results were catastrophic.

Notes

1. Martin Gilbert, *A History of the Twentieth Century*, vol. III (Toronto: Stoddart, 1999), p. 496. *The World Almanac, 2005* (p. 771), agrees that 200,000 died and estimates East Timor's population as 1,019,252, 90% of whom are Roman Catholic.
2. Confidential report prepared by Ambassador William R. Kinter at the State Department, 3 October 1975, John Marsh Files, 1974-1977, Box 4, Folder: Asian-Pacific Area–US Policy Interests, 10/3/75 (1).
3. Memorandum for the President from Robert S. Ingersoll, 1 July 1975, HENRY KISSINGER and BRENT SCOWCROFT Collection, Box A2, Folder: 7/5/75–Indonesia–President Suharto (1), Presidential Briefing Material for NSC Visits, GFPL.
4. Document on the Law of the Sea and its impact on Indonesia and the Bahamas, National Security Adviser, Presidential Country File for Latin America, 1974-1977, Box 2, Folder: Bahamas–State Department Telegrams to SECSTATE (Secretary of State).
5. Cited by W. R. Symser of the National Security Council in a briefing paper prepared for his boss, Henry Kissinger, 4 March 1975, National Security Adviser, Presidential Country Files for East Asia and the Pacific, Box 6, Folder: Indonesia (2), GFPL.
6. Scowcroft to Nessen, n.d. but before 9 Dec. 1975, National Security Adviser, Presidential Country Files for East Asia and the Pacific, Box 6, Folder: Indonesia (5), GFPL.
7. Gilbert, p. 332.
8. *Yearbook of the United Nations, 1975*, pp. 856-858.
9. The *New York Times*, 11 August 1975.

10. Briefing Paper "Meeting with Indonesian President Suharto, Saturday, July 5, 1975" in HENRY KISSINGER and BRENT SCOWCROFT Collection, Box A2, Folder: 7/5/75–Indonesia-President Suharto (4); Presidential Briefing Material for VIP Visits, GFPL. Cited hereafter as Kissinger briefing.

11. Memo of Conversation, 5 July 1975, HENRY KISSINGER and BRENT SCOWCROFT Collection, Box A3, Folder 12/75—Far East Briefing—Indonesia, GFPL. Cited hereafter as Ford-Suharto July conversation.

12. Ford-Suharto July Conversation.

13. Ford-Suharto July Conversation.

14. Ford-Suharto July Conversation.

15. Jussi Hanhimäki, *The Flawed Architect: Henry Kissinger and American Foreign Policy* (New York: Oxford University Press, 2004), p. 389.

16. Scowcroft to Ford, n.d., Memorandum "Your Visit to Indonesia and Meeting with President Suharto," HENRY KISSINGER and BRENT SCOWCROFT Collection, Box A3, Folder 12/75—Far East Briefing—Indonesia, GFPL. Cited hereafter as Visit and Meeting.

17. Visit and Meeting.

18. Visit and Meeting.

19. Visit and Meeting.

20. Visit and Meeting.

21. "Talking Points with President Suharto, 5 and 6 December 1975," HENRY KISSINGER and BRENT SCOWCROFT Collection, Box A3, Folder 12/75, GFPL. Cited hereafter as Talking Points.

22. Talking Points.

23. Intelligence Summary, Dale Van Atta Papers, Box 9, Folder: Intelligence Documents, 1 December 1975, GFPL.

24. Intelligence Summary, Dale Van Atta Papers, Box 9, Folder: Intelligence Documents, 3 December 1975,GFPL. Cited hereafter as Intelligence Summary, 3 December.

25. Intelligence Summary, 3 December.

26. Memorandum from Kenneth Quinn of the National Security Council to Scowcroft, 4 December 1975: Subject: Presidential Talking Points on Portuguese Timor, National Security Adviser: Presidential Country Files for East Asia and the Pacific, Box 6, Folder: Indonesia (Number 4), GFPL. Cited hereafter as Quinn to Scowcroft.

27. Kissinger, pp. 836–837.

28. National Security Adviser: MEMORANDA OF CONVERSATIONS, 1973-1977, Box 16, Folder: October 25, 1975—Ford Kissinger, GFPL. Cited hereafter as Ford-Kissinger (Oct. 25).

29. http://www.gwu.edu/~nsarchiv/news/20050629/index.htm

30. Ford-Kissinger, Oct. 25.

31. Hanhimäki, p. 402.

32. Scowcroft to Ford, n.d., National Security Adviser, Presidential Country Files for East Asia and the Pacific, Box 6, Folder: Indonesia (number 5), GFPL.

33. Quinn to Scowcroft.

34. Memo from Paul Walsh, White House, to Scowcroft, 8 December 1975, National Security Adviser, Presidential Country Files for East Asia and the Pacific, Box 6, Folder: Indonesia (number 5), GFPL.

35. Thomas J. Barnes of the National Security Council to Scowcroft, 9 December 1975, National Security Adviser, Presidential Country Files for East Asia and the Pacific, Box 6, Folder: Indonesia (number 5), GFPL.

36. Do Amaral, Dili, to Ford, 5 December 1975, WHCF Subject File, Box 24, CO 67 Indonesia, Folder 7/6/75-1/20/77, GFPL. The date of the telegram may be a mistake, as Ford's visit to Jakarta took place 5 and 6 December. The invasion occurred as he was flying between Jakarta and Hawaii. See

Hanhimäki, p. 477. Alternatively, it may refer to the Indonesian military actions which took place in the days before the presidential visit.

37. Intelligence Summary, Dale Van Atta Papers, Box 10, Folder: Intelligence Documents, 10 December 1975, GFPL.

38. National Security Adviser, MEMORANDA OF CONVERSATIONS, 1973-1977, Box 16, Folder: December 10, Ford, Kissinger, Simon, Republican Congressional Leadership, GFPL.

39. Davis to Springsteen, 13 December 1975, WHCF Subject File, Box 24, CO 67 Indonesia, Folder 7/6/75-1/20/77, GFPL.

40. Ford, Washington, to Malik, Jakarta, 9 Jan. 1976, Folder 7/6/75-1/20/77, GFPL.

41. National Security Adviser, MEMORANDA OF CONVERSATIONS, 1973-1977, Box 21, Folder: October 7, 1976—Ford, Indonesian Foreign Minister Adam Malik.

42. The quotation comes from Barnes memo to Scowcroft, 12 December 1975, National Security Adviser, Presidential Country Files for East Asia and the Pacific, Box 6, Folder: Indonesia (4), GFPL.

43. Director of the CIA (William Colby) to Barnes, 12 December 1975, National Security Adviser, Presidential Country Files for East Asia and the Pacific, Box 6, Folder: Indonesia (4), GFPL.

44. The report appears in the Dale Van Atta Papers, Intelligence Chronological File, Box 9, Folder: Intelligence Documents, 3 December 1975, GFPL.

45. National Security Adviser, Memoranda of Conversations, Box 21, Folder: 4 January 1977, GFPL.

46. Hanhimäki, p. 402.

47. Transcripts of the Ford-Whitlam conversations are available in National Security Adviser: MEMORANDA OF CONVERSATIONS, 1973-1977, Box 6, Folder: October 5, 1974—Ford, Kissinger, Australian Prime Minister Whitlam; and Box 11, Folder: April 25, 1975, Ford, Kissinger, Australian Prime Minister Gough Whitlam, GFPL. For more information on Whitlam's policies on East Timor, see David Goldsworthy, David Dutton, Peter Gifford, and Roderic Pitty, "Reorientation," in David Goldsworthy (editor), *Facing North: A Century of Australian Engagement with Asia*, Vol. 1 (Melbourne: Melbourne University Press, 2001), pp. 352-370.

48. Record of Meeting between Whitlam and Soeharto [sic], Jakarta, *Documents on Australian Foreign Policy: Australia and the Indonesian Incorporation of Portuguese Timor, 1974-1976* (Melbourne: Melbourne University Press, 2000), pp. 95-98. The quotation comes from p. 96. Cited hereafter as *DAFP*.

49. W.R. Smyser, National Security Council, to Kissinger, 4 March 1975, National Security Adviser, Presidential Country Files for East Asia and the Pacific, Box 6, Folder: Indonesia (2), GFPL.

50. Telegram American Embassy Jakarta to Assistant Secretary of State Philip Habib, Washington, 22 December 1975, National Security Adviser, Presidential Country Files for East Asia and the Pacific, Box 6, Folder: Indonesia (6), GFPL.

51. Telegram American Embassy Lisbon to State Department, 17 Decewmber 1975, National Security Adviser, Presidential Country Files for East Asia and the Pacific, Box 6, Folder: Indonesia (6), GFPL.

52. The wording of the resolution appears in the *Yearbook of the United Nations*, *1975*, p. 866; on 23 December, the day after the vote, the *New York Times* reported that the Security Council vote had been unanimous.

53. Submission to [Andrew] Peacock (Minister for Foreign Affairs in Fraser's government), Canberra, 17 March 1977, *DAFP*, pp. 829-834, esp. p. 830.

54. On 30 December, the *New York Times* reported the Indonesian government's refusal to admit the United Nations officials.

55. Dale Papers, Intelligence Chronological File, Box 11, Folder: Intelligence Documents, 1-2 February 1976, GFPL.

56. Clinton E. Granger of the National Security Council to Scowcroft, 12 Dec. 1975, National Security Adviser, Presidential Country Files for East Asia and the Pacific, Box 6, Folder: Indonesia (6), GFPL.

57. Edelgard E. Mahant and Graeme S. Mount, *An Introduction to Canadian-American Relations* (Toronto: Nelson, 1989), pp. 50-51, 53, 56.

58. The *New York Times*, 13 Dec. 1975.

59. Gary Hart to Donald Rumsfeld, 16 Dec. 1975, National Security Adviser, Presidential Country Files for East Asia and the Pacific, Box 6, Folder: Indonesia (6), GFPL.

60. Draft letter of Rumsfeld to Hart, tentatively dated 31 Dec. 1975, National Security Adviser, Presidential Country Files for East Asia and the Pacific, Box 6, Folder: Indonesia (6), GFPL.

61. This is certainly a feature stressed by Yanek Mieczkowski, *Gerald Ford and the Challenges of the 1970s* (Lexington: University Press of Kentucky, 2005).

62. Barnes to Scowcroft, 30 Dec. 1975, National Security Adviser, Presidential Country Files for East Asia and the Pacific, Box 6, Folder: Indonesia (6), GFPL.

63. Barnes to Scowcroft, 17 May 1976, National Security Adviser, Presidential Country Files for East Asia and the Pacific, Box 6, Folder: Indonesia (7), GFPL.

64. Quoted by Barnes and Janka in their Memo to Scowcroft, 4 May 1976, White House Central File—Name File, Box 1534, GFPL.

65. Barnes and Janka to Scowcroft, 4 May 1976, WHCF Name File, Box 1534, GFPL.

66. McCloskey to Humphrey, 26 April 1976, WHCF Subject File, Box 23: Folder CO 67—Mutual Security/Indonesia, GFPL. Cited hereafter as McCloskey to Humphrey.

67. McCloskey to Humphrey.

68. McCloskey to Humphrey.

69. McCloskey to Humphrey.

70. Humphrey and Case to Kissinger, 28 April 1976, WHCF Subject File, Box 23: Folder CO 67–Mutual Security/Indonesia, GFPL.

71. Barnes to Bill Hyland, 2 June 1976, National Security Adviser, Presidential Country Files for East Asia and the Pacific, Box 6, Folder: Indonesia (7), GFPL.

72. Barnes to Scowcroft, 7 July 1976, National Security Adviser, Presidential Country Files for East Asia and the Pacific, Box 6, Folder: Indonesia (7), GFPL.

73. Ian Taylor to Scowcroft, Subject: Your June 29 Luncheon with Indonesian Foreign Minister Adam Malik and Secretary Kissinger, National Security Adviser, Presidential country Files for East Asia and the Pacific, Box 6, Folder: Indonesia (7), GFPL.

74. National Security Adviser, MEMORANDA OF CONVERSATION, 1973-1977, Box 11, Folder: May 8, 1975—Ford, Kissinger, Singapore Prime Minister Lee Kuan Yew, GFPL.

75. The *New York Times*, 8 December 1975.

76. Hanhimäki, pp. xxii, 478.

77. Christopher Hitchens, *The Trial of Henry Kissinger* (New York: Verso, 2001).

Chapter Eight

INDEPENDENCE FOR MOZAMBIQUE[1]

As a direct result of the events in Portugal, Mozambique gained independence 20 September 1974. This event had an enormous impact on the rest of southern Africa. Since 11 November 1965, Mozambique's inland neighbor, Rhodesia (known as Southern Rhodesia until Northern Rhodesia gained independence as Zambia 1964) had been in a state of rebellion. Its European population—219,000 in 1965 but 241,000 by 1975[2]—had enjoyed internal self-government since 1923. To those people, it was a travesty that the less developed British colonies of Northern Rhodesia and Nyasaland (now Malawi) could achieve independence in 1964, while Southern Rhodesia could not. The British government of Harold Wilson had adopted the NIBMAR policy: No Independence Before Majority African Rule. Most Euro-Rhodesians considered most of the more numerous Afro-Rhodesians—3,600,000 in 1965 and 4,920,000 in 1975—incapable of self-government. What they saw elsewhere in Africa reinforced this idea. Accordingly, Prime Minister Ian Smith of Rhodesia—chosen by a largely European electorate—issued a Unilateral Declaration of Independence (UDI) in 1965. Paraphrasing the United States Declaration of Independence of 1776, Smith indicated that Rhodesians were prepared to go where Americans had led—away from the obstinate British.

The British government of Harold Wilson responded with economic sanctions. It persuaded most friendly countries, excluding Portugal and South Africa, not to trade with Rhodesia. The world would not buy Rhodesian products nor sell to Rhodesians. For almost a decade, nevertheless, Euro-Rhodesians prospered and increased in number. Although theirs was an inland country, access to the ocean lay through Portuguese Mozambique. Rhodesian-bound goods arrived in the Mozambican port of Beira, but after UDI, Portuguese middlemen purchased goods on behalf of Rhodesians and then sold them to Rhodesians. Rhodesians who lived near the border drove their cars into Mozambique to purchase fuel. Rhodesian goods went through Mozambique and into the outside world disguised as merchandise from Mozambique. The mighty Zambezi River, which widens into Lake Kariba, separated Zambia from Rhodesia, and the Zambia-based forces of the Zimbabwe African People's Union (ZAPU) could not readily attack targets in Rhodesia. ("Zimbabwe" was the African name for "Rhodesia.") Portuguese forces maintained law and order on the eastern border. This situation prevailed as long as Antonio Salazar (1932-1968) and Marcello Caetano (1968-1974) led Portugal.

Then on 25 April 1974, Portuguese officers ousted the Caetano régime and prepared both Portugal's transition to democracy and the dismantling of the overseas empire. Not quite five months later, Mozambique became an independent country governed by black Africans of the FRELIMO Movement ("FRELIMO" being the Portuguese acronym for the "Front for the Liberation of Mozambique"). One-sixth of Rhodesia's railway freight cars were inside Mozambique at the time of the change of sovereignty, and the new Mozambican government refused to return them. Henceforth, Rhodesia's only link with the outside world would be through South Africa, governed at the time by its European minority. The military balance of power also changed. From the interior of the continent where it formed the border between Zambia to the north and Rhodesia to the south, the Zambezi River flowed through Mozambique before reaching the Indian Ocean. The Mozambican government welcomed insurgents of the Zimbabwe African National Union (ZANU) led by Robert Mugabe, and ZANU could henceforth cross the Zambezi River on friendly territory and then pentrate deeply into Rhodesia. The war between Rhodesian forces on the one hand, ZANU and ZAPU on the other, became deadly, and Rhodesia's economic position more precarious than ever.

White House correspondence states the Ford administration's position on Rhodesia very clearly. Draft letters dated 18 May 1976 to interested parties quote Ford, "We have to be on the right side morally, and the right side morally is to be for majority rule." The anonymous writer of the draft letter continued:

> It is precisely because we want to avoid a bloodbath that we are pressing Rhodesia, and urging South Africa to do the same, to negotiate a speedy, peaceful change to majority rule but with protection of minority rights. We believe such an approach promises a future of

shared economic prosperity, about which you are rightly concerned. Majority rule achieved only afer a long and bloody guerrilla campaign would be one in which minority rights would be swept away.

Accordingly, the United States is exerting its leadership in taking a strong stand in favor of peaceful, negotiated transition to majority rule in Rhodesia. If we do not take significant action in this direction, the Soviets and Cubans will have continued pretext for intervention in southern Africa—something we all wish to avoid.[3]

For the Ford administration, the situation became one of damage control. As with so many other problems, Ford had inherited this one, and it was too late to avert catastrophe. Perhaps the situation might have been happier if Garfield Todd, Premier of Southern Rhodesia from 1953 to 1958, had been more successful. In 1953, Southern Rhodesia's African population was approaching 2.5 million, while its European population was about 150,000. At that point, black Africans did not hold a single seat in the Legislative Assembly of Southern Rhodesia. Todd himself did not seek universal suffrage, but he believed it a matter of enlightened self-interest for Europeans to take the initiative and involve Africans in the political system as they met certain standards of education or capital accumulation. If Europeans continued to exclude Africans, he warned, the day would come when Africans would use every means at their disposal to take control. A multiracial partnership open to all qualified Southern Rhodesians would create a happier country than one with South African-style racial confrontation. If such a society were to materialize, it would have to begin at once, he believed, for, should an exclusively Euro-Rhodesian government continue to hold office when the neighbouring countries gained independence, rational reform would prove impossible. Todd could not convince even his own cabinet, lost credibility and left office warning that his failure would mean war.[4] In the ensuing elections, he lost his own seat, and every member of his United Rhodesia Party suffered defeat. Whether Todd's formula could have averted the horrors to come remains speculative, but the determination to maintain Euro-Rhodesian supremacy produced a series of nightmares.

In his memoirs, Henry Kissinger explained the position of the Nixon and Ford administrations. Like the Euro-Rhodesians and Euro-South Africans, the Nixon and Ford administrations had doubts about the ability of black Africans to govern what had become modern societies. While the Cold War lasted, the Euro-Rhodesians and Euro-South Africans seemed more reliable as allies than the pro-Soviet ZAPU, the pro-Chinese ZANU, or South Africa's African National Congress. Moreover, even during the sanctions, the United States imported chrome from Rhodesia. Ford inherited this exception from Nixon, and within days of his taking office as President, the Black Caucus approached the White House to request full enforcement of the sanctions.[5] Ford agreed,[6] but the votes to repeal the Byrd Amendment—the legislation which maintained the purchases of Rhodesian chrome—simply were not there.[7] By 1976, however, the military balance of power had changed irrevocably, and a black African government for Rhodesia, to be renamed Zimbabwe, appeared inevitable. If such a government were going to take power, Kissinger reasoned, it should take power sooner rather than later. The faster Rhodesia/Zimbabwe made the transition, the more reasonable and less bitter the African leadership would be. Perhaps it might even be friendly to the United States and to U.S. interests, including companies which wanted to do business in the region.

In order to promote that transition, Kissinger held meetings during the summer of 1976 in Germany and Switzerland with South African Prime Minister Balthazar Johannes Vorster, then visited South Africa in September. Ian Smith joined Kissinger and Vorster in Pretoria. The meeting with Smith required some strange footwork because the Ford administration's policy was to respect the sanctions in matters other than chrome, and the sanctions policy had led authorities to deny a visa to Smith when he wanted to visit the United States.[8] The solution was to pretend that Smith was going to Pretoria for a soccer match and just happened to "drop in" on his friend Vorster when Kissinger was there.

Kissinger distinguished between the Euro-South Africans, who had lived near the Cape of Good Hope since the mid-seventeenth century, and the Euro-Rhodesians, who had begun to occupy Southern Rhodesia only in 1890. He was not on a mission to persuade Euro-South Africans to accept immediate multiracial government. Kissinger's argument was that the time had come for a change of policy toward Rhodesia. Yes, in the past it had made some sense to regard the Zambezi as the most defensible border between countries dominated by black Africans and those governed by people of European extraction. The border between Rhodesia and South Africa was the Limpopo River, a mere stream by comparison. However, if Rhodesia were to become Zimbabwe with a black African government, it was in South Africa's interest that the Africans should be friendly. The longer the fighting continued, the less likely this was to be.[9] Vorster saw the logic. At the Pretoria meeting, Ian Smith felt the heavy hand of his southern neighbor. Smith realized that he could not count on access to the outside world through South Africa.

"I could defy the British," he said later. "I could defy the Americans. I could not defy the South Africans, because they controlled our lifeline."[10] Smith agreed to negotiate with British authorities, ZANU, ZAPU, and other Rhodesian Africans, and the result was the Lancaster House agreement of December 1979. An independent Zimbabwe led by ZANU leader Robert Mugabe emerged in 1980.

Unfortunately, it was too late to achieve a government led by moderate Africans. Mugabe clung to power into the 21st century by means fair and foul, by which time he had destroyed the economy, impoverished Zimbabwe's people, intimidated his opponents, established one of the world's worst tyrannies, and frightened most Euro-Rhodesians into leaving. The Commonwealth suspended Zimbabwe from active membership. As for the minority rights about which the Ford administration expressed concern, by the twenty-first century—after two decades as Zimbabwe's leader—Mugabe was encouraging his followers to invade farms owned by Euro-Zimbabweans and seize them. Any compensation to the Euro-Zimbabwean owners, said Mugabe, should come from the British government. The United Kingdom had illegally occupied part of Africa and distributed land which belonged to someone else. (In the process, productive farms became barren and tens of thousands of black African agricultural laborers lost their jobs.) Even the fears about Communist penetration of South Africa were justified.

As indicated in Chapter Three, historian Piero Gleijeses, who is one of the few outsiders to have seen Cuban diplomatic correspondence, has written convincingly that Fidel Castro sent Cubans to Africa on his own initiative, not at the behest of the Soviet Union,[11] but Ford could not have known this. Ironically, the Cubans erected their huge embassy, shaped like a cracker box on its side, right next door to Ian Smith's Harare home–with a forest of aerials on its roof. Cuban intelligence could undoubtedly eavesdrop on South Africans, among others. This was hardly the fault of President Ford. He and Kissinger had tried to engage in damage control, but by the time they did, it was too late. Any attempt at ending the Euro-Rhodesian control of the country before the Portuguese revolution of April 1974 and Mozambican independence in September would probably have fallen on deaf ears in any event. There was not much that Ford and Kissinger could have done to produce a better outcome.

Notes

1. In 1997-1998, Laurentian University student John Beech wrote his Honours Essay (undergraduate thesis) on the Ford administration's policies in Southern Africa. Mount and Gauthier thank him for his insights.

2. A.J. Wills, *An Introduction to the History of Central Africa: Zambia, Malawi, and Zimbabwe* (Oxford: Oxford University Press, 1987), pp. 495-496. This was also the source of the figures for the Afro-Rhodesian population.

3. Draft letters to Harold P. Stern and John Bladen, n.p., 18 and 24 May 1976, White House Central File, Subject File, CO-124 (Rhodesia), Box 43, Folder: 8/9/74-5/31/76, GFPL. WHCF: Subject File.

4. Todd explained his views and the cabinet struggle to Mount during an interview at his home in Harare, Zimbabwe (formerly Salisbury, Southern Rhodesia), 14 June 1990.

5. Kenneth Rush, Counsellor to the President for Economic Policy, to Charles C. Diggs, Jr., Chairman, House Foreign Affairs Sub-Committee on Africa, 19 Aug. 1974, WHCF: Subject File. See also documents on a White House meeting with Congressmen John Buchanan and Donald Fraser; Memorandum with Congressmen Buchanan and Fraser, 23 or 24 Sept. 1975, WHCF: Subject File, GFPL.

6. Jerald F. terHorst, White House Press Secretary, to Senator Harry Byrd, 28 Aug. 1974, WHCF: Subject File, GFPL.

7. Friedersdorf to Ford, 15 Nov. 1975, File: Countries—Rhodesia, Presidential Handwriting File, Box 7, GFPL.

8. Memorandum for Roland Elliott from Jeanne W. Davis, NSC, 29 Dec. 1975, WHCF: Subject File, GFPL.

9. Kissinger, pp. 958-1016.

10. Said to Mount during an interview at his Harare home, 2 June 1990.

11. Piero Gleijeses, *Conflicting Missions: Havana, Washington, and Africa, 1959-1976* (University of North Carolina Press: Chapel Hill, 2002).

Chapter Nine

THE DEATH OF FRANCISCO FRANCO[1]

Spain made the transition to democracy during Gerald Ford's presidency. The primary concern of the United States was that in the aftermath of the death of its perennial leader, Generalíssimo Francisco Franco, Spain should become a Western European democracy and a U.S. ally. That this would happen was far from certain. The key players were Spaniards, whose democratic traditions were fragile, and Spain had had a lengthy adversarial relationship with the United States—from the 1850s, when the administrations of Presidents Franklin Pierce (1853-1857) and James Buchanan (1857-1861) had sought to detach Cuba from Spain, until the Spanish-American War of 1898, when President William McKinley's administration (1897-1901) succeeded in doing so. In the aftermath of that same Spanish-American War, the United States also annexed three other Spanish possessions: Puerto Rico, Guam, and the Philippines.

For reasons unrelated to the United States, King Alfonso XIII and Queen Victoria Eugenia went into exile in 1931, and Spain became a republic. Key republican policies—such as the political involvement of new elements of society, the degree of regional autonomy, and the status of the Roman Catholic Church—became so controversial that in 1936, Franco launched an uprising. The fighting lasted from July 1936 until April 1939, and with assistance from Hitler and Mussolini, Franco triumphed. His government lasted until his death in November 1975.[2]

There were several reasons for Franco to support the Axis powers. For the first few years of World War II, it appeared that Hitler might win. As a Spaniard, Franco could be hostile to the United States because of the Spanish-American War and to Great Britain, which had annexed Gibraltar in 1713 and was still oc-cupying that peninsula off the Spanish mainland. While Hitler and Mussolini had provided warriors and equipment during the Civil War, the Soviet Union had aided Franco's opponents. Franco offered Hitler, Mussolini, and Imperial Japan more than sympathy during World War II. The Spanish Blue Division fought alongside German troops on the Soviet front. Spanish diplomats smuggled messages useful to the German war effort from countries where Germany no longer had diplomatic relations.[3] German ships refueled and purchased supplies in Spanish ports. Germany's spy service, the *Abwehr*, had outposts in Spain. The Luftwaffe attacked Allied shipping from bases in Spain.[4]

Above all, Franco was an opportunist, and as it became increasingly probable that the Allies would win, he distanced himself from the Axis. When the Cold War followed World War II, U.S. administrations were inclined to overlook Franco's earlier diplomacy and co-opt him as a Cold War ally. After all, like the United States, Franco and his associates disliked the Soviet Union. In 1953, Spain and the United States signed the Pact of Madrid, which allowed the U.S. to establish air bases at Torrejón, Morón, and Saragossa. In 1959, Eisenhower visited Madrid and met Franco. At a time when other European allies refused to accept Spain as a member of the North Atlantic Treaty Organization, Eisenhower found Franco "personable and agreeable."[5] The Eisenhower administration participated in the Spanish stabilization plan of July 1959, an initiative which sought to promote the Spanish economy.

Lyndon Johnson's administration (1963-1969) faced an awkward situation when on 17 January 1966, a B-52 bomber collided with a refueling aircraft near Palomares and in the process littered four hydrogen bombs. Salvage crews recovered three of them quickly, but early in 4 February, with one still missing off the Mediterranean coast, protesters marched through Madrid and called upon their government to "negotiate a rapid and progressive elimination of American bases in Spain."[6] However, Franco allowed the United States Air Force to retain its bases.

As Vice-President of the United States, on 20 December 1973, Ford received a report which foreshadowed Spain's imminent transformation. The Department of State Briefing Paper summarized the political situation in Spain and discussed the scope of U.S.-Spanish relations. Noting that although Franco was 81 years of age, it noted that his family enjoyed longevity. Political change was unlikely while he lived, but his death would enable Spain to become "increasingly answerable to the Spanish people."[7] The document reflected the attitude of President Richard Nixon (1969-1974) that"by working with the government in place, he could best influence the events to come."[8] Nixon's policy was to (1) co-operate with Franco until his death, in order to retain the air bases; and (2) prepare for Franco's successor by developing relationships with prospective leaders. The document doubted whether Franco's envoys would be welcome at NATO gatherings, and prior to 1975, neither Nixon nor Ford tried to push the issue.

The document expressed concern regarding the upcoming negotiations for an extension of the air bases treaty, which would expire in September 1975. The document warned of potential problems concerning its extension, specifically with the possibility that Spain would demand U.S. intervention in the Anglo-Spanish quarrel over Gibraltar as a *quid pro quo*. In an effort to exert pressure, in 1969 Franco had closed the border between Spain and Gibraltar. U.S. negotiators warned their Spanish counterparts that the Senate would probably withhold the required two-thirds vote of approval if any new treaty obliged the U.S. government to take a stand against the United Kingdom, for the UK was the most loyal American ally. Spain's Foreign Minister, Laureano López Rodo, appeared another possible obstacle to the conclusion of a treaty. His attitude to the United States, according to the document, was, "What have you done for us lately?" There was no guarantee that the negotiations would end successfully.

Within the file were briefing papers which explained in detail Spain's role in the Law of the Sea negotiations as well as the Spanish's government actions affecting the U.S. use of the air bases during the Arab-Israeli war of 1973. The document stated that Spain had opposed one major U.S. objective, "an international agreement on a right of free transit through and over international straits," including Gibraltar, during the Law of the Sea talks. Vice-President Ford read that Franco's government believed that only non-military ships should have free transit and that a special Spanish-U.S. accord assured passage for the U.S. Navy and the United States Air Force. This was not official U.S. policy. The document also reviewed Spanish actions during the 1973 war and noted that Franco was considerably less supportive of Israel than the United States had been:

> The primary GOS [Government of Spain] objective during this period was to establish a clear position of noninvolvement in the conflict and to disassociate Spain from any U.S. operations in support of Israel. At the same time, the Spanish sought to avoid a head-on confrontation with us over the actual use of the bases by the tankers [tanker aircraft]. The GOS also hoped to avoid actions and speculation that might pro-

voke adverse domestic reaction by curtailing speculation in the media about our use of basing facilities in Spain. Finally, the GOS had to be able to tell the Arabs and domestic critics that the Spanish position opposing use of the bases for Middle East operations had been made clear to the United States in the formal framework of the Joint Committee.

In order that Vice-President Ford might be fully aware of the situation, the document confided that tankers had actually used the bases at Torrejón. It stated that the tankers refueled aircraft heading to the war zone in the Middle East, contrary to specific instructions from Franco's government. Spain's primary interest had been protection of its Arab oil supply. The document advised Ford of the approach he would take when it concluded that Spain was "uneasy about the use of the bases in any form connected with the Middle East situation, and we [the U.S. government] cannot take for granted future tacit acquiescence in such operations."

In 1973, while Nixon remained President, Henry Kissinger traveled to Madrid to resolve any anxieties over the fuel tankers. For the United States, Kissinger's visit also ensured the initiation of the new air base negotiations. Historian Stanley Payne thought that Franco regarded good ties with the United States as a source of prestige,[9] and Kissinger's visit reinforced that belief.

On 20 August 1974, two weeks after Ford became President, General Scowcroft briefed the President on the latest Spanish developments. Scowcroft had in hand a document prepared by the National Security Council which outlined the current background in Spain, the location of the military bases, and the economic advantages of the Spanish-U.S. relationship. With Franco ailing but still in control, the document anticipated a smooth transition. It predicted that Prince Juan Carlos would most likely be Franco's successor, and in order to avoid military involvement, it suggested that anti-Franco groups would avoid political confrontation.

The remainder of the document focused on the strategy surrounding the extension to the bilateral U.S.-Spanish Agreement of Friendship and Cooperation.[10] The U.S. had limited short-term goals, but Spain's were long-term. For its part, the U.S. wished to renew the existing agreement without an obligation to pay increased rent to Spain. By signing a Joint Declaration of Principles in June 1974, the United States had pronounced Spain as an important state in Europe and as a major U.S. ally."[11] Spain, on the other hand, sought to pursue the security guarantee from the United States. This joined Spain's other requests of "further technology, closer military cooperation and continued concessional sales of American military equipment." The report identified the problems of security agreements within the new agreement and again warned Spain that Congress would be reluctant to approve new defense agreements. The document noted that if Spain stood firm on this issue and refused to sign an agreement short of a security guarantee, the administration would have to "consider whether the Senate would endorse such a commitment." These words that U.S. concessions might be possible. After all, the bases in Spain *were* important. The report explained "that our ability to satisfy fully Spanish demands for a security guarantee may lead them [Spaniards] to raise their demands for direct military and other compensation." The document concluded that the Joint Declaration had satisfied security measures, and that the Ford administration should extend the agreement with its current terms unchanged.

Clearly, the Ford administration was willing to await Franco's death before changing its Spanish policy. Further integration into the North Atlantic community of nations could wait. For the moment, an extension of the 1953 bilateral accord would suffice. President Ford also hoped that Franco's government would agree to a "12-mile territorial sea on a guaranteed right of transit through and over international straits."[12] This would allow the United States Air Force and the United States Navy unrestricted passage through the Strait of Gibraltar. The other major concern was the Anglo-American relationship. How could the Ford administration satisfy both its British partner and Franco at the same time on the Gibraltar issue? The solution seemed to be silence, interpreted as acceptance of the status quo.

Negotiations for a new U.S.-Spanish treaty began 15 September 1975, and initial reports indicated that there was a significant chasm between the parties' respective positions. The Spanish team resisted agreement without a security guarantee from the United States or military ties with NATO. In addition, Franco's government sought $1.5 billion in military aid, in contrast to the $500 million which the U.S. negotiators were prepared to offer. The bottom line for the United States was loss of the air base at Torrejón. This would be a last resort, but it would be better than some of the alternatives.[13]

Franco died 20 November 1975, three weeks after President Ford had stripped Kissinger of his role as National Security Adviser. Scowcroft, previously Kissinger's immediate subordinate, would take that position, but Kissinger would remain Secretary of State. As predicted, Prince Juan Carlos, grandson of Alfonso XIII, ascended the Spanish throne (which had been vacant since Franco restored the monarchy in 1939) as King Juan Carlos I. The fact that most European heads of state boycotted Franco's funeral but attended the king's coronation a few days later confirmed that Spain was no longer a pariah. On 24 January 1976, Kissinger went to Madrid and signed a Treaty of Friendship and Cooperation, which extended the previous agreement for another five years. Scowcroft outlined its major points. First, the U.S. would have no obligation to provide a specific security guarantee to Spain, but it did recognize and reaffirm the importance of strong military ties between Spain and the United States. A Question and Answer document prepared for use with the official announcement of the signing of the treaty underscored this point: "In the President's view, the treaty establishes a strengthened relationship between the United States and Spain, including the provision for military coordination and planning related to Western Defense matters."[14] Secondly, U.S. payments to Spain amounted to roughly $770 million—a compromise. In return, the United States retained control of all the military bases, including Torrejón. In the aftermath of the tanker aircraft controversy of 1973, the treaty included the removal of all tanker aircraft from Spain. The change of personalities in the United States probably mattered less than the change of command in Spain.

Franco's death facilitated improved U.S.-Spanish relations. Pete Cenarrusa, the Secretary of State in Idaho, wrote Ford one month before Franco's death and requested "the immediate withdrawal of all military and economic aid to Spain and the recall of our ambassador to Spain."[15] An American of Spanish-Basque descent, Cenarrusa argued that Franco was responsible for abandoning a just criminal court system and relying on a tyrannical firing squad. Stating that Basque history had been peaceful, Cenarrusa pleaded for President Ford to forbid further U.S. collaboration with the injustice taking place in Spain. Given that the Basques' "peaceful history" is controversial, Ford's response yielded nothing of substance but politely thanked Cenarrusa for his input. However, after Franco's death, President Ford received a letter written by journalist William L. Shirer and historian Barbara W. Tuchman, and endorsed by twenty-four other prominent Americans who formed the Ad Hoc Committee for a Democratic Spain.

The Shirer/Tuchman letter called for "a fundamental review of United States policy toward Spain looking for a restoration of democracy in Spain, with political and personal freedoms for its people."[16] The letter urged continued U.S. involvement in post-Franco Spain and warned, "In the event of such an eruption [a violent uprising in Spain] there can be little doubt that other outside nations, the USSR included, will not maintain the stance of neutral observers." Shirer and

Tuchman argued that King Juan Carlos was not free to ensure the liberty of the Spanish people, as Spain would still be operating under Franco's rules and Franco's advisers. Shirer and Tuchman stated:

> As the leader of the free world, the United States has a significant obligation to discharge: to help assure freedom in Spain without threat of the kind of violence which could lead to a new civil war. Freedom is a right, not a privilege to be doled out at royal whim.

Shirer and Tuchman argued, with justification, that Spain's Axis partners —Germany, Italy, and Japan—had become democracies after their defeat, but that Franco's Spain had remained intact, and that "a thirty year [U.S.] embrace of the Spanish dictator [Franco] began." They highlighted the 1953 bases treaty and Spain's 1956 entry into the United Nations as evidence. The letter concluded that the United States should not stand idly by a second time but should seize the opportunity that existed in the aftermath of Franco's death.

Ford's reply was non-committal. It explained that Spain must become a democracy through the efforts of its own people; that other countries might encourage steps toward democracy but that Spaniards had to make the most important moves. Ford wrote that "overt pressure would only contribute to the most dangerous outcome, that of greater polarization and deeper divisions, and we see only a few extremist groups wanting to run this risk." The draft recognized the urgency of the issue but maintained that "we [the U.S. government] cannot advocate a pace of change which would be beyond the social or political tolerance of the Spanish system."[17]

King Juan Carlos has been a force for democracy in Spain, having learned from his Bourbon ancestors in Spain and relatives in France that absolute monarchy was passé. Closer relations with other democracies would assist the transition from the authoritarianism of Franco to something acceptable in the contemporary North Atlantic community, and the Ford administration proved one of the beneficiaries. It was in the interests of the King's government to bring the treaty negotiations to a successful conclusion.

On 17 May 1976, Scowcroft and Max Friedersdorf—Assistant to the President for Legislative Affairs—prepared a document recommending that Ford place a telephone call to the Chairman of the Senate Foreign Relations Committee. That Committee would recommend to the full Senate whether or not to approve the new treaty, and its recommendation would have considerable influence. The document advised that Ford urge the committee to act quickly so that the Senate could give its consent before King Juan Carlos visited the United States in June 1976. It is not altogether clear whether Ford made the call, but in any event, the Committee approved by a margin of 11:2. At the time, there was no guarantee that the King would promote either democracy or Spain's integration into Western Europe, but Spaniards might have interpreted a negative vote as a rejection and chosen to remain isolated and undemocratic.

By promoting close relations with Juan Carlos, Ford took a gamble that proved rewarding. Clearly, Franco's chosen successor understood the unique opportunity which Franco's death had provided to him and his country. On 21 June 1976, the Senate—controlled by Democrats—approved the treaty by a margin of 84:11, although not before the King's arrival.

The King and the President used the visit to advance the common agenda. When they met early in June, they discussed Spain's transition to democracy and NATO membership for that country. Scowcroft advised Ford to capitalize upon the momentum of the moment to "build a more open, just and modern society" in Spain. He did, and he succeeded. When Spaniards voted in 1977, the Spanish Socialist Workers' Party and the Union of the Democratic Center captured almost two-thirds of the votes, while Communist candidates fared badly.[18]

After Washington, King Juan Carlos went to New York and offered encouragement to the investment community:

> We [the Spanish Government] are determined to maintain order and
> stability, political and social, so that capital, management and labor
> may work together harmoniously for the good of the whole society.[19]

This effort too proved successful. Historians Richard R. Rubottom and J. Carter Murphy reported, "The flow of direct foreign investment into Spain grew with few setbacks in a steady crescendo in the later 1970s."[20]

The next step was Spanish membership in NATO. This proved vital to the democratic transition, for the Spanish Army remained a bastion of the Falange (Franco's movement) and Fascism. For more than another decade, Toledo's mighty fortress, the Alcazar, served as a military museum which depicted Spain's republicans as Communists and displayed friendly greetings from questionable admirers, including veterans of the Blue Division; officers of the Chilean army (in January 1973, nine months before it ousted the constitutional government of Salvador Allende and installed the régime of Augusto Pinochet, now indicted for murder and other crimes); and the Chilean air force (1975) and the Chilean carabineros (police, 1976), both controlled at the time by Pinochet. Picture taking outside or inside was forbidden.[21] Thinking that Spain was moving too quickly toward democracy, Spanish army officers attempted a coup d'état in 1981 but returned to their barracks on the orders of the King. Juan Carlos had prestige which a mere President of Spain would probably have lacked, and his role in the transition was essential. Entry into NATO would further educate the Spanish Army. Fraternization with brother officers from other NATO countries could not but have a liberalizing effect upon Spanish officers, many of whom remained mentally in the late 1930s.

On 28 September 1976, the State Department prepared a memorandum for President Ford entitled "Spain and NATO." It explored questions and possibilities surrounding Spanish membership in NATO. Under the heading "The Problem," the memorandum argued that the United States must "ease Spain's way into NATO with Europeans."[22] Secondly, the document stated that the U.S. Government must decide "how best to influence the evolution of Spanish thinking about NATO." After all, important members of NATO included the United States, which had stripped Spain of four of her colonies in 1898, and the United Kingdom, which still occupied Gibraltar. It would be wise, the memorandum suggested, to await the results of Spain's first post-Franco elections. Another section of the memorandum, entitled "Spanish Views," noted that while some Spaniards wanted to align their country with Western values, others sought to promote Spain as a partner of the Arab world. Perhaps the European Community (which carried less negative historical baggage) might be more persuasive than the United States in luring Spain into NATO. Under the heading "Spanish Roles in NATO," the memorandum said: "It is not in our interest [i.e., the interest of the United States] to encourage further fragmentation; allowing a new partial member to enter on such terms would in effect sanction partial membership." To allow Spain to have the benefits of NATO membership without assumption of the full responsibilities would, according to the memorandum, bring Spain no closer to the Western community. The report concluded with a set of guidelines to accompany plans for Spanish membership.

Time justified Ford's Spanish policies on all fronts. Ideologues might have rejected the Spanish monarchy as an anachronism, promoted by the discredited Franco. However, King Juan Carlos—who had the necessary prestige among important Spaniards—selected the right advisers, arranged elections, and orchestrated the transition to democracy as few if any others could have. In 1982, Spain joined NATO. Five years later it joined the European Community (now the European Union), and in 2002 it adopted the Euro as its currency. Patience proved practical.

Notes

1. This chapter is a revised version of the undergraduate Honours Essay (thesis) of Sean Lougheed, accepted by Laurentian University's History Department in 2003.

2. The classic on the Spanish Civil War is Hugh Thomas, *The Spanish Civil War* (London: Eyre and Spottiswoode, 1961). For further information on Franco's government, see Maria Jesus Cava Mesa, *Los Diplomáticos de Franco* (Bilbao: Universidad de Deusto, 1989); Max Gallo, *Spain under Franco: A History* (New York: Dutton, 1974); Christian Leitz, *Nazi Germany and Neutral Europe during the Second World War* (Manchester: Manchester University Press, 2000), pp. 114-143; Stanley G. Payne and Delia Contreras (editors), *España y la Segunda Guerra Mundial* (Madrid: Complutense, 1996); Stanley G. Payne, *Franco's Spain* (New York: Crowell, 1967); Paul Preston, *Franco: A Bibliography* (London: Fontana, 1995); Richard R. Rubottom and J. Carter Murphy, *Spain and the United States since World War II* (New York: Praeger, 1984); M. Tuñón de Lara, *El primer franquismo: España durante la segunda guerra mundial* (Madrid: Siglo Veintiuno, 1989); Angel Viñas, *Guerra Dinero, Dictadura: Ayuda fascista y autarquí en la España de Franco* (Barcelona, 1984); Arthur Preston Whitaker, *Spain and Defense of the West: Ally or Liability?* (New York: Harper and Brothers, 1961); Neville Wylie (ed.), *European Neutrals and Non-Belligerents During the Second World War* (New York: Cambridge University Press, 2002).

3. For example, see Graeme S. Mount, *Chile and the Axis* (Montreal: Black Rose, 2001),pp. 113, 146-152.

4. Leitz, pp. 199-120.

5. Dwight David Eisenhower, *Waging Peace: The White House Years* (Doubleday: Garden City, N.Y., 1965), p. 510.

6. The *New York Times*, 4 Feb. 1966.

7. Vice-Presidential Events, 12/20-21/73, GFPL. Quotations from "the document" cited on pages 118-120 also came from this source.

8. Rubottom and Murphy, p. 106.

9. Payne, 573.

10. Briefing Paper on Spain, 20 Aug. 1974, File: Spain (1), NSA, GFPL.

11. Cited in the same Briefing Paper. The remaining quotations in this paragraph also come from the Briefing Paper.

12. Vice-Presidential Events 12/20-21/73, Briefing Paper on Spain and the Law of the Sea Negotiations, GFPL.

13. Memorandum prepared by A. Denis Clift, Area Director for Europe on the NSC, for General Scowcroft, 15 Sept. 1975, Folder: Spain (2), NSA, GFPL.

14. U.S.-Spanish Treaty of Friendship and Cooperation, Q&A, White House Central File (WHCF), Country File, CO 139 (Spain), Folder: 10/11/76-1/20/77, GFPL.

15. National Security Memorandum for James H. Falk, Folder: 7/1/75-3/31/76, WHCF, GFPL.

16. Ad Hoc Committee Letter, WHCF, GFPL. This letter is also the source of the next three quotations.

17. Draft Reply to Ad Hoc Committee Letter, WHCF, GFPL.

18. José Maravall, *The Transition to Democracy in Spain* (St. Martin's Press: New York, 1982), p. 151.

19. Rubottom and Murphy, p. 116.

20. Rubottom and Murphy, p. 147.

21. Mount visited the Alcazar in July 1986.

22. "Spain and NATO," File: Spain (6), NSA, GFPL. This is the source of the other quotations in this paragraph as well.

Chapter Ten

THE HELSINKI ACCORD OF 1975[1]

In 1975, the heads of governments of the United States, Canada, and thirty-three European countries (all except Albania) signed an agreement in Helsinki, Finland. The deal was that all thirty-five would accept each other's existing boundaries and make no attempt to change them by force. At the same time, all thirty-five agreed that journalists from any of the other thirty-four signatories could operate on their territory. There were other commitments to human rights.

Although such an agreement would lessen tensions in Europe, it was bound to be controversial. Several boundaries had changed during World War II, and each of those changes produced winners and losers. During the war, the Soviet Union had annexed lands previously belonging to neighbours, from Finland in the north to Romania in the south, as well as the three Baltic republics—Estonia, Latvia, and Lithuania—in their entirety. To compensate Poland for lands annexed to the Soviet Union, Stalin insisted that Germany forfeit its lands east of the Oder and Neisse Rivers, what would be called the Oder-Neisse Line. An estimated 12 million Germans, whose families had lived there for centuries, would lose their property, and the land would become Polish territory. Most ethnic Germans would leave almost empty-handed, and Poles would replace them. (Of these twelve million, eight million would move to West Germany, where they would form a significant bloc of that country's electorate, and four million to East Germany.[2])

Stalin, of course, felt no sympathy for Germans in 1945, and the Oder-Neisse Line might push Poland into permanent dependence upon the Soviet Union for defence against an irridentist Germany. Germans émigrés from the lands lost to Poland remained emotional about their misfortunes into the twenty-first century. After his death, Stalin's successors wanted to maintain tighter control over their own people and the citizens of Warsaw Pact countries

(Bulgaria, Czechoslovakia, East Germany, Hungary, Poland, Romania, and the Soviet Union) than other signatory governments considered desirable. As recently as August 1968, armies of all Warsaw Pact members except Romania invaded Czechoslovakia and replaced a liberal Communist government whom the others considered less than reliable. A deal was far from certain.

As any agreement on boundaries and human rights was bound to be controversial, Ford and Kissinger considered the Helsinki Accord somewhat embarrassing. However, with benefit of hindsight, it became one of the proudest moments of the Ford presidency, and justifiably so. Helsinki hastened the collapse of the German Democratic Republic, otherwise known as East Germany, and facilitated German reunification. It turned out to be a major factor in ending the Cold War. Out of office, former President Ford came to regard Helsinki as a major reason for the fall of the Berlin Wall, a piece of which he displays in his museum at Grand Rapids, Michigan.

President Ford does not deserve *all* the credit. People in all thirty-five countries played a role, especially Germans. West German Chancellor Willy Brandt, who assumed office in 1969, played a vital role. Since the creation of the Federal Republic of Germany, otherwise known as West Germany, in 1949, successive West German governments had refused to accept either the legitimacy of the Soviet-occupied German Democratic Republic or the Oder-Neisse Line. With his policy of opening to the east or *Ostpolitik*, Brandt did both. He met the East German prime minister, Willi Stoph, at Erfurt in East Germany and persuaded the West German Parliament or *Bundestag* to accept the Oder-Neisse Line as Germany's eastern boundary. For his efforts he received the Nobel Peace Prize in 1971. To critics who charged his government with the loss of German territory to Poland, Brandt responded that it was Hitler's government, not his, that had lost those lands. Once West Germany had accepted East Germany's right to exist, West Germany's allies could do so as well. In 1972, the three Western Powers which had soldiers on German soil since 1945 recognized the German Democratic Republic in exchange for acceptance of ties between West Berlin (occupied since 1945 by the British, French, and U.S. armies) and West Germany. Henceforth, Soviets and East Germans would not interfere with ground traffic along the corridors between the two. Without the West German change of policy orchestrated by Willy Brandt, the Helsinki Final Act of 1 August 1975 would have remained an impossibility.

East Germans also deserve credit for the fall of the Berlin Wall. The Helsinki Accord permitted West German journalists to travel throughout East Germany in search of news. East Germans heard their reports on West German radio and television. East Germany's government lost credibility, and throughout the late summer and autumn of 1989, East Germans fled west by the tens of thousands through Hungary and Czechoslovakia, whose governments chose the path of least resistance and let them go. Tens of thousands of other East Germans engaged in protest marches through the cities of the German Democratic Republic, and East German authorities permitted them to do so. On 9 November, those same authorities authorized travel to West Germany in the hope of stopping the exodus. Perhaps, they reasoned, if East Germans knew that they could travel back and forth, they would not make a once-for-all dash out of the country. The following year, the Communist government led by Hans Modrow allowed multiparty elections, and the new non-Communist East German government negotiated a union with West Germany which took effect 3 October 1990. Whether any of this would have been feasible without Helsinki is doubtful, and whether the Helsinki Final Act would have been achievable without President Ford is also doubtful. Regarding Helsinki, Ford did what was right, but he risked many and won few votes for doing so.

The Nixon administration had managed to conclude some significant agreements with the Soviet Union, led at the time by Leonid Brezhnev. In 1972, both countries concluded the Anti-Ballistic Missile Treaty, which George W. Bush would abrogate early in his administration almost thirty years later. Strategic Arms Limitation Talks (SALT I) began under Nixon and reached a successful conclusion by July 1974. Good will from those agreements paved the way for the Helsinki Conference. The Soviets had been promoting a Conference on Security and Cooperation in Europe (CSCE) since 1954, the year after Stalin's death, but Western countries found it unfeasible until the era of Brandt's *Ostpolitik*.

One major U.S. concern was the right of Soviet Jews to migrate. Communist governments believed that citizens who had had an education at public expense must discharge their obligation to the society which had paid for their education before they could move elsewhere. However, anti-Semitism in the Soviet Union arguably put the Jewish community into a special category, and U.S. diplomats demanded that Soviet authorities allow 60,000 Jews to immigrate to the United States. A problem arose. The number of Jews wanting to leave the Soviet Union was substantially lower than 60,000. A report from the Soviet Minister of Internal Affairs indicated that only 14,000 Jewish people wanted to leave.[3] This figure appeared incredible to U.S. authorities.[4]

In connection with the CSCE, Brezhnev complained that the pace was unnecessarily slow. He believed that the Helsinki Conference would open the possibility for a reduction in armed forces and armaments in Europe.[5] At the State Department, Executive Secretary George S. Springsteen (the Deputy Assistant Secretary of State for European Affairs since August 1973), told President Ford that the Soviets "viewed the CSCE as a vehicle for promoting a general sense of détente euphoria, especially among [the] European Allies."[6]

In 1971, Kissinger and other Allied officials met the Soviets for talks on Berlin. As a condition of Allied support for the CSCE, Kissinger insisted that East Germany must negotiate transit routes into West Berlin. The Soviets agreed, but they wanted some commitment on specific borders.[7] Later that same year, West German Secretary of State Egon Bahr met Soviet Foreign Minister Andrei Gromyko in Moscow. Their talks proved successful, and the result was agreement among East Germany, West Germany, and the Soviet Union. The document arising from the talks recognized "the Oder-Neisse line and the frontier between the Federal Republic and the GDR [German Democratic Republic]."[8] (That was East Germany's official name.)The Bahr-Gromyko agreement set a precedent for solutions to disputes between West Germany on the one hand, Czechoslovakia and Poland on the other. The result was a non-aggression pact which confirmed the inviolability of the borders, and a CSCE. On 7 August, both West German Foreign Minister Walter Scheel and Gromyko signed the treaty, and by 12 August, both Brandt and Soviet Premier Alexey Kosygin added their signatures. The signing of the Treaty of Moscow confirmed acceptance of political reality in the West and led to pressure from Moscow upon Warsaw Pact countries to be more flexible towards West German demands.[9]

Problems between the two Germanys as well as Soviet-American economic and financial problems made the CSCE appear a route toward a possible solution. Other Western European governments agreed. To them, the CSCE looked appealing because it offered an opportunity to negotiate the freer exchange of peoples, ideas, and information. Western Europeans could gain rights regarding the reunification of families, access in the East to Western publications, and improved working conditions for journalists in Eastern Europe.[10] The United States and Canada became involved at the request of NATO. European members of NATO insisted that the United States and Canada must participate for the sake of balance. Governments of those two North American countries obliged.

The first CSCE meeting took place in Helsinki, Finland, in September 1972. It established the agenda for the next three years. A ceremonial gathering of the thirty-five leaders met to sign a document which converted the CSCE into a reality. The Second Phase, dealing with détente and dialogue between Warsaw Pact and NATO countries, would last two years, with talks on security and human rights alternating between Helsinki and Geneva.[11] The climax was the Final Act of the CSCE signed 1 August 1975 in Helsinki, after three days of speeches in the Finnish capital.

The CSCE grouped the issues into Baskets. Western European governments, Eastern European governments, and the government of the United States all had specific objectives. Basket I dealt with security, Basket II with promotion of international trade, Basket III the right of people to travel and to disseminate ideas. The deal was to be all or nothing. The three Baskets would have to be part of the final accord. Signatories could not select one or two and reject what they did not like.[12]

For their part, the Western Europeans insisted on procedures. Through general debate, lengthy speeches, and the creation of subcommittees, they thought that they could influence the outcome. Freer movement was for them a high priority,[13] although they also hoped for improved relations between themselves and the Soviet Union. Détente would be a step in the right direction and would lessen Cold War tensions and problems.

For his part, Kissinger sought a low profile. The U.S. delegation arrived at one of the Geneva meetings without instructions or objectives. It supported the Western Europeans on issue of human rights but assumed no leadership role.

In return for greater respect for human rights on the part of the Soviet Union and its Warsaw Pact Allies, the Western Europeans knew that they would have to recognize and accept existing European boundaries. The German Democratic Republic would gain unqualified legitimacy, and the Oder–Neisse Line would be the unquestionable boundary between East Germany and Poland. Soviet conquests of Polish, Romanian and Finnish territory, and the Soviet incorporation of the Baltic States would become permanent. While the East Germans wanted recognition, the West Germans did not want to seal the division of Germany permanently. For their part, the Soviets considered a divided Germany a lesser potential threat to their own security than a united one might be.[14] Reconciliation of the conflicting points of view on Germany would be a challenge. The United States suggested that a principle of the Final Act of the CSCE might be to leave "open the possibility of peaceful border changes."[15]

On 19 June 1973, Brezhnev described the purpose of the CSCE as far as his country was concerned. According to Brezhnev, the United States and the Soviet Union should take the first steps toward détente. If U.S.-Soviet relations improved, the international climate would ease, thereby creating a more relaxed international environment.[16] Some key Americans disagreed. John Maresca, a member of the U.S. delegation, claimed that it was the will of the Soviets to "lull the West into relaxing its defense efforts while the USSR continued its massive military buildup, and to create a situation where Soviet military dominance could be used to pressure Western Europe."[17]

Certainly Kissinger saw the CSCE as

...a Soviet initiative, seen by Moscow originally as a way to confirm in a summit-level final gathering Western acceptance of the territorial and political status quo in Eastern Europe, including the division of Germany...[and] as a vehicle for promotion, a general sense of détente euphoria, especially among our European allies.[18]

Historian William Korey agreed. According to Korey, America's European allies hoped for a compromise which might lead to exchanges of people and ideas, exchanges of information, and advances in "science, technology, art and culture."[19]

Preparations for the CSCE began in Helsinki in September 1972. Delegates from all thirty-five nations attended the preliminary phase of the Conference, held in Helsinki in December of that year. Not surprisingly, the Soviets did not like the human rights section of the deliberations.[20] For their part, the U.S. delegation tried to avoid controversy. The formal sessions began 3 July 1973 with a gathering of foreign ministers, again in Helsinki, and at the first meeting, the delegates approved the agenda for subsequent meetings. Gromyko was the first to address the delegates, who would deliver speeches to teach other over the next five days. He warned, not unreasonably, that without resolution of border disputes, there could be no guarantee of peace. Gromyko submitted a document, the "General Declaration on the Foundations of European Security and the Principles of Relations among States in Europe," which stated the issues to be discussed.

While the foreign ministers debated, a group of civil servants known as the Working Group discussed issues upon which the foreign ministers disagreed. One such issue was a Maltese proposal to invite the governments of Algeria and Tunisia to participate. Rather than fail by trying to do too much, Western European delegations were determined to restrict the conference to Europe and European matters, and they prevailed.[21] With regard to the U.S. role, Secretary of State William Rogers was reportedly nonchalant. He is supposed to have said, "Anything they would work out among themselves will be all right with us."[22] It appears that the Nixon administration participated largely to satisfy the

NATO allies, not because it had high hopes. The controversy aroused by the Mediterranean issue led to the creation of the Principle of Consensus. It was that no one country could override the voice of any other country, thereby establishing a measure of equality. Henceforth, for a motion to be accepted, all countries would have to agree. Unanimity appeared a necessary prerequisite for détente.

Despite this procedural agreement, progress at the first session was slow. The U.S. delegation found the Soviets intransigent.[23] Nevertheless Kissinger, who was still President Nixon's National Security Advisor, thought that solutions to the outstanding issues remained possible.

The second phase of the Conference took place in Geneva and lasted from 18 September 1973 until 21 July 1975. Four days into the Conference, on 22 September 1973, Kissinger replaced Rogers as Secretary of State. The Conference was still in session when Ford replaced Nixon 9 August 1974. President Ford retained Kissinger as Secretary of State, and Kissinger maintained the Nixon policy on the CSCE. The U.S. would participate but not lead. During the second phase, Basket III (human rights) became a contentious issue. The Soviets disliked commitments on this score, especially one to allow the freer movement of people. While debate continued, Soviet authorities arrested the distinguished author, Alexander Solzhenitsyn—a violation of all that Basket III was supposed to represent. Reluctantly Brezhnev's government allowed him to go to Switzerland so that his fate would not disrupt the CSCE. In 1976, Solzhenitsyn moved to the United States.

The Solzhenitsyn matter was not the only complication. President Ford faced a learning curve when he assumed office. New governments also assumed office in 1974 in France, Portugal, and the United Kingdom. Yet, the CSCE remained on track. In May 1975, Kissinger complained to President Ford about what seemed to him Soviets delaying tactics:

> Soviet reluctance to reach reasonable agreements on sensitive subjects and the general unwillingness to give up important points has slowed the Conference progress and will add to negotiation pressures in the weeks to come.[24]

Yet, delay was not lethal. One memorandum prepared for President Ford suggested that in the end, "The West will come out with more, and the Soviets with less."[25]

The Soviet government had reasons for wanting to end the conference by mid-1975. Success would coincide with the thirtieth anniversary celebrations of the end of World War II. It would also help to launch the Conference of European

Communist Parties later that year. Under the circumstances, Moscow would make concessions on Basket III. With the major issues finalized, the date for the Final Act of the Conference became negotiable. Brezhnev suggested that the Final Phase should convene 22 July. The Finns wanted four weeks advance notice before the heads of government would assemble in Helsinki for the signing, and many leaders had commitments for the month of August. This left less than two months for discussion.

The strong Soviet push to bring the Conference to an early end left Romania, Malta, and Yugoslavia at a perceived disadvantage. The shorter the negotiations, the less leverage it appeared that those countries would have. Unresolved issues included the status of Berlin and ways to enforce agreements after the Conference ended.[26] Yet, even these matters fell into place by 5 July, and the delegates agreed that late July would be a suitable time for the signing.

The third phase began after a proposal from Canada. Canadian Ambassador Tom Delworth had received instructions from Prime Minister Pierre Elliott Trudeau to take the lead in trying to convene the final stage before the end of July in order to achieve maximum success from the Helsinki Conference. The evening of 9 July, Delworth made his proposal before the Coordinating Committee, and by the 10th, twelve Committee members agreed with him. Despite objections from Romania and Malta, the Conference accepted the Canadian compromise. Delegates agreed: "Stage III [would] begin in Helsinki on July 30, provided substantive work was completed by July 15th."[27]

Like the other heads of government, President Ford prepared to travel to Helsinki, despite the fears of those who objected to Stalin's World War II incorporation of the Baltic States and certain other existing boundaries. The President explained that the document which he would sign in Finland was neither a treaty nor a legal document. It was simply a statement which outlined the "political and moral commitments aimed at lessening tensions and opening further lines of communication between people of East and West."[28] The Helsinki accord was a compromise that hopefully would allow European countries to strive for détente and greater international trust. Ford noted the wide range of countries in attendance at Helsinki: NATO members, members of the Warsaw Pact, and neutrals. The presence of Canada and the United States confirmed a level playing field for the European members of NATO, who might otherwise have felt overwhelmed.

Ford addressed other concerns. The United States was not about to surrender land to the Soviets. The United States and its allies did not do what the Helsinki

Agreement was about to prohibit and had no intention of starting. A lessening of tensions would promote trade and contribute to world peace. Agreement by thirty-five nations indicated progress and compromise. These agreements included such significant developments as "greater human contacts and exchanges, improved conditions for journalists, reunification of families and international marriages, freer flow of information and publications, and increased tourism and travel."[29] He concluded, "If the Conference fails, Europe will be no worse off than it is now. But if even a part of it succeeds, the lot of people in Eastern Europe will be that much better and the case of freedom will advance at least that far."[30]

Ford and Kissinger faced serious opposition from certain immigrant groups and from former California Governor Ronald Reagan, known to be a serious contender for the Republican presidential nomination in 1976. Reagan agreed openly with Americans whose families had migrated from the Baltic States. The *Wall Street Journal* editorialized, "Jerry, don't go." The liberal *New York Times* regarded Ford's presence at Helsinki as "misguided and empty." Washington Senator Henry Jackson, who would seek the presidential nomination for the Democratic Party, accused Ford of "taking us backward, not forward, in the search for a genuine peace." Reagan commented, "I am against it [the Helsinki conference], and I think all Americans should be against it."[31] Whatever the merits of the Helsinki Agreement, the CSCE could become a political liability for President Ford, already vulnerable after his pardon of Richard Nixon.[32] By Ford's own reckoning, the White House received 558 letters opposed to the Helsinki Agreement, only thirty-two supportive. Lithuanian, Latvian, and Estonian groups staged a vigil in front of the White House.[33] Demonstrating strong leadership and statesmanship, President Ford went to Helsinki nonetheless.

When the heads of government assembled in the Finnish capital, each had an opportunity to make a speech. In his, President Ford extolled the cause of peace:

> We owe it to our children, to the children of all continents, not to miss any opportunity, not to malinger for one minute, not to spare ourselves or allow others to shrink in the monumental task of building a better and safer world.[34]

The Conference, said Ford, was but the first step toward global peace. Many unresolved problems remained. He continued:

> Peace is not a piece of paper…This Conference is a part of that process —a challenge, not a conclusion. We face unresolved problems of military security in Europe; we face them with very real differences in val-

ues and in aims. But if we deal with them with careful preparation, if we focus on concrete issues, if we maintain forward movement, we have the right to expect real progress.[35]

Ford noted that it was appropriate for the United States and Canada to have representatives at Helsinki. Those two countries were peaceful neighbours. He then said:

Stability in Europe requires equilibrium in Europe. Therefore, I assure you that my country will continue to be a concerned a reliable partner. Our partnership is more than a matter of formal agreements. It is a reflection of beliefs, traditions and ties that are of deep significance to the American people.[36]

He concluded, "History will judge this Conference not by what we say here today, but by what we do tomorrow—not by the promises we make, but by the promises we keep."[37]

After the speeches, the representatives sat around a table according to alphabetical order: Austria, Belgium, Bulgaria, Canada, Cyprus, Czechoslovakia, Denmark, Finland, France, the German Democratic Republic, the Federal Republic of Germany, Greece, the Holy See, Hungary, Iceland, Ireland, Italy, Liechtenstein, Luxembourg, Malta, Monaco, the Netherlands, Norway, Poland, Portugal, Romania, San Marino, Spain, Sweden, Switzerland, Turkey, the Union of Soviet Socialist Republics, the United Kingdom, the United States of America, Yugoslavia. Nevertheless, the first to sign the Helsinki Agreement was Helmut Schmidt, Chancellor of the Federal Republic of Germany, followed by Erich Honecker of the German Democratic Republic. Allowing the leaders of those two countries to be the first to sign symbolized the peace achieved by the CSCE.

Once Yugoslav President Josip Broz Tito added his signature, the document was complete. The delegates applauded. Finnish President Urho Kekkonen, the host, offered a brief message. Otherwise, the end of the Conference was anti-climactic. Many in attendance drank a fast glass of champagne before hurrying to catch their planes and return home to deal with domestic problems. Maresca commented: "There were no cannons, no formal salutes, no honors rendered...there were no celebrations, no parades, no dancing in the streets."[38] The reality of this moment of triumph was delegates rushing into the limousines which would take them to the airport.

President Ford regarded his return to the United States as another anti-climax. Such an embarrassment had Helsinki become that he mentioned it only twice for the rest of his presidency. On 22 September 1975, he had no choice because someone raised it during a question-and-answer session.[39] In the course of a speech about his support for freedom in Eastern Europe 2 April 1976, he made a passing reference to the CSCE.[40] However, almost thirteen years after his enforced departure from the presidency, the Berlin Wall opened, and in short order, a piece of it became an exhibit at the Gerald Ford Presidential Museum in Grand Rapids, Michigan. Gerald Ford lived to see the day when he could claim some credit for having helped to dismantle it, and by extension, the Soviet Empire. Any such claim rests upon his accomplishments in connection with the CSCE between September 1972 and August 1975. With its emphasis on human rights and the removal of boundary disputes, Helsinki facilitated the work of journalists from signatory countries. Through radio and television, residents of the German Democratic Republic had access to outside sources of news. The information acquired lessened the credibility of the East German government, leading to the opening and dismantling of the Berlin Wall 9 November 1989 and thereafter.

Ronald Reagan, the fortieth President of the United States, also claims credit, and a piece of the Berlin Wall stands on display in the Ronald Reagan Trade Building in Washington, D.C. Soviet leader Mikhail Gorbachev (1985-1991) also deserves credit for having established the tone of a more human version of Communism. As mentioned earlier in this chapter, many Germans also share the right to glory. However, it began during the Nixon and Ford administrations. Without the process begun by Nixon and concluded—despite the risks—by President Ford, the Wall would probably have survived many years longer.

Notes

1. This chapter is adapted from the Honours Essay (undergraduate thesis) of Laurentian University student Constance Rossi, 2004-2005.
2. For background on the controversy over the Oder-Neisse Line, see the article by R. Gerald Hughes, "Unfinished Business from Potsdam: Britain, West Germany, and the Oder-Neisse Line, 1945-1962" in *The International History Review*, XXVII, 2 (June 2005), pp. 259-294. The estimates of the numbers of Germans who relocated appear on p. 262.
3. William Burr, *The Kissinger Transcripts* (New York: The New York Press, 1999), p. 332.
4. For more information on Jewish immigration, see Noam Kochavi, "Insights Abandoned, Flexibility Lost: Kissinger, Soviet Jewish Emigration, and the Demise of Détente," *Diplomatic History*, XXIX, 3 (June 2005), pp. 503-530.
5. Robin Edmonds, *Soviet Foreign Policy: The Brezhnev Years* (New York: Oxford University Press, 1983), p. 114.
6. Memorandum for Lieutenant General Brent Scowcroft, 01/14/1975, NSA, Box 44, Folder 1, NSA, GFPL.
7. M.E. Sarotte, *Dealing with the Devil: East Germany, Détente and Ostpolitik, 1969-1973* (Chapel Hill: University of North Carolina Press, 2001), p. 114.

8. Michael Freund, *From Cold War to Ostpolitik: Germany and the New Europe* (London: Oswald Wolff Paperbacks), 1972, p. 103.

9. Roger Tilford, *The Ostpolitik and the Political Change in Germany* (Westmead, England: Lexington Books, 1975), p. 82.

10. Memorandum for Scowcroft, 01/14/1975, NSA, Box 44, Folder 1, NSA, GFPL.

11. William Korey, *The Promises We Keep* (New York: St Martin's Press, 1993), p. 6.

12. Korey, pp. 8–9.

13. John Maresca, *To Helsinki: The Conference on Security and Cooperation in Europe* (Durham: Duke University Press, 1985), p. 43. Maresca was a member of the U.S. delegation.

14. Maresca, p. 81.

15. Memorandum: Issues Paper on CSCE for Scowcroft, 01/14/75, NSA, Box 44, Folder 1, NSA, GFPL.

16. Leonid I. Brezhnev, *Our Course: Peace and Socialism* (Moscow: Novosti Press Agency Publishing House, 1974), p. 48.

17. Maresca, p. 55.

18. Memorandum: Issues Paper on CSCE for Scowcroft, 01/14/1975, NSA, Box 44, Folder 1, NSA, GFPL.

19. Korey, p. 4.

20. Korey, p. 9.

21. Maresca, p. 40.

22. Maresca, p. 41.

23. Memorandum for the President, 04/02/1975, NSA, Box 44, Folder 2, NSA, GFPL.

24. Report: Untitled, 05/1975, NSC: Europe, Canada and Ocean Affairs Staff: Files, Box 44, Folder 2, NSA, GFPL.

25. Briefing Item: Soviet Policy after CSCE, 04/29/1975, NSA: Europe, Canada and Ocean Affairs Staff: Files, Box 44, Folder 2, NSC, GFPL.

26. Maresca, pp. 165–166.

27. Maresca, p. 187.

28. Statement, Gerald Ford, 07/25/1975, NSA: Europe, Canada and Ocean Affairs Staff: Files, Box 44, Folder 4, NSC, GFPL. Information in the balance of this paragraph as well as the next comes from this source.

29. Statement, Gerald Ford, 07/25/1975, NSA: Europe, Canada and Ocean Affairs Staff: Files, Box 44, Folder 4, NSC, GFPL.

30. Memorandum, for Secretary Kissinger from Mr. Clift about the proposed reply to Mr. Backaltis, 07/31/1975, NSA: Europe, Canada and Ocean Affairs Staff: Files, Box 44, Folder 4, NSC, GFPL.

31. Ford, p. 300.

32. Ford, p.295.

33. Ford, p. 301.

34. *Public Papers of the Presidents of the United States*, 1 Aug. 1975, p. 1075. Cited hereafter as *PPP*.

35. *PPP*, 1 Aug. 1975, p. 1076.

36. *PPP*, 1 Aug. 1975, p. 1079.

37. *PPP*, 1 Aug. 1975, p. 1081.

38. Maresca, p. 197.

39. Luncheon Meeting of the World Affairs Council in San Francisco, 22 September 1975, *Public Papers of the Presidents*, pp. 1505–1506.

40. Question and Answer Session with Representatives of Greater Milwaukee Ethnic Organization, 2 April 1976, *Public Papers of the Presidents*, p. 892.

Chapter Eleven

REFORMS IN THE CENTRAL INTELLIGENCE AGENCY[1]

According to the biblical story of the Conquest of the Promised Land, Joshua —the Hebrew commander-in-chief—sent two spies to explore the city of Jericho. The men sought refuge for the night and found lodging in the house of Rahab the harlot. Ordered by the Canaanite king to surrender the two men, Rahab hid them and lied that they had left the city at dusk. The men rewarded her with a promise to protect her and her family because she had helped them to scout and seize the land. This incident at Jericho depicts one of the oldest stories of deception, lies, cover-ups, promised protection and secretive pacts, placing spy work among the world's oldest professions.[2]

In what is now the United States, in 1753 George Washington joined a native American on a scout mission to discover whether the French were trespassing on land claimed by the British in the Ohio valley. Instructed to spy on French forts and observe communications, Washington recorded one of the first American espionage assignments.[3] Thus began the history of American intelligence and covert operations.

Not until 8 September 1947 during the administration of Harry Truman (1945-1953) was the Central Intelligence Agency (CIA) formally established. The establishment of the Office of State Security (OSS) to spy on Nazi Germany and Imperial Japan in June 1942 was the first step in creating an agency outside the armed forces that could work with them as well as cooperate effectively with outside foreign intelligence and secret organizations. The mission of the CIA, a response to the perceived Soviet threat, was and remains to provide accurate evidence based comprehensive and timely foreign intelligence related to national security, and to conduct counter-intelligence activities and other functions as directed by the President.[4]

During the Eisenhower administration (1953 to 1961), the CIA's motives changed from the collection of information to pre-emptive action, and its authority included the assassination of foreign leaders considered opposed to U.S. interests. The first indication that the CIA had the capacity for assassination occurred during the last few months of Eisenhower's presidency. Four foreign leaders—Fidel Castro of Cuba, Patrice Lumumba of the former Belgian Congo, Rafael Trujillo of the Dominican Republic, and Sukarno of Indonesia— became targets of political assassination. Eisenhower also authorized the CIA to overthrow unfriendly governments in Iran (1953), Guatemala (1954), and Cuba (1960-61). The first two attempts succeeded, while the effort against Fidel Castro proved a dismal failure. [5] In the aftermath of the Nixon scandals, the Rockefeller Commission of 1975, created by President Ford and headed by Vice-President Nelson Rockefeller, acknowledged allegations that the CIA had participated in assassination plots against certain foreign leaders, but it did not inquire into those allegations very deeply. It recommended that another Commission investigate the allegations, and the President agreed.[6] David W. Belin, the executive director of the Rockefeller Commission, acknowledged that there was a plan against foreign leaders and stated that earlier Presidents and their advisers knew of the plots to assassinate them. According to Belin, the CIA did not work alone. In January 1962, when John F. Kennedy was President, William Harvey of the CIA headed a broader special assassination group to kill Fidel Castro.[7]

Kennedy was taking the path established by Eisenhower. In November 1957, Eisenhower provided rebel Indonesian weapons to overthrow Sukarno. Moreover, the CIA produced a pornographic film which featured a man who looked like the Indonesian leader.[8] Yet Sukarno survived. In 1960, on very short notice, Belgium granted independence to the Belgian Congo at the heart of sub-Saharan Africa. Chaos followed, and Belgian paratroopers landed to protect Belgian citizens. At Lumumba's request, the United Nations sent troops to restore order. A secessionist movement led by Moïse Tshombe attempted to detach the mineral-rich province of Katanga, and Lumumba accepted Soviet military aid to ensure that his country would stay together. This convinced Eisenhower and his advisers that Lumumba was dangerous, and they planned his assassination.[9] Lumumba's opponents managed to kill him in 1961, and many blamed the CIA.[10]

At the same time, the Eisenhower administration feared Rafael Leonidas Trujillo, the abusive and repressive dictator of the Dominican Republic. Assassins did kill him 30 May 1961, but the role of the CIA is unclear. In the aftermath of the failed CIA attempt at the Bay of Pigs to overthrow Castro's government in Cuba, the CIA received instructions carefully to monitor weapons sent to Dominican dissidents. The dissidents who despatched Trujillo used CIA-supplied weapons.[11]

Documents released by the National Security Archive in Washington confirm the role of the Nixon administration in the 11 September 1973 coup d'état against Salvador Allende, the constitutional President of Chile. The CIA financed a truckers' strike so that the stores would lack consumer goods, and the general population would panic. Allende died during the coup, led by Augusto Pinochet. The Santiago newspaper *El Mercurio*, Chile's *New York Times* or *Globe and Mail*, published articles written by the CIA as though they were newsitems. In the aftermath of President Nixon's resignation because of scandalous behavior, suspicions of CIA involvement in the aforementioned activities created a wave of revulsion across the United States and a suspicion of U.S. government agencies, especially the CIA. In response, President Ford ordered Vice-President Rockefeller to head an investigative Commission, which published its report in June 1975.

The Commission acknowledged receipt of information regarding assassination but did not include the information in its report. The Senate, controlled by Democrats, then established a Committee headed by Senator Frank Church (Democrat-Idaho) and known as the Church Committee. Its aim was to investigate the legalities of the CIA's covert operations and to make recommendations for the future. In March 2002, the Gerald Ford Presidential Library declassified additional documents about the CIA's own study about the use of assassination. This documentation is new, unpublished material, which provides additional insight into what the White House knew and ordered.

This chapter, however, will deal specifically with the questions surrounding President Ford, what he knew, and what he wanted the public to know. He hoped that the Rockefeller Commission and the Church Committee would not alter the CIA. Public opinion was such that he had to appear to be taking action, but White House inter-office memoranda indicate that he wanted publicity of past actions and future changes to be minimal.

Seymour Hersh, an investigative reporter for the *New York Times*, released the proverbial cat among the pigeons, with a story on alleged CIA wrongdoing.[12] CIA director William Colby confirmed the allegations, and on 22 December 1974, an article appeared on the newspaper's front page. It said that the

Central Intelligence Agency, directly violating its charter, conducted a massive, illegal domestic intelligence operation during the Nixon Administration against the anti-[Vietnam] war movement and other dissident groups in the United States.

Although Hersh did not identify Colby as his source, days later Colby admitted to Ford that it was he who had fed Hersh the information. The article also stated that for some years, the CIA had exceeded its statutory authority by eavesdropping on the telephone conversations of U.S. citizens, breaking and entering into private properties and businesses, keeping citizens under surveillance, and other illegal activities. (The CIA's legal role was to watch foreigners, not Americans.)

The Ford administration was not prepared for the ensuing furor. Colby was angry at the tone of the story, and Ford, who had no prior knowledge of Operation CHAOS—the CIA's collection of information of Americans through telephone taps and the opening of mail—was caught off guard. In an interview years later with historian John Greene, Colby confessed that "no one thought to brief the President."[13]

The CIA even had a file on Hersh. In a document dated 24 September 1974, Lawrence S. Eagleburger and Robert J. McCloskey prepared a State Department memorandum. Eagleburger and McCloskey noted that Hersh was about to publish a story about CIA involvement in Chile the previous year. Colby had told Scowcroft, they said, that Hersh's information was untrue. Under the circumstances, they thought, there should be a rebuttal, and the rebuttal would have greater credibility if it came from Colby rather than from someone at the State Department.[14] Colby did not provide the rebuttal. Indeed, it would be fair to assume that he had an inherent need to confess and that Seymour Hersh was his confessor.

In his memoirs, Ford says that Colby warned him that Hersh would be releasing embarrassing information. The wrongdoing, Colby assured Ford, had ended.[15] The day after publication of the 22 December 1974 article, Ford demanded from Colby a written explanation of the article, and perhaps an explanation of his own actions. On Christmas Eve, Colby produced a six-page letter. He attempted to discredit the article, and while he admitted that the CIA had made mistakes, he said that it was not responsible for "massive domestic intelligence activity." The CIA, he said, had 9,944 files on U.S. citizens, a number which he evidently considered less than "massive."[16]

Colby's letter identified some of the most alarming individual cases. In 1963, the CIA wiretapped two columnists, Robert Allen and Paul Scott, after CIA Chief Jon McCone, Attorney General Robert Kennedy, and Secretary of Defense Robert McNamara had granted approval. From 15 February to 12 April 1972, during Richard Nixon's presidency, the CIA had maintained surveillance on columnist Jack Anderson and members of his staff under the authority of the current CIA director, Richard Helms. With Helms's authority, it had also monitored a *Washington Post* reporter from October 1971 to January 1972. In 1971, the Office of Security—a branch of the CIA—suspected a female CIA employee who was living with a Cuban national. It searched her house and office for documents but found nothing. Between 1953 and 1973, from the Eisenhower presidency until Nixon's, the CIA Counterintelligence Staff opened mail to and from the Soviet Union as it passed through the Kennedy Airport Mail Depot. Colby terminated that practice in 1973, but at least three Postmasters General had approved it.

Colby's Christmas Eve letter admitted to CIA assassination plots against Castro, Lumumba, and Trujillo, but denied any CIA role in Lumumba's murder 17 January 1961. Colby indicated that the CIA played "no active part" in Trujillo's death but admitted "a faint connection" with Trujillo's assassins. He also said that the CIA occasionally tested experimental electronic equipment on U.S. telephone circuits.

Other advisers made Ford even more aware of specific allegations and "mistakes." Early in the new year, Ford received a memorandum from Laurence Silberman, under orders from Philip Buchen (Ford's legal adviser and Silberman's superior) concerning possible Federal Postal Law violations and violations of the Federal Statute Prohibiting Interception of Wire Communication.[17] That same day, Ford received a memorandum from James Wilderotter, Associate Deputy Attorney General, that admitted to the CIA kidnaping of a Soviet defector in 1964 who subsequently spent two years in a Virginia prison.[18]

The illegal activity, the assassination plots, and the enormity of Operation CHAOS within the United States caused alarm in the media. On 3 January, Ford met Colby in the Oval Office and heard more about the "Family Jewels," the documents about the proposed assassinations of foreign leaders. There was no easy escape. He could call for a massive overhaul of the CIA and publicize its wrongdoing, or he could engage in a cover-up. Full disclosure could cripple the CIA and blacken the U.S. reputation across the planet. It could also discourage foreign governments from sharing information. Yet, said Ford, the Watergate affair demonstrated the perils of a cover-up.[19]

It did not take long for Ford to decide what to do. The very next day, the Office of the White House Press Secretary released news of the establishment of a Commission on CIA Activities Within the United States (hereafter known as the Rockefeller Commission). It would evaluate facts relating to activities within the United States and make recommendations within three months. Responding to Hersh's publicity and unpleasant realities rather than to inner convictions, Ford did not believe in the need for the Rockefeller Commission and hoped that secret information could remain secret. That same day, 4 January 1975, Ford received Kissinger, Scowcroft, and Counsels to the President John Marsh and Philip Buchen at the Oval Office. In numerous memoranda, they voiced their concern, fears, and expectations of the Rockefeller Commission. In a memorandum declassified 20 April 2000, Kissinger warned that Ford would "end up with a CIA that does only reporting and not operations." Ford agreed.[20] The consensus was that the Rockefeller Commission, if too honest, could seriously debilitate the CIA. Kissinger warned that none of the assembled company, including President Ford, could be certain what would be unearthed. Kissinger stated, "Helms said all these stories are just the tip of the iceberg. If they come out, blood will flow." Later in the day, according to a memorandum of conversation declassified 5 May 1999, Ford said:

> The Commission will look at the Colby Report and...make recommendations to me. It is a good commission. I hope they will stay within their charter, but in this climate we can't guarantee it. It would be tragic if it went beyond it because the CIA needs to remain a strong and viable agency. It would be a shame if the public uproar forced us to go beyond and to damage the integrity of the CIA.

Contrary to what Ford stated in his memoirs, the Rockefeller Commission would not seek truth. It would placate the press and public and represent a staged investigation into the intelligence community. Ford wanted to uphold the reputation of the United States and the CIA, despite the 9,944 "mistakes" and assassination plots against foreign leaders. Despite President Nixon's forced resignation after he had tried to hide evidence of the Watergate burglary, there would be yet another Republican cover-up.

Some were immediately suspicious. Judge Henry J. Friendly, a circuit judge from the U.S. Court of Appeals, refused to serve on the Rockefeller Commission because he did "not want criticism of any extra-judicial action...to become even a slight factor in such a controversy."[21] Richard Dellums, a member of the House of Representatives (Democrat-California), noted that the Rockefeller Commission was rather unrepresentative. All its members, he observed, were elderly white men. Its findings, he feared, would be more cautious than they should be.[22]

Ford attempted to keep all information regarding the Rockefeller Commission confidential. Between February and June 1975, not once did the Cabinet discuss the Commission's achievements and progress. (As minutes of the January meeting of the Cabinet were inaccessible, it was impossible to determine whether the Cabinet had any input at that time.) In addition to his duties as Vice President and head of an important investigation, at Ford's initiative Rockefeller also became Vice-Chairman of the Domestic Council. That role demanded daily reports from Rockefeller, preparation of which presumably required time. The cabinet had time to discuss the tax bill (15 April), the economic situation (15 April), the Federal Payroll Savings Bond Campaign (20 February), Kissinger's European trip (7 August), and the use of plastic liners in wastepaper baskets (24 June), but not the Rockefeller Commission.[23] How much time Rockefeller had for his own Commission is a matter for speculation. Ford and Rockefeller did correspond privately. On 9 May 1975, Ford sent a private memorandum to Rockefeller allocating a further sum of $95,000 to the Commission for "unanticipated personnel needs" and any other necessary expenses.[24] Nobody else seems to have discussed this expenditure.

Published 6 June 1975–months later than its initial deadline, the Rockefeller Commission's report favored the Agency but could not retain credibility without some mention of the assassination plots. It said:

> Allegations that the CIA had been involved in plans to assassinate certain leaders of foreign countries came to this Commission's attention shortly after its inquiry was under way. Although it was unclear whether or not those allegations fell within the scope of the Commission's authority, the Commission directed that an inquiry be undertaken. The President concurred in this approach. The Commission staff bean the required inquiry, but time did not permit a full investigation before this draft was due.[25]

One of the most interesting documents that the Commission had in its possession and chose not to disclose was a 37-page report written by James Jesus

Angleton. The Commission requested a written critique of the counter-intelligence function of the Agency. Tom Mangold's *Cold Warrior: James Jesus Angleton, the CIA's Master Spy Hunter*, describes Angleton as the powerful chief of the CIA's counterintelligence staff, the man responsible for protecting U.S. secrets overseas. He had a fearsome reputation and spent twenty-seven years in charge of the CIA's counterintelligence staff, serving effectively as spy catcher for the entire Western world. His primary task was to prevent other countries from learning the secrets of the United States and its allies.[26] The report, sanitized and declassified 24 May 2000, discussed the authority under which the CIA conducted counterintelligence activities, the nature of those activities, a summary of critical developments in the history of United States counterintelligence from 1945 to 1975, and recommendations. Angleton argued the CIA's need for vast strengthening of the defense and noted that without further funding there would be a decline in the quality of foreign relationships. Although the report remains sanitized, Angleton stated:

> Now the fabric of our counterintelligence liaison relationships shows some fraying because of clamor in the American press and a consequent change of atmosphere. Our partners are no longer sure that we can act decisively in concern with them or even keep their secrets.[27]

Angleton warned that the reputation and status of America hung on the decision to disclose the information. He further protested Colby's actions on the grounds that he "managed CIA affairs without consulting [him] or other highly experienced counterintelligence officers about Agency operations, programs, or priorities. Tension in the White House and from within the CIA created strain. The Rockefeller commission did not have a choice about disclosure of any pertinent information. Disclosure would destroy the CIA and the reputations of former Presidents. Ford agreed with Angleton and both avoided the assassination issues and refused to release the final report to the public. However, the response of press and public proved other than docile.

Open America, a national non-profit corporation promoting the public welfare, and the Citizens Commission of Inquiry wrote both Ford and Rockefeller to request the release of information in the Rockefeller Report, especially regarding plots to assassinate foreign leaders. They did so in accord with the Freedom of Information Act (5 U.S.C. Sec 552). James Wilderotter, Associate Council, composed the White House response using a legal loophole to deny the requests:

It has been determined that the Commission is not an "agency" as defined in section 552 (e), title 5 of the U.S. Code. Therefore, the Commission is not subject to the Act and it is not possible to comply with your request for information.[28]

It is debatable whether the White House had the legal right to refuse the requests. In November 1974, in the wake of the Watergate disclosures, Congress amended the Freedom of Information Act over Ford's veto. The new provisions took effect 19 February 1975 and obliged the Executive Branch to disclose information of importance to public debate on national security issues. Ford's veto in such a matter hardly improved his reputation. In the aftermath of the Rockefeller Report, he no longer even pretended to cooperate with those who believed in the public's right to know.

Despite Ford, the Rockefeller Report became public. Some demanded that the CIA be punished for Operation CHAOS and the invasion of privacy. Those aware of the assassination plots found the Rockefeller Report less than credible in the matter. They demanded a full investigation. Congress responded with the creation of the Senate Select Committee to Study Government Operations with Respect to Intelligence Activities,[29] with Senator Frank Church as its Chair. Church believed in the public's right to know. He also believed that despite short-term damage to the reputation of the United States, foreign leaders would have more respect for the United States if its leaders disclosed the truth and avoided lies and cover-ups.

An adversarial relationship quickly developed between Church and the White House. The Committee demanded access to executive documents. Ford ordered that some of the documents not be released. Church went public with his demands. To prevent further embarrassment, the White House sought to give the appearance of cooperation without providing any substantial documents. By making him Chairman of the Intelligence Coordinating Group, Ford placed Jack Marsh, his presidential counselor for National Security and International Affairs, in charge of deciding which documents to send to Church. Marsh was to give the impression of cooperation while supplying documents of little or no consequence.

Between 12 March and 14 November 1975, Church wrote repeatedly to Ford demanding full texts of legal authorities and other relevant documents under which intelligence agencies have operated, as well as specific documents [such as Director Colby's January 1975 report, written 24 December 1974] which are central to the critical issues which our mandate requires us to explore…With the recognition of the Committee's right to review the documents requested…I have been asked by the Committee to express the hope that the remainder of the documents requested will be promptly turned over.[30]

The Gerald Ford Presidential Archives contains no return correspondence in the Frank Church Congressional Mail File, and it is unclear whether Church received full acknowledgment for his attempt to fulfil his mandate. In the end, he managed without White House cooperation. Colby testified to Church, who was then able to piece together a relatively full picture of the assassination plots. Colby's cooperation with Hersh and the Church Committee cost him his job, and George H.W. Bush (who later succeeded Ronald Reagan and became 41st President of the United States) replaced him in November 1975.

There are extensive accounts of unwillingness to release the information among the White House memoranda. On 13 October, Ford wrote that he never thought that the information would be published, and on 31 October, he wrote to Church and asked him not to release the reports on the assassination plots because such information would damage the reputation of the United States.[31] Ford said that he too was appalled that there had been plots to assassinate foreign leaders, and he attempted to reassure Church that he had disclosed all information relevant to the Senate Select Committee. He also argued that disclosure to the Select Committee was entirely different from publication of the materials.[32]

The letter reached Church six months after his numerous requests for information and after Church had managed to unearth the information without White House assistance. Under the circumstances, Church was not concerned about Ford's wishes. Arguably Ford had used the letter to deceive Church. Although he stated that he was willing to help Church, he had already put Marsh in charge of suppressing information which Church wanted. Ford contacted Church only once he was threatened with the release of the information. Only then did he attempt to cooperate, and "cooperation" meant convincing Church that release of the materials would be contrary to the interests of national security. Ford's gamble to create the Rockefeller Commission had clearly backfired. Because of that fiasco, the Church Committee appeared. Yet Ford wanted to demonstrate that the White House had nothing to hide and that *he* would not be part of a cover-up. Now, with Senator Church in control of the release of information, Ford could but plead that the findings be withheld from public knowledge.

Even Colby, who had initially divulged the information, agreed that publicizing it would be hazardous to the United States. On 20 October 1975, he wrote a three-page letter to Ford. He stated, "I urge in the strongest terms possible that this report not be published...Reports and recriminations with respect to the past can only be destructive to our country." Why did Colby change his mind? Perhaps he feared loss of his position. Perhaps he was sincere and concerned about the national interest. Perhaps he regretted that he had confessed in December 1974 and did not want to leave office as the CIA's snitch.

Other inter-office memoranda indicate that Jack Marsh, Philip Buchen, James Schlesinger, Henry Kissinger, and others opposed the release of information. In order to maximize the political effect, the Church Committee published its information in pieces throughout the investigation, and the effect might have been more significant than the information itself. By a vote of 8:3 on 9 December 1975, the Committee decided to begin the release process without White House approval. On 15 December, the Intelligence Community received the document, along with notification that it would have an opportunity to respond to them 18 December. As well, the Church Committee gave President Ford the opportunity to express his views whether the reports would be dangerous to national security. (He did respond that the reports were indeed dangerous to national security.)

In response to the Church Committee's wishes to release select information, Otis G. Pike, Chairman of the Select Committee on Intelligence, wrote 15 January 1976 that the Church Committee should "draw up an informed, final report, without revealing the existence of, or details concerning, programs that should, in the national interest, remain unacknowledged."[33] A further memorandum of unknown origin cites national security and communist gains as reasons against release the information.[34] Regardless, all attempts to keep the documents within the White House proved useless.

Before the end of 1975, the Church Committee published its investigation of CIA plots to assassinate foreign leaders. The report—now accessible on the internet[35]—included voluminous information suppressed by the Rockefeller Commission. It discussed Lumumba, Castro, and Trujillo, as well as Ngo Dinh Diem of South Vietnam (assassinated in 1963) and Rene Schneider of Chile (assassinated in 1973). The conclusions recommended that the United States should not be involved in assassination plots and argued the need for a statute on such matters.

The Church Report found that the United States Government plotted to kill Castro from 1960 to 1965, with the help of American underworld figures and others hostile to revolutionary Cuba. Concerning Trujillo, the report found three pistols and three carbines furnished by Americans, but there was conflicting evidence as to whether the weapons were knowingly supplied for the assassination plot. Concerning Diem, the President of South Vietnam whose popularity was obviously in decline, the report recorded that Diem and his brother were killed 2 November 1963 during a coup d'état, but the report acknowledged that there was no evidence that U.S. officials favored the assassination. The report found the assassination a "spontaneous act" during the coup, which did have the support of U.S. officials. Concerning Schneider, the report stated that the Commanding Officer in Chief of Chile died from gunshot wounds three days after an attempted kidnaping. This happened after the Chilean presidential election, in which none of the three candidates received a majority of the votes, but before Congress met to break the deadlock and choose a winner. Schneider was prepared to allow the political process to proceed without military interference, even if this led to the selection of Salvador Allende, a leftist untrusted by the Nixon administration. Although the U.S. played a role in the coup that ousted Allende and supplied financial aid and machine guns, the Church Report found no evidence that the CIA wanted to kill Schneider. However, the report did find that the CIA supported the coup plotters who were responsible for the shooting Schneider and his subsequent death. In its words, "the intention of dissidents and the United States officials was to abduct General Schneider, not to kill him."[36] The report make no connection between the CIA and Sukarno.

The publication of the Church Report was one of the most traumatic events of Ford's presidency. By then, George H.W. Bush had replaced Colby as Director of the CIA. Bush's task was to prevent the leak of any additional information. Colby, who had launched the process, no longer had access to confidential information, and Church faced an additional challenge in determining the truth.

Recent disclosures indicate that in mid-June 1975, the CIA prepared its own report, declassified in May 2000 and March 2002. It found no evidence of direct CIA participation in Lumumba's death but admitted that CIA officials had discussed plots to assassinate him. There were various plots against Fidel Castro dating from the Eisenhower and Kennedy presidencies, and the CIA provided weapons to Dominicans who would remove the appropriate undesirables. No Americans participated in the actual killing.[37] All this happened before Ford's presidency.

Although Ford participated in the cover-up—for reasons which are debatable but understandable—it appears that publicity provided by Seymour Hersh and the Church Committee had an impact. Assassination ceased to be a weapon of U.S. diplomacy for a generation. The CIA's reputation suffered, but more than a decade before he became 41st President of the United States, George H.W. Bush became the official most responsible for damage control. During the administration of the 43rd President of the United States, George W. Bush, assassination has returned to the diplomatic arsenal. The second President Bush has openly sanctified the kidnaping of terrorists "in order to break their cells or kill them."[38] In November 2001, the CIA deployed a remote controlled Predator drone armed with 1.5 meter-long Hellfire missiles to assassinate Mohammed Atef, lieutenant of Osama bin Laden, mastermind of the 9/11 attacks. The missile missed Atef but killed an al-Qaeda commander and five of his men.[39] Twenty-five years after the Rockefeller Commission and the Church Committee, the second President Bush reversed the decision not to authorize assassination and indicated that he would view the deaths of Osama bin Laden and Iraq's Saddam Hussein with the greatest of pleasure. In the aftermath of the 9/11 attacks, George W. Bush has considerable support.

Notes

1. This chapter is an edited version of the undergraduate Honours Essay (thesis) of Rebecca Vergunst, accepted by Laurentian University's History Department in 2003.
2. Joshua 2:1-7.
3. Christopher Andrew, *For the President's Eyes Only* (New York: Harper Collins, 1995), p. 6. Besides Andrew's book, there have been other classics on the CIA, most notably J. Ranelagh, *The Agency: The Rise and Decline of the CIA*, London: Weidenfeld and Nicholson, 1986); and Rhodri Jeffreys-Jones, *The CIA and American Democracy* (New Haven: Yale University Press, 1989). This chapter, however, benefits from documents declassified since Andrew, Jeffreys-Jones, and Ranelagh researched those books.
4. http://www/cia.gov/cia/information/mission.html
5. Andrew, pp. 199-256.
6. Report to the President by the COMMISSION ON CIA ACTIVITIES WITHIN THE UNITED STATES, June 1975, GFPL.
7. Andrew, pp. 257-306.
8. Andrew, pp. 250-251.
9. See David Doyle, *True Men and Traitors, from the OSS to the CIA: My Life in the Shadows* (New York: John Wiley & Sons, 2001), p. 135; Sarah Foster, *World Net Daily* (http://www.heart.net/mcf/meet_sidney.htm; James Srodes, *Allen Dules, Master of Spies* (Washington: Regnery Publishing, 1999), p. 495.
10. Srodes, p. 495.
11. Srodes, p. 543.

12. Ford mentions the role of Hersh in his memoirs, p. 229.

13. John Robert Greene, *The Presidency of Gerald Ford* (Lawrence: University Press of Kansas, 1995), p. 104. Colby made this assertion to Greene in 1989.

14. Eagleberger and McCloskey to [the President's] Secretary, 24 Sept. 1974, GFPL.

15. Ford, p. 229.

16. Colby to Ford, 24 Dec. 1974, White House Operations: Richard Cheney File, 1974-1977, Box 7, GFPL. Cited hereafter as WHORCF.

17. Silberman to Ford, 3 Jan. 1975, WHORCF, GFPL.

18. Wilderotter to Ford, 3 Jan. 1975, WHORCF, GFPL.

19. Ford, p. 230.

20. Memorandum of Conversations, 4 Jan. 1975, Oval Office, 1973-1977, NSA, Box 8, GFPL. The next two quotations come from this same source.

21. Letter, Friendly, U.S. Courthouse, New York, to Ford, 6 Jan. 1975, WHCF: Legal Services Corporation, FG 392, Box 205, GFPL. Cited hereafter as WHCF:LSC.

22. Letter, Dellums to Ford, 7 Jan. 1975, WHCF: LSC, GFPL.

23. Federal Government Organizations: Cabinet Meeting Minutes, The Presidential Handwriting File, Box 9, GFPL.

24. Memo, Ford to Rockefeller, 9 May 1975, WHCF:LCS, GFPL.

25. Report to the President by the COMMISSION ON CIA ACTIVITIES WITHIN THE UNITED STATES (The Rockefeller Report), 6 June 1975, GFPL, p. i.

26. Tom Mangold, *Cold Warrior: James Jesus Angleton, the CIA's Master Spy* (London: Simon and Schuster, 1991), p. 6.

27. Angleton's Report to the Presidential Commission on CIA Activities Within the United States, pp. 29-30, Richard Cheney Files, 1974-1977, Box 7, GFPL.

28. James Wilderotter in a memorandum for approval, 16 June 1975, Richard Cheney Files, 1974-1977, Box 7, GFPL.

29. Greene, p. 109.

30. Letter, Church to Ford, 9 April 1975, Frank Church Congressional Mail File, Box 14, GFPL.

31. Greene, p. 111.

32. Letter, Ford to Church, 31 Oct. 1975, Robert K. Wolthius, Special Assistant to the President Files, 1974-77, Box 2, GFPL.

33. Letter, Pike to Ford, 15 Jan. 1976, White House Cabinet Secretary, James E. Conner Files, Box 56, GFPL [declassified 8 May 2000].

34. Unknown author memorandum, White House Cabinet Secretary, Conner Files, Box 56, GFPL [declassified in sanitized form 3 July 2000].

35. http://www.history-matters.com/archive/church/contents.htm "Interim Report: Alleged Assassination Plots Involving Foreign Leaders."

36. Church Report, p. 5.

37. Central Intelligence Agency, "Summary of Factgs: Investigation of CIA Involvement in Plans to Assassinate Foreign Leaders," n.d. but c. June 1975, Richard Cheney Files, 1974-1977, Box 7, GFPL.

38. "The CIA's Secret Army," *Time Canada*, 3 Feb. 2003, p. 14.

39. *Time Canada*, 3 Feb. 2003, p. 17.

Chapter Twelve

FORD AND KISSINGER VISIT CHINA[1]

Arguably, it would be easy to ignore President Ford's policies with the People's Republic of China (PRC). He and Secretary of State Kissinger continued what Nixon and Kissinger had begun and what the Carter administration concluded. The Ford administration had no distinctive China policy of its own. To appreciate what happened (or, more accurately, what did *not* happen), consider the counterfactual. Imagine what might have happened if Ford had bowed to right-wing pressures within the Republican Party and sacrificed Kissinger, as he sacrificed Kissinger's mentor, Vice-President Nelson Rockefeller. (Due to pressure from the Republican right, Ford replaced Rockefeller with Kansas Senator Robert Dole as his running mate in 1976.[2]) Nixon's opening to China might have been a passing blip, and the Carter administration—obsessed as it was with the Panama Canal negotiations, an Israeli-Egyptian accord, the kidnaped diplomats in Iran, and the Soviet invasion of Afghanistan—could have been so involved with other priorities that it would have avoided any controversy regarding China. Indeed, it might have lacked the political capital to reverse course on China. The ideological Reagan administration would have been most unlikely to launch any overtures in the direction of Beijing, and relations between China and the United States might well have remained as hostile as ever, even as relations with the Soviet Union were improving. Indeed, improved U.S.-Soviet relations might have created a perception that there was no need to hurry in order to resolve outstanding problems between Beijing and Washington. What Ford did *not* do—replace Kissinger and reverse his China policy—proved vital to a relaxation of tensions in Asia and the co-option of the PRC as a diplomatic and commercial partner.

Since Mao Zedong had proclaimed the People's Republic of China 1 October 1949, relations between the PRC and the United States had been adversarial. The

Truman administration (1945-1953) had supported Chiang Kai Shek (Jiang Jieshie), leader of Mao's adversaries. Mao's army had proved a formidable adversary to forces led by the United States during the Korean War (1950-1953). Chiang's Republic of China (ROC), based in Taiwan, became a *de facto* ally of the United States–protected from PRC attack by the U.S. Seventh Fleet. Truman's successors maintained that policy, and the U.S. had diplomatic relations with the ROC, not the PRC. Mao's government regarded Taiwan as a renegade province of China to which, governed by the PRC, it must return.

The Johnson administration (1963-1969) recognized that it had no choice but to respect the PRC, even to communicate with it. As President Johnson escalated U.S. involvement in Vietnam, he took every precaution to guarantee that PRC and U.S. forces would not again be fighting each other, as they had in Korea. The United States Air Force would stay away from China's borders, and U.S. ground troops would not enter Communist North Vietnam the way they had gone into North Korea in October 1950. PRC and U.S. diplomats consulted regularly in Warsaw and communicated with high level British and Pakistani intermediaries so that there would be no misunderstanding.[3] Yet, the U.S. maintained a formidable consulate-general in the British enclave of Hong Kong and an embassy in Taipei, provisional capital of the ROC, but no diplomats inside the PRC.

When Richard Nixon became President 20 January 1969, the Cold War was becoming triangular. The United States and its allies remained armed for action against the Soviet Union and its allies, and a military coalition led by the United States was deeply involved fighting Communist North Vietnam. At the same time, the PRC and the Soviet Union were entering a period of armed confrontation. Along the 4,380 kilometer border, 658,000 Soviet troops faced 814,000 Chinese soldiers. On 2 March 1969, Chinese forces ambushed a Soviet patrol on an island (Damansky Island in Russian, Zhen Bao Island in Mandarin) in the Ussuri River, which separated the two countries. There were casualties: 31 Soviets dead and 14 wounded then, 800 Chinese and 60 Soviets dead or injured two weeks later when the Soviets counter-attacked.[4] It was not illogical for the Nixon White House to assume that the Chinese might appreciate a powerful ally. Perhaps the Chinese might return the favour and serve as intermediaries with the North Vietnamese.

Quietly Nixon lifted the travel ban which prevented U.S. citizens from visiting the PRC. In 1971, his administration allowed Americans to participate in a ping pong tournament which took place in China.[5] Kissinger, who was then Nixon's National Security Adviser, arranged a secret visit to Beijing via Pakistani President Yahya Khan. At the same time, the U.S. government quietly allowed Americans of Chinese origin to send money to their relatives inside the PRC and permitted ships registered in the U.S. to go to ports on the Chinese mainland. Prime Minister Zhou Enlai used the occasion of Kissinger's visit to invite President Nixon and his entourage to visit China,[6] and from 21-28 February 1972, they did so. The main result of the trip was the opening of liaison offices (quasi-embassies) in each other's capitals. As the United States maintained formal diplomatic relations with the Republic of China, they could not establish formal embassies in Beijing and Washington.

When Ford became President, he appointed George Herbert Walker Bush–later 41st President of the United States–to head the U.S. liaison office in Beijing. Also, when Ford became President, a 1974 Gallup Poll showed 72% of Americans opposed the establishment of diplomatic relations with the PRC.[7]

Following a summit meeting at Vladivostok with Soviet leaders, Ford sent Kissinger to Beijing from 25 to 29 November 1974 to brief the Chinese leadership. By then, Deng Xiaoping had replaced Zhou Enlai as the principal interlocutor in China. Kissinger described Deng as having a more no-nonsense style, and according to Kissinger, Deng immediately voiced his displeasure with the U.S.-Soviet meeting which had just taken place. As a peace offering, Kissinger offered to accept an invitation for President Ford to visit China in 1975. Without consulting Mao, Deng immediately extended the invitation.

Kissinger returned to China 19 October 1975 in order to plan Ford's visit. The issue of Taiwan arose, and Deng rejected Kissinger's proposal that the U.S. could have an embassy in Beijing and a liaison office at Taipei on the grounds that such an arrangement would grant too much prestige to the renegade province.[8] Later Mao told Kissinger what he had told Nixon in 1972—that the Taiwan issue could remain unresolved for another 100 years.[9] Meanwhile, it appeared, the PRC and the U.S. could join forces in dealing with their common adversary, the Soviet Union.

On 1 December 1975, *Air Force One* landed in Beijing. For the first time, President Ford would meet Mao Zedong and Vice Premier Deng Xiaoping. Zhou Enlai was too ill to participate and died one month later. Deng later told Ford that although Taiwan remained a problem, dealing with "Soviet expansionism" was a higher priority. Deng even drew a parallel between Hitler's expansion in the

1930s and current Soviet actions. Ford replied that the United States was better prepared to deal with aggression in 1975 than were Germany's neighbours at the time of Hitler. Ford also indicated that U.S.-Chinese co-operation would help in the effort against Soviet expansion.[10] (Of course, concern about Soviet expansionism was to some measure justified. While it was understandable that neighbours would have boundary disputes, the Soviet Union had invaded Czechoslovakia as recently as 1968 and would invade Afghanistan in 1979.)

Later that day Ford met Mao, accompanied by Kissinger, Bush, Scowcroft, and Winston Lord of the State Department. Mao asked what they had discussed with Deng, and Ford replied that they had discussed the Soviet Union. Mao predicted improvements in Sino-American relations, and Ford suggested that the PRC and the U.S. co-ordinate their plans and policies on the Soviet Union. Ford and Mao agreed that bilateral talks with the Soviets, whether U.S.-Soviet or PRC-Soviet, had not been rewarding. After discussions on their countries' relations with Japan and Angola, Mao and Ford parted on what seemed to be friendly terms.[11]

At another meeting the next day, Deng told Ford that his government had been encouraging both the Japanese and Western European governments to improve their relations with the United States. Deng warned that the Soviet Union had more military muscle than Western Europe and the U.S. combined. Stopping Soviet expansionism would be difficult, especially if the U.S. and the Soviets continued to promote détente, a relaxation of tensions. Ford was not as pessimistic as Deng about the vulnerability of Western Europe to Soviet attack but promised that the U.S. would resume arms sales to Yugoslavia and co-operate with Romania as well.

They then discussed the Middle East and South Asia. Deng indicated concern that the Soviets might have some influence in Iraq and South Yemen. Kissinger expressed optimism that Iranian pressure (from the Shah's government) would keep Iraq from the Soviet orbit, and he said that the U.S. was trying to lessen Soviet influence in Somalia. Such influence appeared strongest in Libya, but with Egyptian assistance, it might be contained even there. Ford said that the U.S. would be supplying arms to Pakistan while trying to minimize Soviet influence in India.[12]

On the last day of the visit, Ford and Deng again discussed Taiwan. Ford said that while the U.S. had a commitment to Taiwan, it would discourage the ROC government from declaring Taiwan an independent country, no longer part of China. He also noted that the U.S. was reducing its armed forces on Taiwan. Deng saw no solution to the Taiwan dilemma but thought the problem less than urgent.[13] The morning of 5 December, Ford left Beijing.

Two weeks later, U.S.-PRC relations suffered a blow. In the aftermath of the events in Vietnam, Congress was less than enthusiastic about a military intervention in Angola, and on 19 December, it endorsed an amendment from California's Democratic Senator John Tunney banning military assistance to Angola's UNITA forces. The Chinese, eager to prevent a victory by the MPLA (backed by Cuba and seemingly backed by the USSR), were most displeased.[14] Information released from the Cuban archives confirms that Angola was of greater interest to Castro's Cuba than to the Soviet Union,[15] but appearances can be more important than realities. When they are available, Chinese archives may indicate that the Tunney Amendment lessened the credibility of Ford and Kissinger. For the moment, however, the train remained on the rails and President Carter would be able to establish full diplomatic relations with the PRC in 1979.

Actually, Chinese leaders were willing to soft pedal the Taiwan issue during Nixon's presidential visit of 1972, at least in part because Kissinger reassured them that the U.S. and the PRC could normalize their relationship shortly after that year's presidential election, certainly during the first half of Nixon's second term.[16] However, the Watergate scandal destroyed Nixon's political capital, and Taiwan proved more contentious than anticipated.[17] Only after the Iranian Revolution of 1979 removed America's southern window on the Soviet Union did China's value as a possible ally become so obvious that, despite Taiwan, normalization could proceed.

Notes

1. This chapter is an extract from the Honours Essay (undergraduate thesis) of Laurentian University student Trevor Mouhan, 2004–2005.
2. Ford, pp. 296–297, 327–328.
3. James G.. Hershberg and Chen Jian, "Reading and Warning the Likely Enemy: China's Signals to the United States about Vietnam in 1965," *The International History Review*, XXVII, 1 (March 2005), pp. 47–84.
4. http://en/wikipedia.org/wiki/Damansky_Island_Soviet-Chinese_Border_Conflict. See also Evelyn Goh, "Nixon, Kissinger, and the 'Soviet Card' in the U.S. Opening to China, 1971-1974," *Diplomatic History*, XXIX, 3 (June 2005), pp. 475–502.
5. Henry Kissinger, *White House Years* (Boston: Little, Brown, and Company, 1979), pp. 709–710. For more on relations between the U.S. and the PRC in the Nixon era, see Charles W. Freeman, Jr., "The Process of Rapprochement: Achievements and Problems," in Gene T. Hsiao and Michael Witunsky

(eds.), *Sino-American Normalization and Its Policy Implications* (New York: Praeger, 1983), pp. 1-27, esp. pp. 2-3.

6. Kissinger, *White House Years*, pp. 30, 723, 724, 733-755.

7. Gallup Poll, Americans Oppose Red China, 08/20/74, folder "CO 34-1: Republic of China," Box 12, White House Central Files, Subject File: Box 12-13, CO 34-1—Republic of China (Formosa-Taiwan), GFPL.

8. Henry Kissinger, *Years of Renewal*, p. 879.

9. Kissinger, *Years of Renewal*, p. 886.

10. Memo, Approaches to Dealing with the Soviet Union, 12/02/75, folder "President Ford's Visit to Peking (1), Box 2, National Security Adviser: Kissinger reports on USSR, China, and Middle East Discussions, GFPL.

11. Memo, Conversation with Mao, 12/02/75, folder "President Ford's Visit to Peking (1), Box 2, National Security Adviser: Kissinger reports on USSR, China, and Middle East Discussions. GFPL.

12. Memo, The Soviet Union; Europe; the Middle East; south Asia; Angola, 12/03/75, folder "President Ford's Visit to Peking (2)," Box 2, National Security Adviser: Kissinger reports on USSR, China and Middle East Discussions, GFPL.

13. Memo, Taiwan; bilateral relations; MIA; trade (oil and computers); Dalai Lama; Korea; Chinese minorities; agriculture; Amb. Bush, 12/04/75, folder "President Ford's Visit to Peking (3)," Box 2, National Security Adviser: Kissinger reports on USSR, China, and Middle East Discussions, GFPL. For a summary of U.S. and Chinese positions on Taiwan during Ford's presidency, see Alan D. Romberg, *Rein In at the Brink of the Precipice: American Policy toward Taiwan and U.S.-PRC Relations* (Washington: Henry L. Stimson Center, 2003), pp. 62-75.

14. Kissinger, *Years of Renewal*, pp. 894-895.

15. Piero Gleijeses, *Conflicting Missions: Havana, Washington and Africa, 1959-1976* , pp.246-272.

16. Goh, p. 477.

17. Goh, pp. 495-499.

Chapter Thirteen

THE PANAMA CANAL TREATIES[1]

As President, Ford favored a negotiated end to U.S. sovereignty over the Panama Canal and the Canal Zone, first ceded by the infant Republic of Panama at the turn of the 20th century. Henry Kissinger discussed a possible transfer of the Canal with Panamanian officials and developed guidelines that the Carter administration found useful in its own subsequent negotiations with the Panamanians.

Ford strongly endorsed his successor's efforts.

—from a Tableau in the Gerald Ford Presidential Museum,
Grand Rapids, Michigan

That quotation summarizes one of President Ford's greatest successes: a major step toward defusing tension in Panama. He continued the process launched by Lyndon Johnson after the deadly Panamanian riots of 1964 and concluded by his successor, Jimmy Carter, in 1977-1978. Thanks to statesmanship at its best by Presidents Johnson, Ford, and Carter, the bitter anti-American tensions of Panama's past disappeared along with the fence along the boundary on Fourth of July Avenue between Panama City and the Canal Zone. With an orderly transition, Panamanians learned how to manage the Panama Canal, which runs smoothly, efficiently, and predictably. A new Panama Railroad, constructed since the handover, links Panama City on the Pacific with Colón on the Caribbean, and Panama's middle class has grown enormously. Where the U.S. military once occupied the former Canal Zone, there are now elegant tourist resorts; and beside the Chagres River, where U.S. forces once trained for the Vietnam War, Embará Amerindians live almost as did their ancestors—the men dressed only in loincloths, the women in grass skirts, the food supply in the river and the jungle. Tourist revenues finance their simple lifestyle. Much of the credit for these happy developments goes to President Ford.

The Isthmus of Panama has been of the utmost importance to North Americans (Canadians as well as citizens of the United States) since the United States acquisition of California in the Mexican War of 1846-1848 and the California Gold Rush of 1849. Despite the challenges of tropical diseases, hostile Panamanians, and heat, Panama quickly became the most feasible route between the population centres east of the Mississippi River and the Pacific coast. Steamers sailed south from New York to Colón, and north from Panama City to San Francisco. With the British Columbia Gold Rush of 1858, travelers from Montreal and Toronto made their way to Panama via New York and to Victoria via San Francisco.[2] In 1849, when Panama was still a part of Colombia, the United States Senate approved a treaty with Colombia accepting some responsibility for the defence of the Isthmus in exchange for the right to keep the transportation routes open. By 1855, the Panama Railroad–the first transcontinental railway in the Americas–linked Colón and Panama City. There was no transcontinental railway across the United States until 1869, across Canada until 1886.

There are several books on Panama's secession from Colombia and U.S. acquisition of the Canal Zone, and the details need not be repeated here.[3] In brief, an interoceanic canal proved less than economically viable for most of the 19th century. Costs of construction and maintenance through Panama's dense jungles more than offset any potential saving from avoidance of travel through the Strait of Magellan or around Cape Horn. Then, the Spanish-American War of 1898 threw the matter into a totally different perspective. Strategists in the U.S. Navy thought that they might need the battleship *Oregon* for combat against Spain in Caribbean waters near Cuba or Puerto Rico. The *Oregon* sailed from her base off the Pacific coast to the south of Chile, then up the Atlantic coast of South America to the Caribbean. By the time of her arrival, the U.S. had won the war and her services proved unnecessary. The *Oregon* nevertheless served as a warning. If the enemy had been Germany rather than Spain, the United States might not have been so fortunate. Clearly the canal's usefulness went well beyond commerce. Security was worth a price.

The administrations of William McKinley (1897-1901) and Theodore Roosevelt (1901-1909) thereupon negotiated agreements with the United Kingdom, which had residual rights in the area, and gained British approval for a canal built, controlled, and financed entirely by the United States. A commission headed by Rear Admiral John G. Walker studied feasible routes: across Mexico's Isthmus of Tehuantepec, along the San Juan River between Nicaragua and Costa Rica, and across Panama. For various reasons, the Walker Commission endorsed the Panama route in 1902. In 1903, the head of Colombia's Legation in Washington, Tomás Herrán, negotiated a canal treaty with Secretary of State John Hay, but when the Colombian Senate unanimously rejected the Hay-Herrán Treaty, President Roosevelt's government colluded with Panamanian separatists through a French intermediary, Philippe Bunau-Varilla. Bunau-Varilla was an engineer with a French company which had tried and failed to build Panama Canal, and he had devoted his life to the cause. Bunau-Varilla had frequent talks with Francis Loomis at the State Department and early in October 1903 talked with President Roosevelt at the White House. Bunau-Varilla then told Panamanian separatist Manuel Amador that he would finance a "revolution" against Colombia provided that Amador and his friends proclaimed Panamanian independence no later than 3 November 1903 and appointed him the new country's foreign minister, with full authority to conclude a canal treaty. Armed with Bunau-Varilla's money, Amador returned to Panama City to proclaim Panamanian independence. Before he could return to New York and then travel by train to Washington, Bunau-Varilla and Hay had negotiated a new canal treaty which they insisted that Amador and the Panamanian junta must accept without amendments. Otherwise, the government of Colombia might be allowed to reassert its authority and punish them for treason.

Bunau-Varilla wrote in his memoirs that his goal was to "negotiate" so one-sided a treaty that the United States Senate would be certain to give the necessary two-thirds vote of approval,[4] and the Hay-Bunau-Varilla Treaty of 1903 reflected his generosity. The United States would control the lands and waterways for five miles either side of the forthcoming canal "as if it were...sovereign" and "in perpetuity." The Canal Zone then became a ten-mile-wide swath of land which separated Panama City from most of its populated hinterland and confined the capital to a few blocks between the Zone and the Pacific Ocean. On a map, Panama City resembled a snake. Colón, Panama's second largest city, became an Panamanian island bordered by either the Caribbean or the Canal Zone, without land access to the rest of the Republic of Panama. In other words, the Canal Zone—controlled by Americans who were bigger and wealthier than most Panamanians, of a different colour and a different religious persuasion—was an ever present factor in Panamanian life. In no way was it out of sight, out of mind. Journalist John Gunther, who visited Panama late in 1940 or early in 1941, described it as being "as much a part of the United States as Omaha, Nebraska."[5] Indeed, from the heart of Panama City, a U.S. flag atop a hill in the Canal Zone a few blocks away was clearly and constantly visible.

The administrations of Franklin Delano Roosevelt (1933-1945) and Dwight David Eisenhower (1953-1961) negotiated new canal treaties which increased the annual rent which the United States paid for the Canal Zone and which created additional employment opportunities for Panamanians inside the Canal Zone. Nevertheless, tensions continued to build as Panamanians resented a foreign presence in their midst, and on 9 January 1964 erupted into violence along 4th of July Avenue. During the three days of turmoil, twenty-one Panamanians and four Americans died.[6]

The following morning, President Lyndon Johnson talked by telephone with Panamanian President Roberto Chiari, who was not himself a candidate in the May 1964 elections but whose party hoped to retain the presidency. By then, an estimated eight to ten people had died and more than 200 had gone to hospital. Johnson, who could talk the proverbial birds from the trees during a telephone conversation, told Chiari that talks could begin as soon as the violence ended. Chiari blamed the violence on U.S. intransigence and indifference but agreed that the violence was bad. Johnson said that he would send Thomas Mann as his envoy to Panama within half an hour, and Chiari expressed appreciation for Johnson's speed.[7] Panama's National Guard—a combined army/police force—restored order, and the talks began. Marco Robles, the candidate from Chiari's party, won the 1964 election, but progress was slow, and the main issue in the next presidential election (1968) was which party was more likely to oust the U.S. from the Canal Zone. Tensions in Panama City and other parts of the Republic of Panama were so extreme that soldiers in the Canal Zone received frequent orders, "Avoid Panama Today." On election day, Sunday, 12 May, the military was on alert. Canal Zone police with two-way radios stood at border crossings, ready on short notice to summon soldiers from nearby buildings where they were standing on guard. This time, Arnulfo Arias, the opposition candidate, handily defeated David Samudio.[8]

Arias was a three time president of Panama (1940-1941, 1949-1951, 1968), with each term ended by a coup d'état and well ahead of schedule. His third term (1-11 October 1968) was his briefest. When he tried to dismiss the head of the National Guard, the National Guard dismissed him and retained control until 1989. The dominant personality throughout the Canal negotiations was Omar Torrijos, probably a more sincere nationalist than Arias.

During his first term, Arias had promoted language laws not unlike those in modern Quebec—designed to restrict the use of English and promote the language of the majority.[9] Arias sought to restrict immigration to Panama by people likely to speak English rather than Spanish: Jamaicans and others from the British Caribbean, people from the Indian sub-continent, and other Asians.[10] He admired Generalíssimo Franco of Spain[11] and tried to restrict freedom of the press. The older brother of Arnulfo Arias, Harmodio Arias, had been President of Panama from 1932 to 1936 and had negotiated the revised canal treaty with Franklin Roosevelt's government. Harmodio was also publisher of Panama's leading newspaper, *Panamá América*, and a cattle baron. Arnulfo wanted to bring the media under his control and threatened reprisals if Harmodio would not co-operate. Harmodio refused and found that the slaughterhouse owned by the municipal government of Panama City bought fewer and fewer of his beef cattle. The mayor of Panama City explained that he was "responding to orders."[12] Harmodio had his opportunity in the autumn of 1941 when the United States Navy became involved in an undeclared naval war against Hitler's fleet in the North Atlantic. For reasons of economy, then as now, many shipowners who lived in the United States registered their vessels in Panama. That way they could avoid U.S. safety standards and minimum wage laws. Arnulfo rejected a request to allow U.S.-owned ships of Panamanian registry to arm themselves. As early as 2 July, Harmodio had approached the U.S. Ambassador, Edmund C. Wilson, to ask what the U.S. response might be in the event of a coup d'état. Wilson gave Harmodio no immediate encouragement. However, when the naval armaments dispute arose, Wilson gave the green light, and the coup took place.[13] Arnulfo's successor, Ricardo Adolfo de la Guardia, granted the permission which Arnulfo had denied, and Arnulfo did not return to the presidency until four years after World War II had ended.

Like his first term, Arnulfo's second was highly controversial. In the aftermath of the disputed 1948 presidential election, an electoral jury ruled that the winner was his opponent, Domingo Díaz. Díaz assumed office but died in mid-1949. His successor, Daniel Chanis, assumed office 28 July 1949 but resigned in November "in order to avoid bloodshed" after a quarrel with the head of the National Guard, Colonel José A. Remón. To the dismay of Monnett B. Davis, U.S. Ambassador to Panama, Remón then—despite a Supreme Court decision—insisted that Arias had won the election after all and must assume office. Davis found this "cynical." While he admired non-intervention as a principle, he questioned whether someone who took office despite decisions of an electoral jury and a Supreme Court decision deserved recognition from the United States government.[14] State Department officials reluctantly accepted Arnulfo's return to office with the logic: "[W]e should be careful not to back Arnulfo Arias into a corner and thereby run the risk of making him more anti-American than he has been in the past."[15] Even Davis came to decide that there were worse options than Arnulfo Arias, including his brother, Harmodio. If restored to the presidency, "Chanis," wrote Davis on 3 December 1949, "would have owed his restoration to power to Harmodio Arias and the Communist-dominated youth organizations…"[16] Still, this was damning with faint praise, and Arnulfo's return to the presidency under such circumstances indicates that he was either an unprincipled opportunist or a leader with little confidence in his own country's judiciary. Arnulfo lost the presidency in May 1951 after he lost the confidence of police chief Remón.

Panama was definitely a low priority for Richard Nixon, who became President of the United States 20 January 1969. Vietnam, China, and the Middle East absorbed his attention. The Nixon administration's primary concerns in Latin America were a possible Soviet nuclear submarine base at Cienfuegos in Cuba and the government of Salvador Allende, which assumed office after the Chilean presidential elections of 1970.[17] In turn, Torrijos later told William J. Jorden, who in 1974 became U.S. Ambassador to Panama, that Panama's purpose in the initial talks was to win time to internationalize the problem. By bringing the Canal issue to the world stage, Torrijos thought he could force the Americans to negotiate more seriously. Torrijos told Jorden, "To resolve a problem, the first thing you have to do is make a problem."[18]

In 1967, Presidents Johnson and Robles had signed draft treaties, which proved stillborn. For unrelated reasons, the Panamanian Congress impeached President Robles and thwarted his agenda. Torrijos found the Johnson-Robles treaties inadequate on the grounds that they conceded too much to the United States and too little to Panama. The Torrijos government's refusal to use those treaties as a basis for settlement led Assistant Secretary of State Charles Meyer and Secretary of State William Rogers to fear yet another outbreak of violence, comparable to that of 1964 or perhaps worse. Rogers told Panamanian Foreign Minister Juan Antonio Tack that the U.S. was willing to revive the negotiations, and Tack was interested but warned that the 1967 accord would be an unacceptable starting point.

In October 1970, President Nixon invited Panamanian President Demetrio B. Lakas—in reality, a subordinate of Torrijos—to the White House. Nixon suggested that the U.S. return control of the Canal Zone to Panama but retain defence rights. Lakas thought that a solution was within sight, but Torrijos remained skeptical—and with good reason. That Nixon had no intention of negotiating a mutually beneficial treaty became evident in April 1971 when Ambassador at Large Robert B. Anderson visited Panama and had lunch in the *Presidencia*, Panama's equivalent of the White House. Torrijos asked Anderson whether the United States was really going to negotiate an end to the Canal Zone.

"Well, not really," Anderson replied. "I'm here to see how we can vary, alter, change, modify the agreements which were entered into in 1967."[19] Silence replaced smiles. Feeling betrayed, Lakas left the room. Nevertheless, Torrijos did not abandon hope and agreed to talk.

Nixon directed the U.S. negotiating team to take a hard stand on the talks. National Security Decision Memorandum (NSDM) #64 outlines his instructions:

> In any new negotiations three points are to be considered non-negotiable: (1) effective U.S. control of canal operations; (2) effective U.S. control of canal defense; and (3) continuation of these controls for an extended period of time, preferably open-ended.[20]

Nixon instructed Anderson to propose a smaller Canal Zone but one still under U.S. control. The duration would be open-ended, with provisions for periodic review. The U.S. government was, however, "prepared to seek ways to create substantial additional revenue for Panama."[21] Essentially, Nixon was offering less than the 1967 treaty accompanied by a bribe.

Panama's negotiating team—Ambassador José Antonio de la Ossa, economist Fernando Manfredo, and lawyer Carlos López-Guevara—arrived in Washington 28 June 1971. Their U.S. counterparts were Ambassador Anderson, businessman John Mundt, and lawyer Richard Finn. When Anderson described Nixon's proposals as a "major, giant step" for America, the Panamanians were stunned. De la Ossa responded that the current U.S. position did nothing to resolve the conflict, and the other Panamanians were equally hostile. For the remainder of the meeting, they asked Anderson pointed questions, while the U.S.

negotiators held firm. The outcome surprised both sides. For their part, the Americans did not expect the Panamanian team to be so well prepared. The Panamanians were shocked at U.S. intransigence.[22]

That the Panamanians would not accept Nixon's bribe quickly became evident, and Nixon responded. The U.S. Ambassador to Panama, Robert Sayre, told Torrijos that Nixon would never accept a termination date nor would Congress accept one. Torrijos responded that the Panamanian people could no longer accept the "in perpetuity" provision of the Hay–Bunau–Varilla Treaty. If negotiations failed, the Panamanian people would resort to force. Panamanians could be patient. The termination date could be distant, but at the same time, it must be definite. Torrijos then repeated that message in a letter to Sayre.[23]

What Nixon had intended as a power play to force Torrijos to back down backfired. Nixon then issued NSDM #131, which gave Anderson the flexibility to negotiate a termination date fifty years into the future. If a new or expanded canal were to be built, the U.S. could have an additional thirty to fifty years.[24] This struck Torrijos as unreasonable, and by late 1971, it was obvious that the treaty talks had reached a stalemate. His solution was to create international embarrassment for the United States.

The first opportunity came during the January 1972 United Nations Security Council Meeting in Addis Ababa, Ethiopia. Issues discussed there ranged from poverty and hunger to colonialism and racism. The Panamanian Ambassador to the United Nations, Aquilino Boyd, used this opportunity to publicize his country's conflict with the United States. He said, "Panama suffered side by side with its brothers of Africa from attempts to undermine the independence, sovereignty, and territorial integrity of small nations."[25] Boyd compared the Canal Zone to colonialism in Africa. He told of an exploitative U.S. occupation that used black Caribbean workers to build the Canal and paid them less than Euro-Americans received for doing the same work. He warned of Panamanian determination to resolve the issue, preferably through negotiations.

Boyd's statement caught the U.S. delegation by surprise. The U.S. Ambassador at the time was George H.W. Bush, later the 41st President of the United States. Bush used his right of reply to denounce Boyd for introducing a topic that had not been on the agenda. Bush denied that there was any comparison between the Panamanian situation and Africa. The U.S. presence in the Canal Zone resulted from a treaty (the Hay–Bunau–Varilla Treaty of 1903), whereas colonialism in Africa was a consequence of European racism. Boyd answered, "For the purpose of condemning colonialism and neo-colonialism in the world, any rostrum at any hour of the day was appropriate on African soil."[26]

The success of the Ethiopian gathering persuaded Torrijos to lobby African and other Latin American governments to hold a Security Council meeting in Panama City in March 1973. Despite U.S. and British objections, other Security Council members agreed to go to the Panamanian capital from 15 to 21 March 1973.[27] Torrijos explained his intentions to the *New York Times*:

> I want the moral backing of the world and especially, I want the people of the United States to know how we feel about the canal. The Americans are very decent people and when they realize what is happening here, they will feel a sense of shame, just as they did during the Vietnam War. That war wasn't stopped because of a lack of bombs but because the American people did not want it. I think they can stop the neocolonialism in the Panama Canal Zone in the same way.[28]

The Security Council met at the Legislative Palace, site of the National Assembly until the 1968 coup. The building across from the Palace had a huge sign in five languages, "What country of the world can bear the humiliation of a foreign flag piercing its heart?" Torrijos launched the gathering by attacking U.S. interference in Latin America and supporting Latin American nations that attempted to assert their own rights and sovereignty. It was obvious that he meant to embarrass the United States and promote sympathy for Panama. Torrijos wondered–out loud–how the U.S., the champion of democracy and critic of colonialism, could maintain a colony in the heart of Panama. Torrijos asked the Security Council:

> Could it be moral to deny to a country natural advantages that were inherent and inalienable, purely and simply because the claim to them came from a weak nation? In what legal dictionary was there set forth the concept of perpetuity as the basis for negotiations? Panama had never been, was not and never would be a colony or a protectorate, nor would it add one more star to the United States flag.[29]

Only Great Britain's Sir Colin Crowe sympathized with the U.S. position.

On 19 March 1973, Panama and Peru introduced a resolution that called on both Panama and the United States to conclude a series of agreements, all of which favoured Panama. John Scali, Bush's successor as U.S. Ambassador to the UN, outlined the U.S. position the following day. Scali admitted that the 1903 treaty should be replaced, that the new treaty should have a fixed duration, that Panama should have greater control of the Canal Zone, and that Panama deserved a greater portion of the canal revenues than it was currently receiving.[30] Scali also emphasized that the U.S. wanted to conclude a treaty promptly. However, the U.S. must remain responsible for the operation and defence of the Canal Zone.

In the course of his speech, Scali made a tactical error. He spoke of what the U.S. had contributed to Latin America, and this offended Latin American delegates and observers. Tack exploited this mistake and used it to nullify any gains which Scali might have made. Yes, Tack agreed. Americans had invested in Latin America, but they did not do so from a spirit of generosity. They had reaped profits. Tack continued, "The trend was clear: not to allow the complete development of Latin America in order to maintain it as a source of supply of raw materials or of cheap labor force."[31] Tack then claimed that bilateral U.S.-Panamanian talks had accomplished little because the U.S. government had no intention of abandoning either perpetuity or its military rights.[32]

Eight non-permanent members of the Security Council supported the Panama-Peru resolution. Backed by Guinea, India, Indonesia, Kenya, Sudan, and Yugoslavia, it called for the abrogation of the 1903 treaty and its replacement by one which would respect Panama's sovereignty. The resolution did not acknowledge U.S. responsibility for nor its right to continue the operation or defence of the canal.[33] Scali cast the third U.S. veto in the history of the Security Council. No other country voted negatively, while thirteen voted in favour of the resolution and the United Kingdom abstained.

The Security Council meeting in Panama won the attention of Capitol Hill, where a critic assailed it as a Communist plot "engineered by Castro and backed by Moscow and Peking."[34] Kissinger feared for U.S. prestige.[35] Torrijos had effectively created his "problem." On 3 May 1973, Nixon made his only public statement about the canal situation. He told Congress:

Another important unresolved problem concerns the Panama Canal and the surrounding Zone. U.S. operation of the Canal and our presence in Panama is governed by the terms of a treaty drafted in 1903. The world has changed radically during the 70 years this treaty has been in effect. Latin America has changed. Panama has changed. And the terms of our relationship should reflect those changes in a reasonable way.

For the past nine years, efforts to work out a new treaty acceptable to both parties have failed. That failure has put considerable strain
on our relations with Panama. It is time for both parties to take a fresh
look at this problem and to develop a new relationship between us—one
that will guarantee continued effective operation of the Canal while
meeting Panama's legitimate aspirations.[36]

Nixon said that Secretary of State Rogers would go to Latin America for a
series of meetings with Latin American leaders, and he said that he personally
would make at least one visit.[37]

Torrijos saw this as an opportunity for progress. Not only had Panama at-
tracted high level attention, but the President of the United States was speaking
publicly of compromise. Directed by Torrijos, Tack developed a set of eight principles to guide the talks:

1. The 1903 treaty must be abrogated.
2. A new treaty must have a fixed termination date.
3. U.S. jurisdiction in any part of Panama should end.
4. The United States could use land and water areas necessary to operate and
maintain the Canal and to protect vital installations.
5. Panama must receive "a just and equitable share" in Canal benefits.
6. U.S. government activities should be limited to operating, maintaining,
and protecting the Canal.
7. Military operations could be only those "expressly stipulated in the
treaty."
8. The United States would have the right to build a sea-level canal if (i) the
U.S. decision was made within "a reasonable period"; (ii) Panama retained
full jurisdiction in the new canal area; and (iii) a sea-level canal treaty also
had a fixed final date.[38]

Rogers was interested, but the Watergate scandal intervened. In order to
augment his administration's prestige and credibility, Nixon wanted to appoint
Kissinger as Secretary of State. Rogers and Anderson resigned. Ellsworth Bunker,
previously U.S. Ambassador to South Vietnam, replaced Anderson. On 23 November 1973, Bunker arrived in Panama City for renewed talks. The Panamanians flew him to the resort island of Contadora for a series of parties and
day-long cruises. This approach fostered an atmosphere of friendship and cooperation, and Bunker was able to arrange a few minor modifications to the Tack
principles. The 1903 treaty would remain in force until a new treaty replaced it.

The new treaty would allow a continued U.S. military presence after the termination date, and Panama would have a more equitable share of Canal profits, even if not proportionate to total U.S. and world revenues.[39]

On 7 February 1974, Kissinger flew to Panama to sign the new set of principles which Tack and Bunker had negotiated. He expressed optimism that an accord was possible.[40] However, another serious obstacle surfaced. What U.S. negotiators termed "residual defense rights" appeared to Tack as "perpetuity." Both parties agreed that U.S. defence rights would end with the treaty "unless the two parties agree otherwise through negotiations to be held five years before the expiration of the treaty."[41]

Another contentious issue of the Nixon presidency was the neutrality of the Canal. The U.S. delegates wanted neutrality enforced by both the United States and Panama. The Panamanians were willing to accept a U.S. presence, but they also wanted an international guarantee through the United Nations. While personally understanding, Bunker realized that Congress would never accept a UN guarantee, and he presented a compromise. Panama and the United States would ensure neutrality of the Canal and would "make efforts that such neutrality is recognized and guaranteed by all nations."[42]

Torrijos had been a brilliant strategic, able to win concessions from even the hard line Nixon administration. His government had embarrassed the United States in both Addis Ababa and Panama City, then provided a face-saving solution: the Tack-Kissinger principles. The Tack-Kissinger principles established a Panamanian agenda at the bargaining table. This time, President Ford would inherit a promising hand.

With Ford in the White House, Torrijos continued his strategy to win international support. In some respects the challenge had become more formidable, because Ford had to consider a major anti-treaty force led by presidential hopeful Ronald Reagan and various members of Congress.[43] Moreover, the State Department lacked consensus on the direction of the negotiations, and Ford and Kissinger made conflicting statements. Without the Panamanian government's vigorous campaign and—ironically—Reagan's use of the issue throughout the 1976 Republican primaries, it would have been tempting to relegate Panama to the back burner.

Despite reassurances from Kissinger and Ambassador Jorden that the U.S. would stay the course, Torrijos was skeptical. Unwilling to wait for Ford to make the first move, Torrijos took yet another initiative. He decided to gain U.S.

attention by establishing diplomatic relations with Fidel Castro's Cuba.[44] Another irony was that the Torrijos government's first involvement with revolutionary Cuba came at the request of the United States. Cuba's navy had seized two ships registered in Panama but owned by Americans, the *Lyla Express* and the *Johnny Express*. The Cuban-born captain of the *Johnny Express*, José Villa, was wounded and taken prisoner. Washington denounced the Cuban action and asked the Swiss Embassy, which had represented U.S. interests in Cuba since 1961, to demand the return of the vessels and their crews, but the Cuban government refused the demand. It claimed that the *Lyla Express* and the *Johnny Express* were pirate ships engaged in counter-revolutionary operations. Castro also claimed that Villa admitted to being a CIA agent.[45]

Given the stalemate, the Nixon administration asked the Panamanian government for assistance in the release of the vessels and their crews. Torrijos sent Rómulo Escobar, the left-wing rector of the University of Panama, to talk to Castro. The two men talked for hours, but the *Lyla Express* and the *Johnny Express*, along with their crews, remained in captivity. Dissatisfied with Escobar, the U.S. government asked Torrijos to send someone else, and Torrijos sent his intelligence chief, Colonel Manuel Noriega. Noriega's effort was successful. Cuban authorities released the two vessels and transferred Captain Villa to a Panamanian prison for a face-saving period of time.[46]

On 20 1974, Ford's twelfth day as President, the Panamanian government announced its decision to re-establish diplomatic relations with Cuba. Ambassador Jorden tried to dissuade Torrijos with the argument that if any OAS members were to recognize Castro's government, all should do so simultaneously. Torrijos observed that many had already done so and saw no reason why Panama could not do likewise. Indeed, he suggested, even the U.S. would do so if it saw any benefits. Jorden responded that the reopening of a Panamanian Embassy in Havana would strengthen the hand of those Americans who saw Torrijos as a leftist, and the Canal Treaty negotiations would encounter new difficulties. Torrijos agreed but responded:

> Your people have to understand that we are independent, that we have minds of our own, and that we can go in more than one direction. The only kind of friends worth having are those that stand on their own feet, not those who kneel before you to your face, and curse you behind your back.[47]

Torrijos pre-empted another problem—political glory versus alienation of the Panamanian business and investor community. The solution was to send to Cuba a huge delegation with representation from all sectors of Panamanian society. The free market advocate, Nicolas Barletta, Minister of Economic Planning, led the group, while the presence of Escobar and a few other socialists would appease the left. In this way, Torrijos could send a message to the Ford administration, avoid allegations of being too left-wing, and satisfy Panamanian socialists.

Initial reaction from Washington was negative. Kissinger and the State Department were furious, while opponents of any new Canal Treaty viewed Torrijos's actions as confirmation of his leftist sympathies and agenda. Ambassadors Bunker and Jorden found themselves answering a barrage of questions instead of negotiating a treaty. The Ford administration delayed loans to Panama and minimized diplomatic communication.[48] Happily, it was clear by October that Torrijos was not Castro's puppet, and was spending more time dealing with Panamanian and foreign business groups and bankers than with Cubans. On 28 October 1974, U.S. diplomats returned to Panama for talks, again on Contadora.

Timing and control were the key issues. In earlier talks, Panamanian delegates had demanded jurisdiction over the Canal Zone within five years, while their U.S. counterparts wanted at least fifty. At Contadora, Bunker said that the U.S. was willing to return jurisdiction but not operation of the Canal nor responsibility for its defence within the five year period. Moreover, the treaty would terminate the Canal Zone government, and a Panamanian could fill a new position of counsellor to the President of the Canal Company, an appointee of the U.S. government. The Panamanian negotiating team was happily stunned. Ambassador Nicolas González-Revilla told the Americans, "Look, you've broken the back of the negotiations. This is the treaty."[49]

Yet, complications remained. Despite a Status of Forces Agreement, completed by March 1975, problems between the U.S. negotiating team and the Pentagon caused delays. The American negotiators had offered to double the annuity paid to Panama from $5 million to $10 million and grant another $1 million to Panama's National Guard. Torrijos found this much too little and relegated the price to the back burner.[50] Then, differences between the Pentagon and the State Department led to the collapse of the talks. The Pentagon argued that the negotiating team was offering to transfer too much of the Canal Zone to Panama, thereby jeopardizing its ability to defend the Canal. A Pentagon official explained:

We were being driven out of Southeast Asia. When Saigon fell, the attitude tightened considerably at the Department [of Defense]. A lot of men said, "Why give away something you already have?"[51]

The breakdown of the bilateral talks convinced Torrijos to renew his campaign to internationalize the Canal conflict and maintain global pressure on the United States. He met the Presidents of Colombia, Costa Rica, and Venezuela, and the four Heads of State wrote a "Declaration of Panama" which called for prompt and fair negotiations for the return of the Canal Zone to Panama.[52] When most U.S. media ignored the Declaration, the Presidents published it as a paid advertisement in the *New York Times* of 10 April 1975. The advertisement noted rights that Colombia, Costa Rica, and Venezuela would receive under a new treaty as a reminder that the conflict did not concern only the United States and Panama but other countries as well. Included were speeches from Torrijos and the presidents of the other three countries. The presidents also wrote a letter to President Ford. The OAS adopted a resolution calling for a prompt conclusion to Canal negotiations along the lines of the Tack-Kissinger principles.[53]

This time, changed conditions in Washington lessened the impact of international pressure. During Nixon's time in the White House, the problem had been a disagreeable President of the United States. During Ford's presidency, the primary reason for the stalled talks was the Ford administration's battles with Congress and the Pentagon. On 26 June 1975, the House of Representatives debated a $7.2 billion appropriations bill to the State, Justice, and Commerce Departments for the following fifteen months. Representative Gene Snyder (Republican-Kentucky) proposed an amendment to the bill that would prohibit the use of any funds "to negotiate the surrender of relinquishment of United States rights in the Panama Canal Zone."[54] Snyder argued that there was a conspiracy among Omar Torrijos, Fidel Castro, and the *Front de Libération Québecoise*–a terrorist group which Prime Minister Trudeau had effectively smashed after two high profile kidnappings in 1970. According to Snyder, Castro was masterminding a conspiracy whereby the FLQ would capture the St. Lawrence Seaway and Torrijos would grab the Canal Zone.[55] The Amendment carried 246:164, but the Senate rejected it on the grounds that it was inappropriate or unconstitutional to limit the President's ability to conduct foreign relations. The Senate sent the bill back to the House without the Snyder Amendment, and this time it passed.[56]

With that situation in the United States, Torrijos was fully aware that he must maintain pressure on the Ford White House if he were to prevent the administration from yielding to Congressional critics and the Reagan wing of the Republican Party. Pressure would have to come from third countries. Torrijos's next contact was Mexican President Luis Echevarria (1970-1976), whom he met in the Mexican town of Agua Azul. There the two leaders issued a joint statement which urged the United States to transfer the Canal to Panamanian control. Echeverria also confirmed that Mexico recognized Panama's sovereignty over the Canal Zone.[57] A few days later, both the retiring and incoming Secretaries General of the OAS called upon the United States to resolve the Panama problem as quickly as possible and to respect Panamanian sovereignty.[58]

Behind the scenes, the Ford administration was seeking an escape from the entire issue. The Assistant Secretary of State for International Affairs, William D. Rogers, asked Ambassador Jorden what would happen if (i) there was no treaty; (ii) Panamanian and U.S. negotiators could agree on a draft treaty which the administration did not hurry to submit to the Senate for approval; (iii) the draft treaty went to the Senate but the Senate delayed action. Jorden replied:

> If we fail to get a treaty, the sands rapidly run out and we face confrontation, demonstrations, and probably worse. With a treaty in hand that is not submitted to the Congress, I reckon we get 6 to 8 months, during which I believe there are things we can do to further extend the deadline. If we got a treaty, put it into the Senate and that body—in its wisdom—decided to hold off on any action, I think the leadership here can neutralize and channel the extremists' threats and activities until early 1977. If nothing happens then, batten down the hatches, fasten the seatbelts, and stay away from outside windows.[59]

Torrijos further underlined Jorden's point in a two hour interview which he granted the *New York Times* 24 July 1975. Torrijos warned that further delays in the negotiations would surely lead to violence in Panama. Addressing the possibility of violence the General said, "Two courses of action would be open to me: to smash it or to lead it. I am not going to smash it."[60] Ford faced a dilemma. Failure to negotiate seriously would probably lead to renewed violence. Successful negotiations would jeopardize not only his hopes for a second term but his presidential candidacy as the Republican nominee in 1976.

What Ford *could* try to do was help to end the dispute between the State Department and the Pentagon. A meeting of the National Security Council 9 August 1975 resolved this division with DSDM #302. NSDM #302 modified and supplemented NSDMs #s 115 and 131 from the Nixon administration, which remained in effect. President Ford ordered the negotiating team to separate the duration issue into operation of the Canal and defence of the Canal. The negotiators could still attempt to achieve the longest treaty life possible with a minimum 40-50 year defence duration but with operational rights to terminate no earlier than 31 December 1999.[61]

Other issues covered were Canal expansion, land and waters, negotiation process, the resumption of negotiations, and the creation of a favourable national environment for treaty ratification. A sea level Canal was no longer a serious consideration, but U.S. negotiators were to acquire first rights to build one. The land and waters issue would revert to the position of 18 January 1975, with limited room for compromise. Ford also ordered the negotiators to "seek to obtain Panama's agreement that the negotiations will remain confidential so that the Panama Canal issue will not be injected into the domestic political process in the United States in 1976."[62] Ford had accepted Rogers' second option: "negotiate but [do] not submit the treaty to Senate."

When bilateral treaty talks resumed in September 1975, there was no progress. Bunker proposed a package with four parts: (i) on the future of the Canal; (ii) on Canal neutrality; (iii) on a treaty about Canal defence; and (iv) on the Status of Forces Agreement. The treaty provided for a 25-year duration, exclusive U.S. rights to Canal expansion or the building of a sea-level Canal, and the already agreed upon Status of Forces Agreement that included U.S. Canal Company employees. The Republic of Panama would receive 27 cents for every ton of cargo to transit the Canal, an estimated $35 million each year.

The most contentious issue was Canal defence. The U.S. sought to guarantee the neutrality of the Canal for its lifetime. Unless both parties agreed, only the United States and Panama could maintain forces in Panama. Worst of all from a Panamanian standpoint was the 50-year defence right for the United States with a provision to extend the military presence even longer.[63] The Panamanian government rejected this U.S. proposal, and Tack charged that the American negotiators were trying to disguise "perpetuity." The talks collapsed.

Neither Ford nor Torrijos benefited from the breakdown. In an interview with reporters in Knoxville, Tennessee 7 October 1975, Ford received his first public question about Canal negotiations. What Ford had most feared was coming true; Canal negotiations had become a campaign issue.[64] For his part,

Torrijos was losing support among university students, known to be impatient. A mob of 600 to 800 students assaulted the U.S. Embassy to protest both the American presence in the Canal Zone and displeasure with the Torrijos government.[65] Indeed, cynicism among the Panamanian public at large seemed to be on the rise. One Panamanian office worker told a *New York Times* reporter:

> The [Panamanian] Government keeps promising there will be a new treaty in a month or two, but nothing happens. I don't have any faith in the negotiations. I don't think the Americans will ever leave Panama.[66]

Nevertheless, a new round of negotiations commenced in November 1975, but it too proved as fruitless as the last. On 20 November, Panamanian frustration came to a head. Tack accused the U.S. team of deviating from the Tack-Kissinger Principles and said that the U.S. position "offer[ed] no possible basis for negotiations."[67] Tack argued that U.S. insistence on defence rights was irrational. He reminded the Americans that their forces would be useless against sabotage or a missile attack. The Panamanian Foreign Minister suggested that the real purpose of the U.S. military presence would be to control Panamanians. Upset, Tack left the talks without informing the Americans to attend Franco's funeral in Spain. This appeared a deliberate slap in the face.[68]

Bunker understood the Panamanian frustration and did not abandon the round of talks. Rather, he presented the best option allowed by NSDM #302. He reduced the duration offer on the defence treaty from 50 years to 40 and proposed that the transfer of control could occur 31 December 1999, instead of 25 years into the future. He also dropped residual defence rights.[69] This was not what the Panamanians wanted, but it did represent progress. Tack thought that he could persuade the Americans to terminate defence rights as well by the end of the century, and that was the Panamanian objective at a secret round of talks 17 December 1975.[70] The effort, unfortunately, was in vain because NSDM #302 restricted what the U.S. team could accept.

Negative publicity surrounding the bilateral talks contributed to the rise of the Panama Canal lobby, which included an ex-naval captain, a retired ambassador, a Florida real-estate developer, a presidential candidate (Reagan), members of the House of Representatives, Senators, and 100,000 others. Although lacking in organization, members compensated with intense campaign rhetoric. Residents of the Canal Zone pressured their home state Representatives, Senators, and Governors, and encouraged relatives to do likewise. One of the lobby's bumper stickers read,

"Don't give Panama our Canal: Give them Kissinger instead!" The anti-treaty forces played the Soviet card. They portrayed Torrijos as a Communist and the negotiations as a Soviet plot to gain control of the Canal. They suggested that the return of the Canal to Panama would set a precedent for Mexico to demand the return of the Gadsden Purchase (land in southern New Mexico and Arizona acquired in the 1850s) and for the Soviet Union to demand Alaska.[71]

In December 1975, lobbyist and presidential candidate Ronald Reagan met Arnulfo Arias, still in exile after his dismissal from Panama's presidency seven years earlier.[72] During his brief third presidency, Arias had demanded "the immediate return of the Zone to Panamanian jurisdiction."[73] Yet, it appears that Reagan and Arias managed to reach an agreement. Reagan would support an attempt by Arias to regain his position as President of Panama, and Arias would accept a "softer" Canal treaty.[74] Given Arias's track record, it does appear that ambition trumped principles.

On 21 January 1976, the U.S. government received a communiqué from the government of Panama. The communiqué said that "a vast conspiracy against the revolutionary government [that of Torrijos] was dismantled" by the G-2 [intelligence] section of the National Guard.[75] The conspirators sought to overthrow the Torrijos regime and restore Arnulfo Arias. Torrijos claimed:

> The existing proof demonstrates that all public and private actions sponsored by this group have international roots which link them to displaced politicians who have found encouragement in a U.S. Presidential candidate [Reagan] in exchange for antipatriotic concessions in the discussion of a new Panama Canal treaty.[76]

Reagan campaigned on the Canal issue throughout the Republican primaries, accusing the Ford administration of deceiving the American public and of negotiating a secret formula to give Panama the Canal.[77] In so doing, Reagan nullified any hope of agreement on a draft treaty before the elections, antagonized Torrijos and the Panamanian negotiators, and brought the issue more forcibly than ever to the attention of the U.S. electorate.

As the Republican primaries continued, the Canal negotiations became less and less meaningful. On 1 April 1976, Tack resigned as chief negotiator for personal reasons. Boyd, Panama's Ambassador to the United Nations, replaced him. The departure of Tack was probably the factor which made Torrijos realize that there could be no treaty until the U.S. presidential elections had taken place.[78] He also realized that Panamanians needed to be patient; negotiations were close to success. A *New York Times* article of 11 April 1976 reported that he had made a deal with Panamanian students and workers. There would be no violence unless negotiations broke down. "We have set 1977 as the goal," the *New York Times* quoted Torrijos. "Patience has its limits."

The Carter administration built on the foundations laid by Ford, Kissinger, and their negotiators, and in 1977 managed to conclude two handover treaties with Omar Torrijos. President Carter's memoirs indicate the importance of President Ford to winning Senate approval in 1978 so that the treaties could take effect and the handover take place in a well organized, orderly fashion 31 December 1999. In view of the Constitutional requirement that two-thirds of the Senators must approve any treaty, bipartisan support was vital, and former President Ford lobbied Republican Senators.[79] Enough responded favourably that the Canal continued to operate smoothly and the United States managed to avoid guerrilla warfare against Panamanian insurgents. Both the 38th President (Ford) and the 39th President (Carter) deserve credit.

There have been blips since 1978, not an uninterrupted triumphal procession. In 1989, the *real* ruler of Panama, National Guard leader Manuel Noriega (the man who had gone to Cuba in 1972 at the behest of the Nixon administration), called elections. President George H.W. Bush anticipated fraud and asked former presidents Ford and Carter to go to Panama to monitor developments. Almost all international observers, including Ford and Carter, agreed that the successful candidate was Guillermo Endara. Noriega thereupon annulled the elections and continued to govern.[80] In December and January, the first President Bush sent forces to invade Panama, capture Noriega, and take him to trial for violations of Florida law. Convicted, Noriega remains a prisoner in Florida to this day. Despite the dubious legality of the invasion, the loss of the lives of an estimated 500 to 1000 Panamanian civilians, and the destruction of the homes of some 10,000-18,000 other Panamanians,[81] Operation Just Cause—as Bush called it—restored democracy to Panama and undoubtedly created a more stable environment for the handover. President-elect Endara took his oath of office and reintroduced the constitutional government which had been lacking since 1968. At the time of the handover in 1999, Mireya Moscoso, widow of Arnulfo Arias, was beginning a five-year term as Panama's first female President. Her successor was Martin Torrijos, son of Omar, winner of the presidential election of 2004. Meanwhile, those who died in the 1964 riots have become martyrs, 4th of July Avenue has become Avenida de los Martires (Avenue of the Martyrs), and the occasion of those riots has become a statutory holiday.

Notes

1. The sections of this chapter which deal with the treaty negotiations during the Nixon and Ford administrations are extracts from the Honours Essay (thesis) of Laurentian University student Christopher Bartman, "A Blueprint for Successful Negotiations with the United States: U.S.-Panamanian Negotiations, 1971-1977," 1995-1996. Mount and Gauthier are also grateful to Laurentian University student Tim Greenough, who as this manuscript was going to press was writing an Honours Essay on the Ford administration's Panama policies and who had access to more recently declassified documents at the GFPL.

2. Graeme S. Mount, "Isthmian Approaches: The Contextual Trajectory of Canadian-Panamanian Relations," *Caribbean Studies*, XX, 2 (June 1980), pp. 49-60.

3. Three classics are Walter Lafeber, *The Panama Canal: The Crisis in Historical Perspective* (New York: Oxford University Press, 1978); John Major, *Prize Possession: The United States and the Panama Canal, 1903-1979* (Cambridge: Cambridge University Press, 1979); and David G. McCullough, *The Path Between the Seas: The Creation of the Panama Canal, 1870-1914* (New York: Simon & Schuster, 1977). Perhaps the most succinct and yet complete rendition of U.S.-Panamanian relations until 1964 is that provided by Alex McPherson, *Yankee No! Anti-Americanism in U.S.-Latin American Relations* (Cambridge, Mass.: Harvard University Press, 2003), pp. 77-116. See also Michael Conniff, *Panama and the United States: The Forced Alliance* (Athens: University of Georgia Press, 1992).

4. Philippe Bunau-Varilla wrote two sets of memoirs, first published in French and subsequently translated into English: *Panama: The Creation, the Destruction, the Resurrection* (1914); and *From Panama to Verdun: My Exploits for France* (1940).

5. John Gunther, *Inside Latin America* (New York: Harper and Brothers, 1941), p. 152.

6. Figures vary, but these are the ones which appeared in the Panamanian press during the 1968 election campaign.

7. A recording of the conversation, dated 1/10/64—11:40 a.m., is available in collection WH6401.28, PNO 10, at the Lyndon Baines Johnson Archives, Austin, Texas.

8. Mount was in Panama at the time of the 1968 presidential election. Apart from personal observations, Panamanian newspapers served as sources on the election and its aftermath: *El Estrella, La Hora, El Mundo, Panama América,* and the *Star and Herald*.

9. A summary of Arias's language laws appears in a letter from Attorney-General Ricardo Adolfo de la Guardia, Panama City to all provincial governors, 16 October 1940, Collection of Arnulfo Arias's first term (1940-1941), Box 6, Archivos Nacionales de Panamá. Cited hereafter as ANP.

10. A summary of Arias's immigration laws appears in a letter from the Japanese legation in Panama City to Arias, 23 Oct. 1940, Box 10, File 1, ANP.

11. As a medical doctor, Arnulfo Arias was interested in public health issues and created the Panamanian Red Cross, to be led by his wife. In January 1941, Luis de la Barra Lastarria represented Panama at the 4th Inter-American Congress of the Red Cross, which met in Santiago, Chile. There he went out of his way to sponsor a resolution which by implication praised Franco's government. It wished for "el completo reestabliciemiento de la noble España de que heredemos la sangre" (the complete re-establishment of noble Spain, from which we inherit our blood). Box 1, File 1: Ministerio de Trabajo, Provisión Social, y Salud Pública, ANP.

12. Harmodio Arias to several cabinet ministers, 31 July 1941, Box 5, File 3, ANP.

13. Details of Ambassador Wilson's talks with Harmodio Arias and the other conspirators are available in the Department of State collection, R.G. 59, Series 819.000, Box 3728, at the U.S. Archives, College Park, Maryland.

14. Davis, Panama, to the Department of State, Washington, 25 Nov. 1949, *Foreign Relations of the United States (FRUS)*, 1949, Vol. II, pp. 722-725; and Davis to the Department of State, 25 Nov. 1949–9 p.m., *FRUS, 1949*, II, pp. 725-727. The word "cynical" appears in the second despatch.

15. Memorandum by the Acting Officer in Charge of the Division of Central America and Panama Affairs ([Murray M.] Wise), to the Assistant Secretary of State for Inter-American Affairs ([Edward G.] Miller), 28 Nov. 1949, *FRUS, 1949*, II, p. 729.

16. Davis, Panama, to the Secretary of State, 3 Dec. 1949, *FRUS, 1949*, II, p. 735.

17. Richard Nixon, *The Memoirs of Richard Nixon* (New York: Filmways Company Publishers, 1978). There is no mention of Panama or he Canal conflict anywhere in Nixon's memoirs. See also the memoirs of Henry Kissinger for Nixon's first term, *White House Years* (Boston: Little, Brown, and Company, 1979), where coverage of Chile and Cuba is extensive but Panama does not appear in the index.

18. William J. Jorden, *Panama Odyssey* (Austin: University of Texas Pres, 1984), pp. 175-176.

19. Jorden, p. 154.

20. National Security Decision Memorandum (NSDM) #64, 5 June 1970, *Presidential Directives on National Security: From Truman to Clinton* (Washington, DC: National Security Archive, 1993).

21. NSDM #64.

22. Jorden, pp. 156-158.

23. Quoted from Jorden, pp. 161-162.

24. NSDM #131, 13 Sept. 1971, *Presidential Directives*.

25. *UN Monthly Chronicle* (United Nations Office of Public Information, March 1972), p. 23.

26. *UN Monthly Chronicle* (March 1972), p. 28.

27. Jorden, pp. 173-174, 184.

28. Richard Severo,, "UN Panel Sits in Panama Today: Torrijos Asks Moral Backing of World on Canal Issues," *New York Times*, 15 March 1973, p. 16.

29. *UN Chronicle* (April 1973), p. 17.

30. U.S. Vetoes UN Security Council Resolution on Panama Canal Treaty Negotiations," *Department of State Bulletin* (23 April 1973), p. 494.

31. *UN Chronicle* (April 1973), p. 50.

32. *UN Chronicle* (April 1973), p. 50.

33. UN doc. S/10931/Rev.1; reprinted in *Department of State Bulletin* (23 April 1073), p. 497.

34. Jorden, p. 197.

35. Jorden, p. 198.

36. Richard Nixon, "Fourth Annual Report to the Congress on United States Foreign Policy, May 3, 1973," *Public Papers of the Presidents: Richard Nixon, 1973* (Washington: United States Government Printing Office, 1975), p. 443.

37. *Ibid.*

38. Reproduced from Jorden, p. 204.

39. Jorden, pp. 216, 695-696.

40. Henry Kissinger, "U.S. and Panama Agee on Principles for Negotiation of New Panama Canal Treaty," *Department of State Bulletin* (25 Feb. 1974), p. 182.

41. Jorden, p. 253.

42. Jorden, p. 253.

43. Ford, pp. 374, 375, 380.

44. Jorden, pp. 253-254, 256.

45. "Freighter is Reported Attacked and Seized by Cuban Gunboat," *New York Times*, 16 Dec. 1971, pp. 1 and 25; Tad Szulc, "U.S. Warns Cuba on Ship Attacks," *New York Times*, 18 Dec. 1971, pp. 1 and 15; "Castro Says Freighter Captain Admits Being Agent for CIA," *New York Times*, 23 Dec. 1971, p. 5.

46. Jorden, p. 257.

47. Jorden, p. 259.

48. Jorden, pp. 260-261.

49. Jorden, p. 263.

50. Jorden, pp. 265-274.

51. National Security Council Policy Review Memorandum-1 related: Panama, *Presidential Directives*, tab 9, p. 12. The quotation comes from the *New York Times* of a much later date, 16 Sept. 1975, p. 11.

52. The *New York Times*, 26 March 1975, p. 24.

53. OAS doc, AG/RES. 174 (V-0/75), "Negotiations between the Governments of Panama and the United States of America on the Question of the Panama Canal," *Department of State Bulletin* (23 June 1975), pp. 882-883.

54. The *New York Times*, 27 June 1975, p. 7.

55. Jorden, p. 282.

56. Lafeber, 186-189.

57. The *New York Times*, 6 July 1975.

58. The *New York Times*, 8 July 1975.

59. Jorden, p. 285.

60. The *New York Times*, 28 July 1975, p. 3.

61. Gerald R. Ford, National Security Decision Memorandum #302, *Presidential Directives*, p. 1.

62. *Ibid.*, pp. 2-3.

63. Jorden, p. 304.

64. "Interview with Reporters in Knoxville, Tennessee, October 7, 1975," *Public Papers of the Presidents: Gerald R. Ford, 1975* (Washington: United States Government Printing Office, 1977), p.1614; NSDM #302, p. 3.

65. The *New York Times*, 25 Sept. 1975, p. 3.

66. The *New York Times*, 8 Oct. 1975, p. 2.

67. Jorden, p. 306.

68. Jorden, p. 307.

69. Jorden, p. 308.

70. Jorden, p. 309.

71. The *New York Times*, 5 November 1975, pp. 1 and 10.

72. Stephen Low to Brent Scowcroft, "Memorandum: National Security Council Information, December 16, 1975," White House Central File: Country File, Box 40, Folder #117 (Panama), GFPL.

73. Kissinger, *Years of Renewal*, p. 712.

74. The *New York Times*, 14 Dec. 1975, p. 54.

75. Panamanian communiqué, 21 Jan. 1976, White House Central File: Country File, Box 40, Folder #117 (Panama), GFPL.

76. Panamanian communiqué, White House Central File: Country File, Box 40, Folder #117 (Panama), GFPL.

77. The *New York Times*, 3 March 1976, p. 34.

78. The *New York Times*, 2 April 1976, p. 3; and 19 Sept. 1976, p. 16.

79. Jimmy Carter, *Keeping Faith: Memoirs of a President* (Toronto: Bantam, 1982), pp. 159 and 165.

80. The role of former Presidents Ford and Carter in monitoring the Panamanian election of May 1989 appears on a tableau in the Gerald Ford Presidential Museum, Grand Rapids, Michigan.

81. Stephen J. Randall and Graeme S. Mount, *The Caribbean Basin: An International History* (London and New York: Routledge, 1998), p. 162.

Chapter Fourteen

ARGENTINA ENTERS A NEW DARK AGE[1]

Argentine gets 640 years for atrocities." On 20 April 2005, the *Globe and Mail* appended that headline to a story by Giles Tremlett, datelined Madrid. The report dealt with the verdict of a Spanish court which sentenced Captain Adolfo Scilingo, age 58, of tossing 30 political prisoners from aircraft over the Atlantic at a height of 4,000 meters. Scilingo himself confessed that over a period of two years, as many as twenty prisoners at a time left aircraft drugged and naked under such circumstances. Tremlett also mentioned what Argentine naval officers labeled "barbecues," occasions when Argentine naval officers used electric shocks to burn the flesh of their victims. Henry Kissinger might not have known precisely what was happening at the Naval Mechanical School in Buenos Aires, but recently declassified documents indicate that he was aware of uncivilized behaviour and that he did not object. What concerns he had were not for the well being of the victims but for the way publicity might affect U.S. government support for Argentina's military government.

In 1973, former Argentine President Juan Perón returned from almost two decades of exile in Franco's Spain. His first presidency had been highly controversial, involving the granting of hospitality to fugitives from the Third Reich, developing economic policies which arguably contributed to economic instability, and fighting with the Roman Catholic Church. However, he remained popular, and when he returned, the sitting president, Héctor J. Cámpora, resigned so that new elections could take place. Perón won decisively, along with his wife Isabel, who was his Vice-Presidential running mate. When Perón died in July 1974, Isabel became President of Argentina.

Chaos followed. Isabel had no administrative experience, and Juan himself had always had a polarizing effect. More than 1000 died in political violence in

1975, and politically motivated kidnappings became another unpleasant reality. In March 1976, the Argentine military—for almost half a century the arbiters of Argentine political life—deposed Señora Perón and created a three-man junta. General Jorge Rafael Videla, the head of the triumvirate, became head of state. The State Department had advance notice that the coup might take place, but it appears to have decided to let matters take their course. The Assistant Secretary of State for Inter-American Affairs, William D. Rogers, simply expressed the hope that the new government would be friendly to the United States.[2] Perhaps someone made a calculated decision that Isabel Perón's government did not deserve to survive. Perhaps the conventional wisdom in Washington was that its influence in Argentina was too weak to risk for a lost cause.

Like its opponents in the street, the junta played rough, but Henry Kissinger quickly decided that rough play from the military government was preferable to chaos, the most probable alternative. Professional diplomats at the State Department, however, were somewhat more sensitive to the suffering of innocent people. The first reaction of the U.S. Ambassador in Buenos Aires, Robert Hill, was enthusiastic support for the security measures of the new military government.[3] Nevertheless, the Latin American Bureau at the State Department instructed Hill to protest against "escalating death squad operations, disappearances and reports of torture." Kissinger was furious.[4] This was no fluke. On 3 June, Kissinger was preparing for a conference of the Organization of American States (OAS) in Santiago. William Rogers raised the possibility that while speaking to the Chilean president, General Pinochet, Kissinger might say something about human rights. "I am not on the same wavelength with you guys about this business," said the Secretary of State. "I just am not eager to overthrow these guys." When he met Pinochet face to face a few days later, Kissinger assured him that he had the support of the Ford administration. "I think that the previous government [Allende's] was headed toward Communism," he told Pinochet. "We wish your government well."[5] (See Chapter Eleven.) When he met the Argentine Foreign Minister, Admiral César Augusto Guzzetti, 10 June 1976 at that same OAS gathering in Santiago, Chile, Kissinger said, "If there are things that have to be done, you should do them quickly. But you should get back quickly to normal procedures." Kissinger said that he understood the need for drastic action at a time "when political, criminal, and terrorist activities tend to merge," but that other Americans did not. Hence, whatever had to be done should be done quickly.[6]

According to Washington's National Security Archive, the day before Kissinger's meeting with Guzzetti, Argentine secret police had raided the offices of the Catholic Commission for Refugees in Buenos Aires and removed documents. The day after the meeting, an Argentine-Chilean-Uruguayan "squadron" kidnaped and tortured twenty-four Chilean and Uruguayan refugees, who had been escaping from *their* military governments. Under the name "Operation Condor," the military governments of Argentina, Bolivia, Brazil, Chile, Paraguay, and Uruguay coordinated efforts against dissidents.[7] By 31 December 1976, the estimated death toll included 10,000 Argentines.[8]

Kissinger was aware of the situation, for as early as 6 April that year, Ambassador Hill had notified him from Buenos Aires that human rights violations were becoming more numerous.[9] By 11 May, Hill was losing faith in the junta, lamenting "that what had begun so well [the military government] was running the risk of being ruined." Hard line officers were more becoming influential than the "moderate" Videla.[10] On 25 May, Hill told Ricardo Yofre, General Under Secretary at the Office of the President in Buenos Aires, that the United States was "very worried" about human rights. Yofre responded that Videla and his associates were more worried about kidnapings.[11]

On 17 July 1976, Harry W. Shlaudeman, Assistant Secretary for Latin America, notified Kissinger that Argentine authorities had arrested some 5,000 Argentines and foreigners. Hundreds had been killed, he said.[12] On 21 July, Kissinger noted that hundreds had been killed, but he blamed the deaths on the weakness, not the malevolence, of the Argentine government. It simply could not cope with a chaotic situation.[13] By 23 July, the U.S. Embassy in Buenos Aires had done a complete about turn and was blaming the Videla government for the atrocities.[14] Certainly by 23 August, Kissinger was aware of Operation Condor.[15] On 27 August, Kissinger notified the U.S. Embassies in Buenos Aires and Montevideo that Amnesty International reported the imprisonment of twenty-three Uruguayans under questionable circumstances.[16] How much of this was known to President Ford is not clear, for his memoirs do not make a single mention of Argentina.

Not surprisingly, then, Argentina's new leaders thought that they had a green light for brutality from Washington. One estimate is that during their six year rule (1976-1982), some 30,000 people died or disappeared.[17] In September 1976, Ambassador Hill visited Washington, where people spoke to him about human rights violations by Argentina's military government and assassinations committed as part of Operation Condor. Hill carried those concerns back to Buenos Aires, where, he said, Foreign Minister Guzzetti expressed total amazement. From his conversation in Santiago with Kissinger, he had the impression that the Ford administration was indifferent to any cruelties which might be perpetrated as long as they were perpetrated quickly.[18]

Four days later, Hill met President Videla and tried to clarify the situation. According to Hill, Videla expressed pleasure when

> Guzzetti reported to him that Secretary of State Kissinger understood their problem and had said he hoped they could get terrorism under control as quickly as possible. Videla said he had the impression senior officers of the USG [United States Government] understood situation his govt faces but junior bureaucrats do not. I assured him this was not the case. We all hope Argentina can get terrorism under control quickly—but to do so in such a way as to do minimum damage to its image and to his relations with other governments. If Security Forces continue to kill people to tune of brass band, I concluded, this will not be possible. I told him Secretary of State had told me when I was in U.S. that he wanted to avoid human rights problems in Argentina.[19]

In October, Guzzetti went to Washington and received a different message. According to Hill, Guzzetti had expected a reprimand for his government's violations of human rights but "returned in a state of jubilation." As far as Guzzetti was concerned, thought Hill, only "certain elements of Congress" and some badly informed Americans cared what the military government was doing. The United States Government certainly did not. Hill concluded that as long as that was Guzzetti's impression, it would be pointless for the U.S. embassy in Buenos Aires to protest human rights violations.[20] It would seem that the Videla government acted on the assumption that whatever it did would be tolerable. In October 1976, an unidentified U.S. citizen in Argentina, one of six Americans arrested in the Videl government's counterinsurgency campaign that year, reported that her captors used an electric prod on her.

> Then they tied me down and threw water on me...They questioned me but it was more just give it to her. There. There. There. In genital area...They said they'd fix me so I couldn't have children.[21]

On 9 December 1976, the State Department prepared a statement on human rights in Argentina. It noted that 2000 Argentinians had died of terrorist violence during the second Perón era (1973-1976). In response, the security forces had taken "drastic" counter-terrorist action, arresting thousands and killing hundreds. Right-wing terrorism continued nonetheless. The most notorious of these, the report said, was the AAA (Alianza Anticomunista Argentina). The security forces themselves were probably involved in some of these right-wing death squads. At any rate, they had taken no effective means to control them. Even clergy and foreign political refugees had fallen victim. While no U.S. citizens had died, two claimed that they had been tortured. Anti-Semitism, which the report identified as a recurrent problem in Argentina, was reviving.[22]

This appears to have had no impact on Secretary Kissinger, who might or might not have informed President Ford. The administration of Jimmy Carter, who became President of the United States 20 January 1977, was concerned about human rights, but faced challenges because of what Kissinger had reportedly said. Carter's ambassador to Argentina, ironically named Raul Castro, complained that Kissinger, as a private citizen who no longer held public office, had just visited Argentina. That visit, thought Castro, had created complications. Kissinger's "repeated high praise for Argentina's action in wiping out terrorism and his stress on the importance of Argentina may have gone to some considerable extent to his hosts' friends." Ambassador Castro expected that the junta would justify whatever it did by citing "Kissinger's laudatory statements."[23]

Notes

1. As this manuscript was going to press, Laurentian University Student Matt Tessaro was writing an Honours Essay (thesis) on the Argentine policies of the Ford administration. Mount and Gauthier thank him for his insights.

2. Memo, William D. Rogers, Assistant Secretary of State for Inter-American Affairs, Washington, to Kissinger, 13 Feb. 1976; Robert C. Hill, U.S. Ambassador to Argentina, Buenos Aires, to State Department, 26 Feb. 1976; both in File: Justicia, verdad y memoria: El Estado terrorista desenmascarado, website of the National Security Archive: http://www/cels.org.ar/Site_cels /ejes/a_justicia/justicia_archivos_estado_t_c.html. Cited hereafter as Justicia.

3. Letter, Hill, Buenos Aires, to Kissinger, Washington, 26 March 1976, Justicia.

4. These and many subsequent quotations were downloaded from the National Security Archive website: http://www.gwu.edu/~nsarchiv/NSAEBB/NSAEBB135/index.htm. (Series: Kissinger State Department Telcons, Document 1, 30 June 1976). Cited hereafter as Telcons.

5. Telcons, Document 2, 3 June 1976.

6. Summarized from http://www.nsarchive.org, distributed in an email from the National Security Archive in Washington, D.C. 27 Aug. 2004. A text of the Kissinger-Guzzetti conversation of 10 June 1976 is available on the website http://www.gwu.edu/~NSAEBB/NSAEBBB133/index.htm. under the heading "Kissinger to the Argentine Generals in 1976: "If there are things that have to be done, you should do them quickly."

7. John Dinges, *The Condor Years: How Pinochet and his Allies Brought Terrorism to Three Continents* (New York: New Press, 2004).

8. Carlos Osorio and Kathleen Costar (editors), "Kissinger to the Argentine Generals in 1976: "If there are things that have to be done, you should do them quickly." National Security Archive website http://www.gwu.edu~nsarchiv/NSAEBB/NSAEBB133/index.htm. Cited hereafter as "Quickly."

9. Letter, Hill to Kissinger, 6 April 1976, Justicia.

10. Letter, Hill to Kissinger, 11 May 1976, Justicia.

11. Letter, Hill to Kissinger, 25 May 1976, Justicia.

12. Memo, Shlaudeman, Washington, to Kissinger, 17 July 1976, File: Justicia, verdad y memoria: El Estado terrorista desenmascarado; http://www.cels.org.ar/Site_cels/ejes/a_justicia/justicia_archivos/estado_t_d.html. Cited hereafter as Justicia, verdad.

13. Memo, Kissinger to Edward H. Levi, Head of the Justice Department, Washington, 21 July 1976, Justicia, verdad.

14. Letter, Maxwell Chaplin, Head of Mission, U.S. Embassy in Argentina, to Kissinger, 23 July 1976, Justicia, verdad.

15. Letter, Kissinger to the Embassies in Buenos Aires, Montevideo, Santiago, La Paz, Asunción, and Brasilia, 23 Aug. 1976, Justicia, verdad.

16. Letter, Kissinger to the Embassies in Buenos Aires and Montevideo, 27 Aug. 1976, Justicia, verdad.

17. Benjamin Keen, *A History of Latin America* (Boston: Houghton Mifflin, 1996), p. 321 Keen estimates that 1100 died violently in the chaos of Isabel Perón's presidency.

18. Series: Argentine Military Believed U.S. Gave Go-ahead for Dirty War," Document 8, 20 Sept. 1976, downloaded from website http://www/gwu/edu~NSAEBB/NSAEBB73/index3.htm. Cited hereafter as Dirty War.

19. Dirty War, Document 9, 24 Sept. 1976.

20. Dirty War, Document 10, 19 October 1976.

21. "State Department Opens Files on Argentina's Dirty War," Document 1, 4 Oct. 1976, http://www.gwu.edu/~nsarchiv/NSAEBB/NSAEBB73/index.htm.

22. State Department, Informe confidencial, 9 December 1976, Justicia, verdad.

23. Dirty War, Document 12, 27 June 1978.

Chapter Fifteen

ISRAELI-EGYPTIAN RELATIONS

A sign in a display case of the Gerald Ford Presidential Library in Ann Arbor, Michigan, summarizes the story. It reads:

> The search for a peaceful settlement of the Arab-Israeli conflict was a pressing American priority after the 1973 Yom Kippur War and the oil embargo that followed. While two historic disengagement agreements—between Egypt and Israel, and Israel and Syria—had been achieved by Secretary of State Kissinger, progress toward an overall settlement had slowed by the spring of 1975. Egypt wanted Israel to withdraw from positions held since the 1967 Six Day War: Israel wanted guarantees that Egypt would not budge.

A proposal to place American civilian observers in a demilitarized zone in the Sinai, and U.S. promises of massive aid to both sides brought further concessions by late summer. On September 1, 1975, Israeli Prime Minister Yitzak Rabin and Egyptian President Anwar Sadat initialed the Sinai accord. Israel conceded two strategic Sinai passes and returned the Abu Rudeis oil fields, and Egypt granted non-military Israeli cargo passage through the Suez Canal. Both sides agreed not to resort to military action. The agreement was as close to a declaration of peaceful intentions toward Israel as any Arab country had come since the founding of the Jewish state.

One can credibly argue that the Sinai accord was the single most brilliant achievement of the Ford presidency. Without it, President Carter would not have had a basis upon which to build the Camp David Accord, which provided for the withdrawal of Israeli forces from the Sinai Desert, the dismantling of Jewish settlements there, the opening of the Egypt-Israel border, and the establishment of embassies in each other's capital city. Camp David effectively neutralized Egypt, the largest Arab nation, in ongoing Arab-Israeli disputes and rendered wars which threatened the survival of Israel next to impossible. The Helsinki Accord, also of the summer of 1975, also made the world a much better place, but the initiative there was a European one. (See Chapter Ten.) By contrast, Ford and Kissinger deserve full credit for defusing the Israeli-Egyptian confrontation. Also, most of the signatories at Helsinki were either Western Europeans who wanted stability and more open borders, or post-revolutionary Communists who sought to hold what they had. The Middle East was home to religious fanatics who would assassinate both Sadat and Rabin. Moreover, like Helsinki, the Sinai Accord was controversial at home and might well have convinced some voters to oppose the re-election of President Ford.

Both adversaries deserve sympathy. Abused, even massacred, for centuries in Europe, Jews understandably wanted a country of their own. Hitler's Holocaust was the proverbial last straw. Yet, unless the homeland were located in Antarctica (a suggestion which nobody seems to have made), creation of a Jewish homeland would inevitably involve the displacement or overwhelming of other people. Emotionally, Zionist leaders—those who favoured creation of a Jewish homeland which included Jerusalem—wanted a return to the place where their Hebrew ancestors had lived in Biblical times. Early in the twentieth century they rejected a British offer to establish a Jewish community in Uganda; had they accepted it, by the 1960s Jewish settlers would undoubtedly have been fighting Black Africans instead of Arabs. Religious Jews believed that three thousand years earlier, God had given land between the Jordan River and the Mediterranean Sea (Palestine) to their ancestors, even though others were already living there.[1] After one too many rebellions, Roman authorities had expelled Palestine's Jews, most of whom moved to Europe, and others replaced them. What the Romans had done was brutal and arbitrary, and Zionists believed that correction of a historic wrong was justifiable. If Hebrew occupation of the land of other people(Canaanites) had been acceptable to God in the era of Joshua and King David, Jewish recovery of those same lands must be acceptable to God in the twentieth century.[2]

Palestinian Arabs also had a strong case. For almost 2000 years, their ancestors had lived in Palestine. Although subjects of other people's empires–Ottoman until the end of World War I and British from then until 1948, the Palestinians had their homes there and developed their way of life. The area between the Jordan River and the Mediterranean was the only home they knew, and after so many centuries, they were legitimate occupants, not settlers or squatters. What Europeans had done to Jews was indeed terrible: attacking them during the Crusades, expelling them from Spain in 1492, staging anti-Semitic pogroms in Czarist Russia, killing millions in Hitler's gas chambers. However, compensation should come from those who had committed the misdeeds, not from Arabs who had done no harm and had provided the happiest safe haven for mediaeval European Jewry—the Islamic communities of Spain. Most Palestinians were Muslims, with a substantial Roman Catholic minority. Both Muslims and Christians had their own sacred sites in Jerusalem. Palestine was a Holy Land for them too.[3] Moreover, one would be hard pressed to find other parts of the world where one-time victims tried to reverse almost two millennia of history. The Welsh were unlikely to recover England, Amerindians the United States, or Aborigines Australia.

Such irreconcilable differences led to a series of wars. The United Nations voted in 1947 to divide Palestine into three parts: almost half Jewish, almost half Arab, with Jerusalem an international enclave. Arab governments in surrounding countries rejected this action as a high-handed imposition by outside powers, and in 1948, hours before the British terminated their mandate, Zionist leaders proclaimed the Republic of Israel. Israel's Arab neighbours attacked, and in the course of the fighting, the Israelis captured more land than allotted to them by the United Nations. Hundreds of thousands of Palestinians fled Israel, and most of them settled in what remained of Palestine, either the West Bank (which Jordan governed) or the Gaza Strip (which Egypt governed). Some went to other Arab countries. Renewed warfare between Egypt and Israel in 1956 saw Israeli forces occupy the Gaza Strip and Egypt's Sinai Desert, but under pressure from the Eisenhower administration, the Israelis withdrew from both Sinai and Gaza. After another round of fighting in 1967—this time against Jordan and Syria as well as Egypt—the Israeli government occupied the West Bank and the Gaza Strip, the Sinai Peninsula right to the east side of the Suez Canal (which ceased to function), and Syria's Golan Heights. In September 1973, President Sadat's government launched a surprise attack upon the Israelis, and for the first time since 1967, the Egyptian flag flew east of the Suez Canal.

After this respectable performance by the Egyptian Army, President Sadat was willing to come to terms with Israel. No longer did he trust the Soviets, who had been the principal suppliers of military equipment to Egypt. His impoverished people could benefit from Suez Canal revenues, and he wanted to regain the Sinai Desert. President Nixon sent Secretary of State Kissinger to engage in "shuttle diplomacy," flying from Israel to capitals of surrounding Arab countries to determine what, if any, common ground there was. Kissinger determined that an Israeli-Egyptian settlement might be possible, but that differences between Israel on the one hand and the remaining Arab governments made further progress impossible for the foreseeable future. A settlement on one front, he concluded, was preferable to none at all, and Presidents Ford and Sadat concurred.

The stakes were high for both Rabin and Sadat. Rabin knew that it would be unwise in the long run to reject peace with Egypt. Arabs outnumbered Israelis; Egyptians alone outnumbered Israelis by a margin of more than 10:1, and if Egypt were no longer an enemy, Israel would enjoy greater security. Israeli commerce could benefit from the Suez Canal. On the other hand, Sadat would not forever be President of Egypt. One way or another, his time in office would end. Sooner or later, a successor might not share his priorities or his values, and Egypt could once again become an enemy. The Suez Canal was a more defensible boundary than any conceivable alternative. Unlike Egypt, Israel could not afford to lose a war. Its territory was so small that a single defeat could render its people once again homeless, or worse. It was no light matter to gamble with Israel's security. Also, as long as Israel controlled the Sinai Peninsula, it had access to a source of oil. Given that Saudi Arabia, Iraq, and Kuwait would not sell oil to Israel and that Iran might some day have a less sympathetic government (as turned out to be the case in 1979), it was risky to lose control. As for Sadat, the reopening of the Suez Canal and regaining of the Sinai Desert would bring significant gains, but at the price of diplomatic isolation, at least temporarily, from the rest of the Arab world. Personally, he risked assassination from someone who considered him a traitor to the Arab cause. Collectively, his people could face reprisals from residents of other Arab countries.

Ford too faced risks, albeit not the disappearance of his country or assassination. (In September 1975, there would be two assassination attempts against President Ford but not because of his Middle East policies.) Israel had a powerful lobby in the United States, and Jewish-American voters could play a significant role in determining the winner of a close presidential race. He was aware of this. On 25 April 1975, after the failure of the first round of Egyptian-Israeli talks, Ford told Kissinger and Scowcroft that he had hosted prominent Republican senators for a dinner, where they had discussed the Middle East. Jacob Javits of New

York said that the U.S. must guarantee Israel; Clifford Case of New Jersey said that this was the year to go for a comprehensive agreement.

Kissinger replied:

Case has really been very good. I think it is better to hit the Jewish Community between the eyes once hard and get it over with. Nahum Goldmann [a prominent American Jew] says the same as Case–a confrontation with Israel and the Jews is unavoidable; there will be two-three months of demonstrations until they know we mean business and then they will go along.[4]

Kissinger resented the idea that because of his Jewishness, he should place the perceived interests of Israel ahead of those of the United States, which had sheltered his family from Hitler's Holocaust and allowed him to become Secretary of State.[5] In Jerusalem during his shuttle diplomacy, he encountered demonstrators who considered him a traitor to the cause. One placard said, "Jewboy, go home!" Another was more sarcastic: "Hitler spared you so you could finish the job!"[6] Conceivably, because of his religion, Kissinger could exert greater pressure on Rabin than could a Secretary of State of a different religious persuasion. Realistically, Ford did lose New York to Carter in the presidential election of 1976. If he had carried New York, he would have won an additional four years in the White House. Admittedly, dissatisfaction in New York's Jewish community is not the only explanation. Ford had not been as generous as many residents of New York thought he should have been when their city faced financial difficulties, and he dropped Vice-President Nelson Rockefeller, a former Governor of New York, as his running mate. The Nixon pardon was another liability, as it was throughout the United States. As indicated in Chapter One, Ford hardly went out of his way to court Irish-American voters. Still, antagonizing New York's Jewish-American voters could be (and perhaps was) costly, and Ford exhibited formidable political courage.

Memoirs of Ford and Kissinger make clear that they considered Sadat more reasonable than Rabin. Ford said that since Israel's birth in 1948, his predecessors had armed Israel and been generous with money for development on the assumption that a strong Israel would feel sufficiently secure that it would make concessions for the sake of peace. Yet, wrote Ford, despite Israel's strength, peace was as elusive as ever. Under the circumstances, he wondered whether the policy of generous support for Israel had failed. "I wanted the Israelis to recognize that there had to be some *quid pro quo*," he said.[7] In return for weapons and money from the United States, Israel must negotiate seriously, and he said so in an interview to *Time* and on NBC-TV. As Kissinger shuttled back and forth in March 1975 between Israel and Egypt, "the Egyptians bent over backward [and]...the Israelis resisted...Rabin...didn't seem to understand that only by giving do you get something in return."[8]

Israeli "stalling" led to the collapse of the talks. "Their tactics frustrated the Egyptians and made me mad as hell." When he returned to the United States, a "deeply disappointed" Kissinger feared that Sadat would not trust the United States again. Repeatedly he had accepted Kissinger's suggestions, only to have the Israelis reject them. Sadat might even form a partnership with Libyan leader Muammar Qaddafi, no friend of the West.[9] The White House voiced its unhappiness, and President Ford braced for a verbal onslaught from American friends of Israel. At the same time he let those friends know that he was willing to be much more forcible and much more blunt.[10] Apart from the survival of Israel, after all, important U.S. interests were at stake. There was always the danger that regional wars could escalate into Soviet-American confrontations, and Arab good will was important to American oil imports.

American friends of Israel accused President Ford of anti-Semitism, a charge he vehemently denied. Israelis tried to discredit Kissinger, on the grounds that as a Jew, he was so worried about appearing overly friendly to Israel that he had become overly friendly to Egypt. President Ford rejected the charges. On 21 May, seventy-six of the hundred Senators wrote the White House to ask President Ford to be as generous as ever with military and economic assistance to Israel. He saw this as an action "inspired by Israel"...and it "really bugged" him.[11] Supported by the seventy-six Senators, the Israelis became more intransigent than ever.

On 1 June, Presidents Ford and Sadat met in Salzburg, Austria. The next day, Sadat suggested what would end the stalemate. Israeli forces would withdraw to the Gidi and Mitla Passes, still well within Egypt but roughly fifty miles (eighty kilometres) from the Suez Canal. Some 200 civilians from the United States could occupy a buffer zone between the two armies and report on any inappropriate troop movements by either side.

Ford's memoirs continue. When Rabin visited Washington ten days later, "shaken by our [the U.S.] decision to 'reassess' our policies in the Middle East,"[12] Ford forwarded Sadat's proposal to him, without saying that it had originated with Sadat or any other Egyptian. Israeli authorities would have preferred U.S.

soldiers to U.S. civilians, but Ford and Kissinger were adamant. If ever the U.S. decided to withdraw its forces, said Kissinger, it would be accused of starting a war. If it did not withdraw its forces, it would be accused of defending Israel. U.S. soldiers in the Sinai would be a lose-lose proposition. Ford agreed.[13]

Kissinger tells the story at greater length. While Israel would continue to occupy most of the Sinai Peninsula, Sadat, after all, would be making major sacrifices. Isolated from leaders of other Arab countries, he had to convince his own people that the Sinai Agreement was but the first step, not an end in itself. At a minimum, he must gain access to the western ends of the Gidi and Mitla Passes and control of the Abu Rudeis oil fields. Kissinger says that the transfer of land made little difference militarily or economically, as Abu Rudeis was thought to have only a four to six year supply of oil. However, the transfer was symbolic. Appearances can be of greater psychological importance than realities, and both the passes and the oil fields were clearly visible.[14] Ford, according to Kissinger, was direct with Rabin when he went to Washington in June 1975 and in an "unusually explicit letter to Rabin" on 27 June. He demanded that Rabin show some evidence of taking the Sadat proposals seriously (without attributing their origin to Sadat) by 11 July, and warned that if Rabin did not do so, Ford would "go public with his own assessment of why the negotiations were stalemating." No President since Eisenhower, said Kissinger, "had...addressed the Israeli government in so abrupt a manner."[15] (When Syrian President Hafiz al-Asad asked Kissinger why Eisenhower could wring concessions from the Israelis but his successors could not, Kissinger replied: "In 1956, Israel was much weaker, and it was not so well organized in America." [16]) On 4 August, Ford sent Rabin what Kissinger terms "a blistering telegram," and after more negotiating of the details, the Sinai Accord of 1 September 1975 proved possible. Three days later, the formal signing took place, and shortly thereafter, Congress approved the necessary funds so that the U.S. could fulfil its part of the deal.

St. Matthew's Gospel quotes Jesus as saying, "Blessed are the peacemakers..."[17] Yet, President Ford's peacemaking certainly did not help and perhaps hurt his bid for re-election. Three years after the Camp David Accord, an assassin killed President Sadat. Prime Minister Rabin would suffer the same fate in 1995, not because of his role in establishing peace with Egypt but because he was prepared to continue the process through concessions to Palestinians. Diplomacy requires courage, a phenomenon which these three men were to exhibit.

Notes

1. Exodus 3:8.

2. For more extensive accounts of the above, see Graeme S. Mount, "Zionism," in James S. Olson and Robert Shadle (editors), *Historical Dictionary of the British Empire* (Westport, Connecticut: Greenwood Press, 1996), pp. 1182-1184; Howard M. Sachar, *A History of Israel From the Rise of Zionism to Our Time* (New York: Knopf, 1979).

3. In his memoirs, Kissinger says that Syrian President Hafez al-Asad said to him in 1975 what the King of Saudi Arabia had said to President Franklin D. Roosevelt late in World War II, "Why should Arabs pay with their territory for the crimes committed in Europe against the Jewish people? Why should Arabs be asked to accept the biblical claim of a religion they do not themselves practice?" (Kissinger, *Years of Renewal*, p. 350.)

4. National Security Adviser, MEMORANDA OF CONVERSATIONS, 1973-1977, Box 11, Folder: Ford, Kissinger, 25 April 1975, GFPL.

5. Historian Noam Kochavi agrees that Kissinger's first priority was U.S. interests, not Jewish causes (pp. 503-530).

6. Kissinger, *Years of Renewal*, p. 452.

7. Ford, p. 245.

8. Ford, p. 246.

9. Ford, p. 247.

10. Ford, pp. 247-248.

11. Ford, p. 287.

12. Ford, p. 291.

13. Memorandum of Conversation—Ford, Kissinger, Scowcroft, Camp David, 5 July 1975, National Security Adviser, Presidential Country Files for East Asia and the Pacific, Box 6, Folder: Indonesia (7), GFPL.

14. Kissinger, *Years of Renewal*, pp. 385-386. For Kissinger's complete account, see pp. 385-459.

15. Kissinger, *Years of Renewal*, p. 446.

16. Memorandum of Conversation, Presidential Palace, Damascus, 9 March 1975, National Security Adviser, Kissinger Reports, File: March 7-22, 1975, Kissinger's Trip—Vol. I, GFPL.

17. Matthew 5:9.

CONCLUSIONS

The record of the Ford administration in these critical events was mixed.

The Ford administration's relations with the United Kingdom were sensible and rendered co-operation feasible for subsequent administrations. Clearly the good will of the British—who controlled Hong Kong and whose military and economic power could assist U.S. interests—was more valuable than the anger of Irish-Americans, many if not most of whom voted Democrat anyway. The bicentennial reception for Queen Elizabeth indicates that affection as well as self-interest was involved. The transition from Franco to democracy in Spain began fifteen months into Ford's presidency, and under the circumstances, it is understandable that the United Kingdom would appear a more valuable ally than Spain. Whatever the historic rights and wrongs, the people of British Honduras differed so decisively from Guatemalans that to have backed the latter in that dispute would have been a demonstration of cynical *Realpolitik* of the highest order of magnitude. This was a situation where duty and interest coincided, and the Ford administration did well.

On Portugal, the Ford administration performed brilliantly. It found just the right balance to encourage the forces of democracy without offending Portuguese nationalists and thereby helping Portuguese Communists. The Ford administration also paved the way for the renewal of treaty arrangements in the Azores.

On Cuba, Ford attempted a policy of reconciliation but Castro's price was intolerably high—especially independence for Puerto Rico and the right to export revolution to African countries. Even if Castro and Ford had reached an agreement, there is no guarantee that it would have survived for very long. Fidel Castro has his own agenda, and others can support him or become his adversaries.

Prime Minister Trudeau certainly sang Castro's praises in a most public way, but Castro persevered in Angola, notwithstanding Trudeau's opinion to the contrary and a reduction in Canadian foreign aid to Cuba. Nor did Castro become more agreeable with age. In 1997, Canada's Foreign Minister, Lloyd Axworthy, visited Cuba, as did his boss, Prime Minister Jean Chrétien, the following year. Chrétien raised the matter of four political prisoners: Marta Beatriz Roque Cabello, Vladimiro Roca Antúñez, René Gómez Manzano, and Félix Bonne Carcassés. After Chrétien returned to Canada, the four received lengthy prison sentences after secret trials. Also, along with the United States, Castro's Cuba was the only Western Hemisphere country to reject the 1997 Treaty of Ottawa banning land mines, a high priority for Lloyd Axworthy.[1] The evidence is that vinegar does not influence Castro, but neither does sugar.

On Canada, the Ford administration rolled with the punches. It could not control Prime Minister Pierre Elliott Trudeau, but it could attempt to exploit his actions. If he was going to Cuba, despite White House policy toward that country, he could at least prove useful as a messenger. If West German Chancellor Helmut Schmidt wanted Canadians at future Economic Summits, the Ford White House saw advantages.

On Vietnam, Ford had inherited a very bad hand, and events on the ground in that country along with the refusal of Congress to vote funds gave him little choice but to evacuate as many Americans and friendly Vietnamese as possible. The *Mayagüez* was costly in terms of human lives, but it was not unreasonable to send North Korea and other countries the message that defeat in Vietnam did not mean a wider United States withdrawal or capitulation.

On Korea, Ford did the best possible under the circumstances. North Korea had the same leader, Kim Il Sung, who had orchestrated the 1950 invasion of South Korea. Since the Armistice Agreement of 1953, North Korea had continued to pursue a series of provocative actions, and it continued to do so into the twenty-first century. Human rights in South Korea would remain a contentious issue long after Ford left the White House. Nevertheless, President Ford's reassurances to South Korean authorities, along with the Operation Paul Bunyan warning to North Korea, prevented worse from happening. South Korea did not acquire nuclear weapons. North Korea did not attempt to invade South Korea. Roughly a decade later, South Korea began the successful transition to democracy.

On Indonesia and East Timor, Ford and Kissinger clearly sent the wrong message. In their determination to assure President Suharto that Indonesia would not become another South Vietnam, they opened the door to an invasion of East Timor which would cost hundreds of thousands of Timorese lives. The Ford administration's policies toward Indonesia and East Timor are the most blatant case of *Realpolitik*, devoid of any hint of idealism on the part of the administration.

On Mozambique's changed situation and the resulting consequences for Rhodesia, Ford did well. He encouraged Kissinger to do what he could to avert catastrophe in Rhodesia, even though he believed that his administration's "betrayal" of Euro-Rhodesians jeopardized his position in the race against Ronald Reagan for the Republican presidential nomination. Conservative Republicans, who were numerous in Southern states, were furious that Ford and Kissinger were not backing Ian Smith.[2] On this issue, Ford and Kissinger both succeeded and failed. They *did* persuade South African Prime Minister Vorster to qualify and, if necessary, terminate his support for Smith and the Euro-Rhodesians. In so doing, they launched the process which led to the Lancaster House Agreement of 1979. However, in so doing they alienated voters whom Ford needed in certain Southern states, and they failed to avert catastrophe (Mugabe's induced famine and tyranny) in Rhodesia/Zimbabwe. It was not the fault of Ford and Kissinger. The time for that, if it had ever existed at all, had passed.

On Helsinki, Ford deserves top marks. He could have done what was popular and boycotted the Conference and withheld his signature from the Agreement. Fortunately, he defied the odds and went to the Finnish capital. The current generation of Americans did not appreciate the gesture, and it did not save him from defeat in the 1976 presidential election. However, subsequent generations—throughout the world, but especially throughout Europe and even more especially in the Baltic countries—can be grateful.

On Spain (in contrast to Vietnam), Ford had good luck. Franco's death ended a stalemate at the negotiating table and facilitated conclusion of a new bilateral U.S.-Spanish treaty. Moreover, as almost any new Spanish leader was bound to be less controversial than Franco, the political climate at home changed to Ford's advantage. Winning the necessary two-thirds vote of approval for such a treaty in the U.S. Senate was bound to become more feasible. Significantly too, the thirty-eighty President of the United States, a Republican (Ford), demonstrated greater patience in the face of desirable régime change than did his Republican successor, the forty-third President, George W. Bush. In the short run at least, the results in Spain have been happier for all concerned than the outcome in Iraq. Spain is not Iraq, and it is certainly possible that what worked in Spain would not have worked in Iraq. What is clear, however, that the Ford formula proved successful in Spain, while the Bush recipe seems to be creating new enemies for the United States in Iraq.

On China, Ford probably did the best he could. Like Nixon, he exploited the Sino-Soviet rift and maintained reasonable relations with the People's Republic of China. He lacked the political strength both in the nation as a whole and within the Republican Party itself to make a drastic breakthrough in relations between Washington and Beijing. However, he did not destroy the process which Nixon had begun—despite the fact that such a course of action would have been popular—and the process of normalization continued. Future generations would be grateful, even if contemporaries were indifferent or hostile. In 1979, when the Iranian Revolution deprived the United States of its listening posts on Soviet borders, the value of a civilized relationship with the PRC became evident. In the 1990s, as North Korea behaved like a rogue state, the PRC proved an invaluable diplomatic partner for the Clinton and George W. Bush administrations.

On reforms in the CIA, arguably Ford was in a position analogous to that of Napoleon's mother. Must she accept some indirect responsibility for the death and destruction which her son inflicted on Europe from Lisbon to Moscow? Must Ford accept *some* indirect responsibility for the war of 2003 against Saddam Hussein because he promoted George Herbert Walker Bush to become Director of the Central Intelligence Agency? Without the high profile which he had there, could Bush have become Vice-President of the United States in 1981 and President eight years later? Without the first Bush presidency, would there have been a second? Is Ford's responsibility increased by the fact that it was he who was first to appoint Rumsfeld Secretary of Defense and Richard Cheney Chief of Staff?

On Panama, Ford facilitated the Carter-Torrijos Treaties which permitted a successful, orderly handover of the Canal Zone. What could have become a battleground comparable to Iraq in the era of George W. Bush became a peaceful, prosperous enclave between less developed countries of Central America (other than Costa Rica) on one side and drug-divided Colombia on the other. The temptation to avoid controversy by stalling for time or reversing course must have been formidable, but the Ford administration did what it believed to be right and what subsequent events have confirmed to be right.

On Argentina, the policies of the Ford administration were abominable, lethal, perhaps criminal. To have allowed the government of Isabel Perón to collapse is understandable. To have maintained support for the military government was despicable.

On Egyptian-Israeli relations, Ford and Kissinger were brilliant and courageous. At considerable political risk, which certainly did not help his bid for re-election, President Ford and Secretary Kissinger achieved the Sinai Accord of 1 September 1975. This involved winning the confidence of Egyptian President Sadat and, despite the powerful Israeli lobby in the United States, cajoling Israeli authorities into making concessions. Without the Sinai Accord, there could not have been the Camp David Accord of 1978. Without the Camp David Accord, the Middle East undoubtedly would have been even bloodier than it has been.

To summarize, the record was mixed—enlightened in some areas, myopic, even brutal in others. There was a certain consistency regarding human rights. In South Korea, Indonesia, and Argentina, Ford and Secretary of State Henry Kissinger did not object to political repression as such but feared only that more sensitive Americans might try to obstruct U.S. relations with those countries. Perhaps one of the most significant aspects of Ford's presidency was his choice of advisers—George Bush, Donald Rumsfeld, Dick Cheney. These people, along with George W. Bush (son of Ford's George Bush) would play prominent roles in subsequent Republican administrations for more than three decades and by invading Iraq and repudiating treaties, would change the world forever. That is a story unto itself.

Notes

1. Lloyd Axworthy, *Navigating a New World: Canada's Global Future* (Toronto: Knopf Canada, 2003), pp. 69 and 143; Sahadeo Basdeo and Ian Hesketh, "Canada, Cuba, and Constructive Engagement: Political Dissidents and Human Rights" in Sahdeo Basdeo and Heather N. Nichol (editors), *Canada, the United States, and Cuba: An Evolving Relationship* (Miami: University of Miami Press, 2002), p. 43; Peter McKenna, John Kirk, and Christine Climenhage, "Canada-Cuba Relations: 'Northern Ice' or *Nada Nuevo*" in Basdeo and Nichol, pp. 62-63.
2. Ford, pp. 380-381.

INDEX

CHILE AND THE NAZIS: From Hitler to Pinochet

Based on documentary evidence from the archives of the Chilean Foreign Office, and from U.S., British, German, and, intercepted, Japanese documents, Mount is one of the first authors to provide evidence of the events and circumstances surrounding Chile's reluctance to sever diplomatic ties with Nazi Germany allowing it to maximize its opportunities there, influencing Chilean politicians, military operations, and the popular media.

Mount's cool, clear prose avoids the expressions of outrage that blunt so many books about the right in Chile. His revelations are enough. —*Guardian*

Mount reveals the conflict, the espionage, and the difficulty with policy which resulted from wide-spread Nazi influence...all issues that continue to be of importance even now. —Professor Florentino Rodao, President of the Asociación de Estudios del Pacifico

A most impressive book, based on a variety of archival and oral historical sources from three continents...about a hitherto little-known, but fascinating aspect of 20th century history. —Stan Hordes, Latin American and Iberian Institute, University of New Mexico

2001: 204 pages, photographs, bibliography, index
Paperback ISBN: 1-55164-192-5 $19.99   ✧   Hardcover ISBN: 1-55164-193-3 $48.99

DIPLOMACY OF WAR: The Case of Korea

with Andre Laferriere

Written with the help of Soviet and Chinese sources which became accessible after the Cold War, U.S., Soviet, and Chinese archival sources, memoirs, and secondary literature, this book examines the course of the Korean War from the perspectives of all the players, including the role of the Commonwealth and the United Nations.

Mount argues convincingly that, while a united Commonwealth might have had some influence on the American-dominated politics and strategy of the Korean War, in practice the Commonwealth was rarely united. The great strength of the *Diplomacy of War* is in the wealth of detail with which Mount charts the course of policy-making in each of the Commonwealth capitals, the very limited coordination between them, and the way in which their individual strategic needs inevitably led to differing policy positions on Korea.

Fifty years on, the relationship of coalition with superpower is as relevant as ever. —Peter Londey, Historian, Australian War Memorial, Canberra

Interesting, readable, and exceedingly well documented. I found it fascinating. —John Melady, author of *Korea: Canada's Forgotten War*

Advances our understanding of the Korean War and makes complex diplomatic history accessible. —Hank Nelson, Professor Emeritus, Australian National University, Canberra

2004: 224 pages, photographs, bibliography, index
Paperback ISBN: 1-55164-238-7 $24.99   ✧   Hardcover ISBN: 1-55164-239-5 $53.99